INDIGENOUS KNOWLEDGE DEVELOPMENT
IN BANGLADESH

INDIGENOUS KNOWLEDGE DEVELOPMENT IN BANGLADESH

Present and Future

Edited by
Paul Sillitoe

ITDG
PUBLISHING

Published by ITDG Publishing
103-105 Southampton Row, London WC1B 4HL, UK
www.itdgpublishing.org.uk

First published in 2000
Reprinted 2004

ISBN 1 85339 518 8

This edition of the book is published jointly with The University Press Limited,
Dhaka, Bangladesh.

A catalogue record for this book is available from the British Library.

ITDG Publishing is the publishing arm of the Intermediate Technology
Development Group. Our mission is to build the skills and capacity of people
in developing countries through the dissemination of information in all forms,
enabling them to improve the quality of their lives and that of future generations.

Typeset by MNS Computer Printers, Dhaka and produced by The University Press
Limited, Red Crescent Building, 114 Motijheel C/A, Dhaka, Bangladesh.

For the poorest of the poor in Bangladesh, may your voice be heard.

"We have for over a century been dragged by the preposterous West behind its chariot, choked by dust, deafened by noise, humbled by our own helplessness, and overwhelmed by the speed ... . If we ever ventured to ask 'progress towards what, and progress for whom', it was considered oriental to entertain such doubts about the absoluteness of progress."

RABINDRA NATH TAGORE 1941 *Rabindra Nath Tagore on rural reconstruction.* Government of India, New Delhi.

Contents

List of Tables

List of Figures

Contributors

Abdul Momen Miah, Associate Professor, Department of Agricultural Extension Education, Bangladesh Agricultural University, Mymensingh, Bangladesh.

Aditi Khisa, Department of Botany, University of Chittagong, Chittagong 4331, Bangladesh.

Anna Miles, Geography Department, University of Durham, Old Elvet, Durham DH1 3HN, U.K.

Antonia Reihlen, Maastrichter Str. 15, 52074 Aachen, Germany (also c/o International Centre for Living Aquatic Resources Management (ICLARM), House 75, Road 7, Banani, Dhaka 1213, Bangladesh).

Ben Angell, Anthropology Department, University of Durham, Old Elvet, Durham DH1 3HN, U.K.

C. C. Wilcock, Forestry Department, University of Aberdeen, Aberdeen, Scotland, U.K.

D. Mazumder, International Centre for Living Aquatic Resources Management (ICLARM), House 75, Road 7, Block H, Banani, Dhaka 1213, Bangladesh.

Dwijen Mallick, Research Associate, Bangladesh Centre for Advanced Studies (BCAS), House 620, Road 10A (New), Dhanmondi, Dhaka 1209, Bangladesh.

H. Zaman, ex-member, Planning Commission, Government of Bangladesh, Dhaka.

Jane Stokoe, Anthropology Department, University of Durham, Old Elvet, Durham DH1 3HN, U.K.

Julian J. F. Barr, Centre for Land Use & Water Resources Research, University of Newcastle, Newcastle-upon-Tyne, NE1 7RU, U.K.

K. Naher, On-Farm Research Division, Bangladesh Agricultural Research Institute, Joydepur, Gazipur-1701, Bangladesh.

M. A. Quddus, Village and Farm Forestry Program, Swiss Agency for Development and Cooperation, Dhaka, Bangladesh.

M. A. Rahman, Professor of Botany, Department of Botany, University of Chittagong, Chittagong 4331, Bangladesh.

M. F. Haq, On-Farm Research Division, Bangladesh Agricultural Research Institute, Joydepur, Gazipur-1701, Bangladesh.

M. I. Zuberi, Professor of Botany, Department of Environmental Sciences, Gono Biswabidhyalay, P.O. Mirzanagaar, Dhaka 1350, Bangladesh.

M. Millat-e-Mustafa, Associate Professor, Institute of Forestry and Environmental Sciences, University of Chittagong, Chittagong 4331, Bangladesh.

Mahbub Alam, Anthropologist, DFID Land/Water Interface Research Programme, Charan, Tangail, Bangladesh.

Mahfuzul Haque, Programme Coordinator, Sustainable Environment Management Programme (SEMP), Paribesh Bhaban, Agargoan, Dhaka 1207, Bangladesh.

Mohammad Abdur Rahman, Professor of Forestry and Wood Technology, Department of Forestry, University of Khulna, Khulna 9208, Bangladesh.

N. Begum, On-Farm Research Division, Bangladesh Agricultural Research Institute, Joydepur, Gazipur-1701, Bangladesh.

Nurul Islam, International Centre for Living Aquatic Resources Management (ICLARM), House 75, Road 7, Block H, Banani, Dhaka 1213, Bangladesh.

P. J. Dixon, Anthropology Department, University of Durham, Old Elvet, Durham DH1 3HN, U.K.

P. Sillitoe, Professor of Anthropology, University of Durham, Old Elvet, Durham DH1 3HN, U.K.

Paul M. Thompson, Technical Co-ordinator, International Centre for Living Aquatic Resources Management (ICLARM), House 75, Road 7, Block H, Banani, Dhaka 1213, Bangladesh.

Philip Townsley, Former Social Anthropologist on Flood Action Plan (FAP 17) Project, c/o Fisheries Research Centre, House 42, Road 28, Gulshan, Dhaka 1212, Bangladesh.

S. B. Naseem, Principal Farming Systems Agronomist, Bangladesh Rice Research Institute, Gazipur 1701, Bangladesh.

S. B. Uddin, Department of Botany, University of Chittagong, Chittagong 4331, Bangladesh.

S. K. L. Mohammed Lalon, Ashoka Fellow, Rajshahi Niskriti (NGO), Sultanabad, Rajshahi 6100, Bangladesh.

Salina Jahan Nuri, Scientific Officer, Bangladesh Agricultural Research Institute, Iswurdi, Pabna, Bangladesh.

Sukanta Sen, BARCIK, 3/7 Block D, Lalmatia, Dhaka 1207, Bangladesh.

T. Islam, Bangladesh Agricultural Research Council, Farm Gate, Dhaka, Bangladesh.

Wajed A. Shah, Monitoring and Evaluation Specialist, International Centre for Living Aquatic Management (ICLARM), House 75, Road 7, Banani, Dhaka 1213, Bangladesh.

Z. Samina, Intermediate Technology Development Group, Dhanmondi, Dhaka 1209, Bangladesh.

Zahir Ahmed, Anthropology Department, University of Sussex, Falmer, Brighton, U.K. (On leave from Jahangirnagar University, Dhaka, Bangladesh).

Foreword

THIS IMPRESSIVE VOLUME on *Indigenous Knowledge Development in Bangladesh* edited by Paul Sillitoe is an important contribution to the fields of both anthropology and development. It will be particularly useful for all those who are directly or indirectly concerned with the problems associated with development in Bangladesh including social scientists, planners, policy-makers, extension workers and both government and non-government workers. Divided into five sections relating to development issues, agroforestry, plant resources, fish resources and methodological issues, the book contains twenty-four valuable articles including an introduction and conclusion and brings together a range of disciplines from anthropology and sociology to natural resource sciences and development studies. Authors are both Bangladeshi and British, and as such the volume encompasses both emic and etic perspectives. Contributions are based on the authors own research experiences of indigenous knowledge with particular reference to Bangladesh. Taken as a whole, the volume provides us with a wealth of information on both the theoretical and practical aspects of indigenous knowledge research. However, the principle aim of this volume is to assess the current situation of indigenous knowledge research and development in Bangladesh. The authors have succeeded in achieving this objective through emphasising the importance and richness of local people's knowledge and by advocating its incorporation as an integral component in the planning and implementation of any development initiative in Bangladesh and elsewhere.

Bangladesh is predominantly a rural country with agriculture being the mainstay economy. The majority of the population is either directly or indirectly connected with agriculture. In such an agrarian society, farmers have relied upon indigenous knowledge for centuries, organising production on the basis of local knowledge handed down from previous generations where it is built upon, modified and refined to suit current circumstances. Today, farmers are exposed to modern knowledge of farming but they have not abandoned their indigenous knowledge, and this remains true for other traditional occupational groups such as carpenters, potters, weavers, blacksmiths, herbal practitioners and fishermen. These groups also continue to draw on their local knowledge heritage, intrinsic to daily life, when producing their goods and products.

I agree with the view that farmers' indigenous knowledge derives from past experiences, is transmitted from one generation to another, evaluated and fine-tuned, as people engage in a continuous process of experimentation and innovation. But today, local knowledge is eroding fast and much has been lost (or at least, dramatically changed) with the modernisation of agriculture and the rapid spread of 'foreign' technology introduced from outside. Thus, as many of the authors emphasise, we need to redouble our efforts to document this knowledge.

We can no longer afford to ignore the value of indigenous knowledge and, as the chapters in this volume demonstrate, by continuing to view the knowledge and practices of local people as 'primitive', unscientific and as a hindrance to development, the desired goal of achieving sustainable development in the country's many sectors (agriculture, forestry, fishery and so on) may continue to remain unrealised. It is essential that planners, policy-makers and development practitioners endeavour to understand the indigenous knowledge and practices of the community in which they are working. At present many are either relatively unfamiliar with such a notion or otherwise suspicious of its worth. Through an understanding they will be better able to integrate local knowledge with modern scientific knowledge, and in doing so instigate development initiatives that are both environmentally and socially appropriate and hence more sustainable. This is the conclusion the reader inevitably reaches after digesting this volume.

Any development endeavour aiming to improve and enrich the lives of the poor and weak ('target group populations') in a country like Bangladesh should incorporate indigenous knowledge and involve local people's participation at all stages of intervention. Such a 'bottom-up' approach — working from the grassroots level — ensures both participation and empowerment of people. The present volume suggests such a development strategy for changing the fate of the millions of poor people in Bangladesh, a strategy with which I am in full agreement.

This volume represents an important contribution to the field of indigenous knowledge and development and should be considered an essential read for all those wishing to pursue further studies in this new and exciting field. I congratulate the editor and all the contributors to the book. We should also thank the Bangladesh Resource Centre for Indigenous Knowledge (BARCIK) for organising the 1998 workshop *The State of Indigenous Knowledge in Bangladesh* at which the majority of these papers were originally presented, and wish it well in the future in supporting this valuable work.

Anwarullah Choudhury
Professor of Anthropology
University of Dhaka, Bangladesh

INTRODUCTION

1 The State of Indigenous Knowledge in Bangladesh

Paul Sillitoe

"WHAT ARE YOU SAYING, that Bangladesh should go back to the stone age?" Although an exaggerated challenge, for it is no more conceivable that Bengal — part of the ancient South Asian civilisation where Harappan metallurgy arrived over 3000 years ago (Clarke 1962; Piggott 1950) — might regress to stone tool technology than the United States of America, this challenge, thrown out at the meeting to launch the indigenous knowledge network in Bangladesh, typifies a widespread attitude to the current promotion of indigenous knowledge research in development. It is a common misapprehension, particularly among scientists and technocrats that it somehow implies going backwards technologically. Another speaker, underlining the stone age challenge, pointed out that without the scientific breeding of high yielding varieties (HYV) of rice and associated technology of fertilisers, biocides and so on, Bangladesh would have been unable to feed its expanding population. The implication was that an interest in indigenous knowledge would somehow undo these advances. The unspoken question was what could indigenous knowledge research do to increase production similarly.

These two comments catch the provocative tone of some of the lively debate that characterised the meeting held in Dhaka in May 1998 to inaugurate the national network of indigenous knowledge researchers under the auspices of the newly founded NGO the Bangladesh Resource Centre for Indigenous Knowledge (BARCIK — see Sen *et al.* chapter 24 for details), which is affiliated to the rapidly expanding international network of indigenous knowledge resource centres (Liebenstein *et al.* 1995). The title of the conference, reproduced in the title of this introduction, was 'The State of Indigenous Knowledge in Bangladesh'. The comments cited above suggest that we need urgently to carry forward the debate initiated at the meeting, to clarify the possible contribution of indigenous knowledge research to development. This volume aims to facilitate this process. It is certainly not the intention of those of us promoting indigenous knowledge research to put communities backwards in any sense. Indeed the reverse. We believe that the relatively small resources that indigenous knowledge research requires will yield a large dividend in furthering poor peoples' advance forwards. There is no reason for scientists to feel threatened, it should not take resources away from their valuable research, nor undermine it. On the contrary it should enrich and improve it.

There is a profound misunderstanding of the indigenous knowledge agenda. There is clearly a need to establish what indigenous knowledge is and how incorporating it into the scientific research process might advance development. Scientists' attitudes reflect the current confusion. Some, far from joining their dismissive colleagues, are trying to incorporate an indigenous knowledge component into their work. Indeed it is these scientists, together with the vigorous NGOs, who are largely furthering indigenous knowledge 'work in Bangladesh — where anthropologists are relatively new to the academy — as reflected in the contributions to this book by foresters, agronomists and fisheries specialists among others (see list of contributors). But even this enlightened minority is undecided what the indigenous knowledge component should amount to, how to access it and incorporate it effectively into their research.

It is important to capitalise on the opportunity that has opened up for this work with the recent dramatic change in approaches to development, with the shift that has occurred from a focus on the 'top down' imposition of interventions to a 'grassroots' participatory perspective. The emergence of local knowledge ideas and practice has depended crucially on this change. The dominant development paradigms until a decade or so ago were modernisation — the classic transfer-of-technology model associated with the political right — and dependency — the marxist informed model associated with the political left. They are both blind to local knowledge issues. The new bottom-up oriented development paradigms that have recently emerged to challenge these top-down perspectives give more credence to local perspectives (Potter *et al.* 1999:43-71; Preston 1996; Närman 1999). They are an attempt to access the very poor, now the explicit target group of aid agencies, which have been searching for some time for more effective approaches with mounting evidence of resources wasted in ill-conceived, frequently centrally imposed schemes that have not only failed to improve matters in lesser developed countries but have on occasion made them worse. The contribution of Haque (chapter 5) illustrates this point with a series of vignettes of what he calls 'development disasters' which failed to access local opinion and indigenous knowledge, from the displacement of people by hydroelectric and forestry projects to misconceived water management schemes. The contributions to this book seek to move us forwards, to promote 'development successes'.

Indigenous knowledge in Bangladesh

Typically the Bangladeshi production system comprises peasant farmers cultivating small intensively managed plots crowded together across the floodplain, a mix of landowners, sharecroppers and landless labourers. Muslim families dominate rural society. Farmers cultivate rice as a staple, together with other crops like mustard, onions and jute, for subsistence and sale at local markets. The number of crops which they are able to take in a year varies from one to three, depending on the extent and duration of the inundation of plots, large areas of the floodplain disappearing under water from a few weeks to several months during the monsoon. At this time many people turn to fishing to supply some of their food. A few persons, largely Hindu of low *jele* caste, are full-time or 'professional' fishermen, although their numbers have been decreasing of late with extensive disruptions to the hydrological cycle, notably with the construction of flood protection devices. They have joined the human flood of dispossessed persons who eke out an existence day labouring, pulling rickshaws, petty trading and so on in towns and rural areas.

Recent strategy documents for environmental management and agricultural extension indicate that the Government of Bangladesh is increasingly interested in seeing some attention given to indigenous knowledge, particularly as it relates to natural resources management. The National Environmental Management Action Plan (1995) includes in its recommended actions on land resources: "study on indigenous

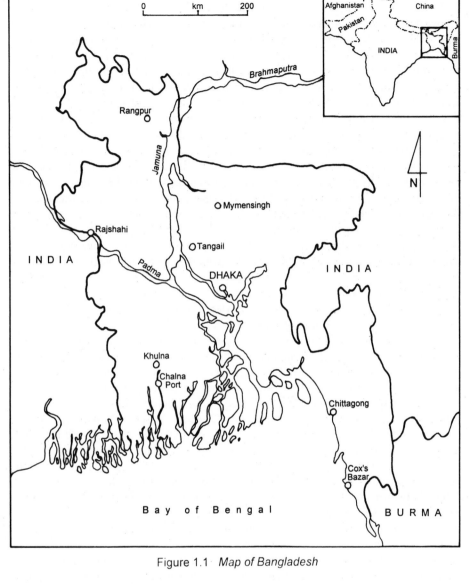

Figure 1.1 *Map of Bangladesh*

land use practices, to increase efficiency of the production system and its application". The New Agricultural Extension Policy (1996) states further that: "It is recognised that farmers' own Indigenous Technical Knowledge is often environmentally sustainable, and efforts should be made to support and learn from farmers, as well as the formal research system", going on that "The New Agricultural Extension Policy also recognises that farmers themselves are actively engaged in their own experimentation, as part of their daily agricultural lives. Efforts to learn from and strengthen such informal research should be made". These sentiments are expressed by many of the contributors to this book. It is clearly an opportune time for us to advance on indigenous knowledge work in the context of development initiatives in the country.

Indigenous technical knowledge

A widespread assumption among scientists and many others is that indigenous knowledge research comprises investigations into local technologies, and associated knowledge of natural resources and their management; for example boats and gears used in fishing and freshwater management, or ploughs and ladders used in farming and crop agronomy. Two recent books on indigenous practices in Bangladesh are excellent examples of this perspective (Bangladesh Academy of Agriculture 1997; Sharma 1998), which a colleague has dubbed the '100 useful indigenous how-to-do tips' approach. The Bangladesh Academy of Agriculture (1997) volume is a model compedium of technologies from around the country divided into sections according to crop production, livestock, fisheries and forestry, comprehensively described with illustrations. The Sharma (1998) volume describes fifty-two techniques and associated tools employed by tribal people in watershed management in the country's eastern hilltracts region. The contribution of Mallick (chapter 6), a review of the literature on Bangladeshi indigenous knowledge, is an good example of this approach, as a compendium of practices pertaining to crop cultivation, fisheries and livestock, and local environmental management. Other contributors give further examples, such as Quddus (chapter 7) who details several indigenous agroforestry practices, Shah and Nuri (chapter 12) on seed storage, and Begum, Haq and Naher (chapter 13) with their inventory of medicinal plant uses. This technologically framed approach has recently become called an 'indigenous technical knowledge' (ITK) perspective, to distinguish it from more culturally encompassing 'indigenous knowledge' (IK).

The definition of indigenous knowledge research in development is not easy. It is a new and fast moving field of enquiry which, in the process of establishing itself, is trying out different approaches to find its proper home. Several of the contributions to this volume address the issue of definition and attempt to clarify the field, and it would be presumptuous to attempt a brief definition in this introduction. It is still open to debate, as some of the coming chapters show. The contribution of Mustafa (chapter 3) is largely a discussion of definition and ensuing methodological issues, and my piece (chapter 19) attempts to move the debate forwards by situating it in the context of a continuum extending from local people to natural scientists. The many terms currently used for indigenous knowledge in development discourse reflect this fluidity (Purcell 1998; Antweiler 1998). The majority of these terms — such as folk, indigenous, peoples', local knowledge and so on — feature as synonyms, and do not clearly specify different fields of enquiry or approaches. They are used confusedly, largely in attempts to achieve political correctness, as writers seek a term that allows them to distinguish between 'other' knowledge and science without implying inferiority. But the distinction between these and terms that specify technology, such as 'indigenous technical knowledge', does not rest on small semantic differences of the sort that fuel many academic debates. The contribution of Miah (chapter 2) offers a good definition of indigenous technical knowledge. When it started to find a place on the development agenda a decade or so ago, indigenous knowledge was interpreted in this narrow technical way, but now wider cultural contextualisation is increasingly recognised as necessary. There is a profound difference (Sillitoe 1998*d*). But this is not to decry interest in local technical issues, which is better than no interest and to be encouraged.

The attraction of technical matters to scientists, including Bangladeshi scientists working in local floodplain communities or hill tract villages, is understandable. They mirror their own disciplines' technically informed approaches to environmental problems. A forester will feel comfortable with agroforestry practices, an aquacultural-ist with fisheries knowledge, a soil scientist with fertility management and so on. It reflects their own specialised reductive training and compartmentalisation of the world. Several of the papers in this volume illustrate this point well, for example Rahman (chapter 8) is clearly comfortable with tree diseases, Rahman, Khisa, Uddin and Wilcock (chapter 10) with botanical catalogues, and Islam, Reihlen and Thompson (chapter 15) focus on the concerns of fisheries scientists. They feel secure in identifying local practices that parallel their own subject areas of expertise and matching them up with their disciplinary understanding and expectations (Sinclair and Walker 1998). It is familiar and they do not feel deprived of their expert status. One of the problems with this approach is that it is what anthropologists call ethnocentric, that is the investigator uses a preconceived model of the world to access and structure others' ideas, even to assess them. And there is a particular danger that 'strong' heavily deductive scientific models will overwhelm 'weak' more inductive local ones, which may be ajudged inadequate when an inappropriate scientific yardstick is applied to them.

It is not only scientists who are beguiled by the narrow indigenous technical knowledge approach to local natural resource management issues, but also many other Bangladeshis involved in development work, policymakers, aid agency staff, extensionists, NGO personel, and so on. The interest that many of these people evince in indigenous knowledge may in part be interpreted as motivated by concerns that are the polar opposite of scientists' interest in it. We have a contradiction of the kind so familiar to Asian philosophy with its interest in the mediation of opposites. Coming to terms with paradoxes is a recurring theme in indigenous knowledge documentation, which should recommend it to Bengali thinkers. Scientists would argue that while their disciplinary specialisms may be narrow, they have contributed to the devising of technological advances that have furthered food production, people's health and so on. The application of these advances is the rationale behind many development programmes. But these development interventions, driven by a largely materialistic Western view of human advancement, albeit in the context of South Asia's complex modernity (Bose and Jalal 1998), are a threat to the integrity of Bengali culture. Threats of this kind have been evident since at least the start of Western colonialism, and were varyingly contained throughout South Asia (Chaudhuri 1998), but they have become progressively more overwhelming, until now, with the identification of the process as globalisation (Waters 1998), many people perceive of them as accelerating juggernaut-like out of control, indiscriminantly crushing cultural differences.

Protecting culture

The perception that Bengali culture is under threat promotes the idea that it needs protection. It is the material possessions of people that change rapidly and most obviously when what they perceive of as more efficient imported technology becomes available. It is what development is all about after all, facilitating such changes and increasing the material standard of peoples' lifestyles. They swop draught ploughs and ladders for mechanical cultivators, earthernware pots for alluminium vessels, large nylon drift nets for locally made fishing devices, and so on. These adopted technologies in turn result in changes in working practices, the manner in which villagers organise themselves to work and the nature of their co-operative arrangements, which in their turn again have wider social implications, perhaps changing the content of relations within extended families, between landlords and sharecroppers, and so on. The social changes take longer to have effect, although they are arguably the more significant in the long term, heralding some changes in peoples' values about life. The technological changes are frequently dramatic, one can see that the use of traditional muscle powered irrigation technology for example has declined markedly in the space of a decade or so with the introduction of diesel pump shallow and deep tube wells.

One way to protect the perceived loss of cultural heritage is to document it. This is a significant incentive in Bangladesh currently for the interest evinced in indigenous techncial knowledge. Several of this book's papers voice this sentiment; Mallick (chapter 6) laments the loss of valuable folkways and the need to save them, arguing that indigenous knowledge research has a role to play here, likewise Quddus (chapter 7), Rahman *et al.* (chapter 10), Zuberi (chapter 14) and Naseem (chapter 18) all talk about indigenous knowledge being lost and the urgent obligation on us to document it. The promotional literature for the Bangladesh Resource Centre for Indigenous Knowledge (BARCIK 1998) catches these sentiments well. It notes that "Today, because of its oral tradition as well as the introduction of new technologies, the preservation of indigenous knowledge is at risk. It has also been eroded by different cultural perversions ... because much indigenous knowledge has never been documented, it is being forgotten as it is replaced by modern education and technology. It is not only important but a much felt need to preserve the indigenous knowledge before they are lost forever". The solution is obvious, these outside induced corrosions must be combatted, and one way is to record knowledge and practices before people forget them. As the Bangladesh Resource Centre for Indigenous Knowledge flyer goes on to explain, the Centre has been established "with a view to preserve, document and for dissemination of indigenous knowledge in the fields of agriculture, environment conservation, food preparation and other development arenas". It is not only Banglas who think this way, but also some Bideshi foreigners working in their country; for example a piece that I was asked to write for a UK Department for International Development publication was retitled by the editor, without any reference to me, "Preserving Indigenous Knowledge" (Sillitoe 1997)!

There are marked parallels here with nineteenth century assumptions and the emergence of anthropology. The rate of change observed among some recently colonised peoples suggested to the Victorians that their cultures were disappearing at an alarming rate. For example one hundred years ago Hunt observed in the *Journal of the Anthropological Institute* "My own experience, gained by ten year's residence in Polynesia and New Guinea, it that the advent of the white man is invariably followed by the gradual extinction of the native race. Unintentionally, perhaps, but none the less certainly, the white man carries with him wherever he goes, causes which ultimately destroy the native population" (1899:18). It became a priority to some scientists, missionaries, and travellers among others, to document this disappearing human heritage before it was too late, and they embarked on what has subsequently become called salvage ethnography. For example, in the same volume of the *Journal of the Anthropological Institute* Cooke reported on the Central Hill Tribes of India "They had lived for countless ages in a state of comparative isolation; it was clear that their origin and distribution suggested a most interesting series of ethnological problems ... . It was obvious, too, that if their social polity and creeds deserved enquiry, no time should be wasted. As the newspaper and Board School are playing havoc with our native folk-lore, so the Hindu missionary, the ascetic, like the Jogi and Sannyâsi, were gradually bringing them within the Brâhmanic fold, and it was certain that before long much that was interesting and characteristic would be utterly lost" (1899:220). Some of the most thorough ethnographic records that we have date from this time. In some places technology and material culture were among the more accessible topics to study, where disruption to the pre-contact lifestyle was so extensive that many aspects of it, such as rituals, ceremonies, warfare and so on, were discontinued. Reduced to relying on what people could recall, sometimes from a previous generation, fieldworkers could find examples of handicrafts (in museums, private collections etc.) and discuss their manufacture, use and symbolism.

We have come to realise that the outcome of the overwhelming change induced during colonial contact was not cultural annihilation. Human reactions have proved far more complex, their cultural responses more flexible, extending an unexpected resilience in the climate of change. A Hopi artist in a recent Survival International[1] brochure (1998:8, 13) observes "Watching a dance .... I thought 'so we're dying are we?' I first heard that when I was two, now I'm 44. People think of the dances as ancient, but in fact they are as contemporary as the jets flying overhead .... We are on a continuum". A Makah filmmaker further catches these sentiments when she observes "I hope we can get to the point where we don't have to be the frozen images of the past". The cultures of the Navaho, Eskimo, Aborigine, Zulu and so on have not 'died out'. They have changed. But there is nothing new in this, societies have been changing for all time. If this was not so, we should never have ventured from our palaeolithic caves to today's skyscrappers. The salvage image encourages stone age misconceptions.

Identity and indigenous knowledge

The tendency to see indigenous knowledge research as saving cultural property from being lost may be related to deep-rooted identity issues in a world perceived to be changing rapidly and in undesireable ways in some respects. While ethnic identities and cultural traditions persist, they do so under constantly and increasingly fast changing circumstances. This was recently conveyed to me during a visit to a friend's house in Dhaka, sitting watching the TV with his daughters who, indoors, were *purdah* free and relaxed, when to their amusement an American musical show came on featuring near naked dancers. The hilarity was not the reaction I expected, feeling somewhat embarrassed, and then it struck me that with global communications the same programme might be watched with quite different reactions, as it meets with different local circumstances in the American mid-West, the Australian outback and African savanna, viewed by US wheat farmers, Aborigines and Masai pastoralists. But when they reflect on these trends some people feel a sense of threat to their own cultural identity: public displays of nudity do not sit well with the tradition of the veil.

We have another intriguing paradox of the kind beloved by Eastern philosophy. People are embracing aspects of Western driven globalisation, particularly evident in the adoption of material things such as TVs, vehicles, PCs, and clothing, iconised in the ubiquitous baseball cap and coke can, which imply exposure, particularly via mass media, to alien lifeways and values. Yet simultaneously they wish to protect what they perceive of as their distinctive cultural heritage, expressed in dances, language ceremonies, ethnic dress and so on.[2] Identity is a concern of human-beings the world over, and there is a fast growing literature on identity and boundaries (Cohen 1994; Woodward 1997). In the Pacific region, for instance, it is common to hear people talk about *kastom*, which derives from the English word 'custom'. While *kastom* appears to exemplify persistence, it is in fact a reponse to social change, it relates the old to the new and as such is a paradoxical blend of convention and invention (Keesing 1992; Foster 1995). It marks a concern to cling to certain traditional ways, for example ceremonial exchanges of wealth, dances, songs and rituals, even sometimes to rediscover or reinvent them, to counter outside influences. When people talk about *kastom* they have in mind something which we can gloss as traditional lore, that is following practices that originate from their own cultural tradition and rooted in their value system as opposed to deriving from elsewhere. People want the best of both worlds, access to cash and material prosperity without the loss of culture and customary rights, aspirations which riddle *kastom* with contradictions. It is an ambiguous notion, demanding sympathetic, and frequently multi-layered and even contradictory, contextual interpretation. Sometimes it is used locally, others regionally and occasionally nationally to differentiate kin, neighbours and strangers, to demarcate boundaries, to lay claim to rights, and assert cultural autonomy.

In the quest for *kastom* we can identify parallels with Bengali interest in indigenous technical knowledge, both relate to people's search for, and defence of identity in the contemporary world. Several of the papers in this volume evidence sympathy with this quest. The review of the indigenous knowledge literature relevant to Bangladesh by Mallick (chapter 6) reflects the theme, as do Zaman (chapter 4) and Begum *et al.* (chapter 13). These apprehensions relate to present concerns, not historical ones to turn the clock back to the stone age or whatever epoch. These customary declarations often feature cultural revivalism and reclamation. They sometimes involve idealisation of the pre-colonial past. They may promote a view that is too romantic. This is evident in another part of the world known well to myself, and many emigrant Bangladeshis too. In England we have people promoting a particularly rosy view of rural life in the past, with morris dancers, craft fairs and folk museums, of communities featuring the local public house, village cricket and church services. It is an industry no less, supported by institutions such as the National Trust and English Heritage, and while partially pandering to tourist expectations, it features a strong element of cultural identity, defining and protecting Englishness against outside threat, one of which is perceived to be a large immigrant population, including the Londonis from Bangladesh (Gardner 1995; Stolke 1995; Grillo 1998).

These overly positive views are a distortion. In many respects life was hard. The indigenous technology and practices — of Bangladesh, England or wherever — associated with hand-scythe harvesting, cattle-drawn tillage, transportation of straw bales on the head and so on, involves heavy and tiring labour. Life is not only hard but also insecure. Before inorganic fertilisers, biocide sprays, mechanical irrigation and so on yields were considerably less and more erratic, and the spectre of famine more common. We have another Eastern brain-teaser of an opposition which we have to try and resolve to come to some operable definition and understanding of indigenous knowledge research. This knowledge harks back to difficult conditions, echoed in queries about returning to the stone age. It is unclear, particularly to many scientists, how such knowledge might feature in development to improve peoples' lives. And yet others are urging its consideration, as in this book.

One counter argument is that indigenous knowledge may include some valuable wisdom that could prove useful in unforseen ways. Shah and Townsley (chapter 17) offer a good example from local aquaculture. A spur to this work is the fear that the introduced technologies, such as the high yielding varieties of rice and associated husbandry practices, may not prove sustainable, even that they are currently damaging the environment, and will need to be reversed. The theme of sustainability informs several of the contributions to this book. Some commentators, such as Zaman (chapter 4), Miah (chapter 2) and Naseem (chapter 18), foresee serious problems in Bangladesh with its expanding population and evidence that the yields of high yielding rice varieties may prove unsustainable. Other problems mentioned by these and other writers include loss of plant genetic material and biodiversity, which can impact particularly hard on the poor, as Stokoe (chapter 11) points out for women and Zuberi (chapter 14) for herbal healers, and declining soil fertility and increasing dependence on inorganic inputs to keep yields up, as I mention (chapter 19). Some fear that a disaster could occur, Zaman for example urging us to learn from history and the collapse of South Asian civilisations in antiquity. The indigenous techncial knowledge needs to be there for people to fall back on, if the the environmental disaster some people fear comes to pass.

Insiders' versus outsiders' knowledge

It is understandable that Bangladeshi researchers should see indigenous knowledge in terms of material culture, technology and associated practices that symbolise something of their Bengaliness, reflecting their own, commonly unspoken concerns, with identity in an increasingly global community. There is a further dimension regarding this subjective tendency that relates to the attraction of the narrow indigenous technical knowledge focus. The inclination to see indigenous issues in these terms may relate in part to these comprising the Bengali commentators own culture. It is an anthropological tenet that it takes outsiders to see things from a holistic perspective, to put them in their broad anthropological context. According to some, anthropological research can only be undertaken by outsiders. It is one of the few defining features of the discipline. An Englishman working in Cornwall or an American in Kentucky are sociologists, unlike a Chinaman in Cornwall or a Pakistani in Kentucky, who are anthropologists. It is a moot point how wide the cultural difference should be between investigator and investigated, but some would argue that an American in Cornwall or Chinaman in Japan would not be anthropologists either because their cultural backgrounds would be too similar to the people among whom they work.

Whatever the status of this unresolved distinction between anthropology and sociology, it is thought that persons view their own culture in different ways to other cultures, that in some senses, as members of it, they are unable to see the 'cultural wood for the personal trees', to distinguish aspects of the collective from their individual experience. In other words, a great deal of what is relevant to understanding a society is too obvious to insiders, who take it for granted as part of their daily lives. It is tacit knowledge. Mustafa (chapter 3) makes some interesting observations about the methodological implications of this and related issues, and the contribution of Dixon, Barr and Sillitoe (chapter 20) likewise has some relevant methodological points. Furthermore, some issues may be beyond questioning for members of a culture; for example, many Bangladeshis would be unwilling to critique their Islamic beliefs and practices in their investigations, holding them sacred and beyond enquiry, even thinking that the idea is blasphemous. Ahmed's contribution (chapter 23) illustrates this point, relating his conflict with a local *imam*, who perceived in indigenous knowledge research a challenge to his religious authority. Islamic beliefs undeniably comprise a central part of Bangladeshi society and from an anthropological perspective cannot be overlooked without distorting overall understanding. It is consequently difficult to situate indigenous technical knowledge in cultural context; members see it from the point of view of their own concerns as members of the society, namely as something to symbolise their threatened Bengali identity.

The narrow notion of 'indigenous technical knowledge', presenting it as culturally disembodied technical knowledge, is dubious. And if the separation of knowledge from the human milieu where created, reproduced and manipulated is questionable, it is doubly dubious to isolate technical information from its cultural context and attempt to match it with Western scientific concepts. In this regard, narrow interpretations of indigenous knowledge, as in the study of the modifications that local people make to introduced technologies, need to be treated with care. Some of the papers in this volume take this restricted view, such as Mazumder, Samina and Islam (chapter 16) who consider how people accomodate to interventions in openwater fisheries and modify introduced aquaculture technology to fit their management regimes, and Rahman (chapter 8) in his account of tree diseases. National scientists involved in development work, Bengalis or whoever, need to beware because the distorted understanding that results may not only promote inappropriate interventions, but also falls into the trap of accepting Western society's and science's definition of development. We find people caught in another paradox. On the one hand they are unable in some senses culturally to contextualise local knowledge because it is a part of their heritage, and yet in failing to do so they are acceding a dominant role to western science. They are falling in with their western scientific education at the expense of allowing expression to their own cultural reality. Ultimately they are furthering development not as a partnership, but as an imposed process continuing Western hegemony.

When decoupled from its socio-cultural context, local knowledge can fall prey to ambiguous science-like representation, which encourages focussing on those aspects thought to mirror science and technology and likely to prove amenable to further manipulation. The conceptual framework of western science and development discourse come to define it. This is seen in the selection of knowledge to reflect our disciplinary distinctions and interests, as in its ordering according to ethnosciences that reflect scientific subjects, such as ethnopedology, ethnobotany or ethnozoology. We see this in some of the papers here, for instance those of Rahman *et al.* (chapter 10), Begum *et al.* (chapter 13) and Islam *et al.* (chapter 15), all are good examples of ethnoscientific accounts, with accompanying catalogues of plants and fish. In this approach the information implicitly becomes a construction of western-trained professionals, claiming to act in the interests of local populations, whereas the status of this knowledge may be different from a local viewpoint. Like any other scientists, Bangladeshi ones need beware of misinterpreting indigenous knowledge. It is mistaken to recodify and interpret it scientifically. If science sets the parameters, it will isolate for analysis specific resource use practices from the broader circumstances that critically inform them, whether agroforestry, crop manipulation, water management, erosion control or whatever. Outsiders decide what is relevant, not those who possess the knowledge.

The imposition of our scientific categories and technological priorities not only threatens to misrepresent knowledge, but also to limit analysis by predisposing us to think certain issues important and to overlook others that may be significant to local understanding and experience (Hobart 1993). Taking knowledge out of cultural context threatens both to misrepresent and devalue it. The 'indigenous technical knowledge' formulation, implying universality, overlooks unique features of particular local knowledge traditions. It defines as irrelevant some issues that might crucially inform others' environmental understandings, notably the non-empirical such as ritual, social and symbolic formulations. It is necessary to accommodate to the notion of the 'cultural construction of the environment', that culture informs understanding of the natural world (Croll and Parkin 1992). People may codify and store the intelligence amassed by their cultures over many generations of trial-and-error in ways alien to science. Indigenous knowledge can be a complex of contexts, and may incorporate supernatural, cosmological, everyday technical, socio-political, and kin factors. The farmers' approach is more holistic, and may reflect wider socio-cultural and economic issues, distinguishing resources according to various uses and associations. The contribution of Islam *et al.* (chapter 15) illustrates this well for fish classification, and Stokoe (chapter 11) illustrates it for wild vegetable resources, prominent in the diet of many poor families. Some of these issues and practices, being local, culturally relative and context specific, may limit the wider use of indigenous knowledge in the development of generic technologies. The implication is not that it is irrelevant and has no value.

The assumption that there exist definable bodies of knowledge independent of socio-cultural context is unacceptable from an anthropological perspective. Understanding is flawed, abstracting knowledge from the milieu that generates and sustains it, giving it meaning in use. This approach is open to the same criticisms as topdown development theory for over-simplifying and generalising complex local problems (Hobart 1993; Fardon 1995), instead of promoting an in-depth appreciation of other people's ideas about their environments and natural resource management, thought necessary for appropriate development interventions. Any indigenous technical knowledge emerges from a particular culturally informed world view, it is a local cultural construction. This is evident with fishing on the Bangladeshi floodplain. It is all very well to give an account of Bengali fishing nets and techniques, but if you overlook to situate the use of this technology within the socio-political and historical context of rights of access to waterbodies like *beel* and *hoar*, and the marginalised position of minority Hindu fisher groups, any understanding of fishing practices will be totally compromised. You will fail to comprehend why certain persons use certain techniques and not others, when they employ them and why, as Shah and Townsley (chapter 17) show. Consideration of these wider issues leads us onto political matters, among others, which critically condition understanding of indigenous technical knowledge, and lie at the root of many of development's problems in attempting to assist the poorest of the poor. Wealthy large landowners frequently monopolise access to the waterbodies that remain stocked with fish after the monsoon floods recede, commonly employing illegal methods to intimidate local fishermen. Fishing is certainly not a case simply of the correct tackle and boats, and knowledge of how to deploy them to best effect.

Politics and indigenous knowledge

The employment of indigenous practices, even their reinvention, to assert cultural identity is common around the world, and may easily shade off into politically motivated acts; as evidenced for example in recent newspaper reports of Makah Indians of the U.S. Pacific coast reviving their traditional seasonal whale hunt after seventy years in abeyance, both to assert their spiritual heritage but also to challenge the global whaling ban with all its commercial implications (Langton 1998). The political dimensions of indigenous knowledge predictably pose further contradictions and anomalies. The implications of politically contextualising knowledge brings up another possible point regarding the attractiveness of the narrow concept of indigenous technical knowledge to Bangladeshi researchers.

Many of those currently interested in indigenous knowledge research, including some academics, still have farming connections through their families and own land in Bangladesh, some of them owning considerable areas by local standards. They may not wish to contextualise indigenous technical knowledge with regards to the wider society as wealthy absentee large landowners. If they can restrict interest to technical knowledge, which is relatively neutral and harmless, and frequently perceived not to have much development potential, even be regressive in some minds with its 'stone age' implications, this can serve to protect their vested interests. If they venture into the wider socio-political domain they will have to deal with the unequal political relations that characterise Bengali rural society, which the national researchers, as relatively privileged and 'wealthy' members of their society relative to peasant farmers, would rather avoid and keep off the agenda. They may not do this consciously, for many of these persons are well-meaning and would like to do something to improve the lot of their fellow poor countrymen. But few would contemplate doing so at the expense of their own families' comfort and security. Zaman (chapter 4) has some sharp observations to make on these political issues, talking about the need for a revolution to overthrow the pernicious hierarchical aspects of Bangla society which cast rural peasants as only one up from beggars and the destitute (Sen and Dréze 1999).

These comments also bear on the self-evident, but often overlooked point that local communities are variable in their composition and not homogenous (Scoones and Thompson 1994). This raises some interesting methodological challenges, namely how we should access and document this individually variable knowledge, as Mustafa (chapter 3) comments in his contribution. The chapters by Stokoe (chapter 11), Shah and Nuri (chapter 12) and Begum *et al.* (chapter 13) illustrate the gender dimensions to this variability in their discussions of wild vegetables, seed storage and medicinal plants respectively, which are largely female domains. The paper by Islam *et al.* (chapter 15) intimates the variability in fisheries and aquatic ecology knowledge both within and between communities. And the contribution of Barr and Sillitoe (chapter 21) suggests a way forwards methodologically to handle this variability using the rapidly developing qualitative database sofware now available.

These political realities illustrate the point made above about members of a society having difficulty undertaking an anthropological investigation of it. They have too many vested interests. It also vindicates the argument that we need to situate technical knowledge in the wider social context to understand it. Ahmed (chapter 23) explores some of the issues, casting his argument in terms of current postmodern critiques of representation and subjectivity. The dimension of power relations raises a further methodological point regarding national researchers engaging in indigenous knowledge work. This relates to the danger of creating national gatekeepers, controlling access to, and interpretation of, indigenous knowledge. These persons will have entrenched interests as members of the society studied and will naturally further these, albeit perhaps unconsciously, if well-meaning persons. They will be tempted to direct development assistance to their own ends. Our experience in Bangladesh suggests that this may be quite blatant. The consultancy culture for example is entrenched among relatively wealthy Bangla university and research institute staff, who expect to receive a generous daily allowance on top of their salaries for any contribution to aid-funded projects. And sometimes their contributions are minimal. Such as the institute staff who, on a trip searching for a field research location, did nothing other than enjoy a chaffeured day out looking at the countryside. Or the corner-cutting scientist who conducted a survey from the verandah of a field house, taking it easy and ordering villagers to bring him material from their fields. They made a mockery of the research while pocketing the money.

These episodes suggest that considerable communication problems may occur between collaborators, as is common in interdisciplinary work, presenting indigenous knowledge research with a further range of methodological problems, as Dixon *et al.* (chapter 20) discuss. These problems may be exacerbated by different cultural expectations, one's graft maybe another's fair recompense. They also suggest attitudes towards poor farmer-fishers, which South Asian hierarchical cultural values may again promote, that could seriously hinder indigenous knowledge research. The contribution of Mahbub Alam (chapter 22) graphically illustrates from an anthropological viewpoint how these can interfere with ethnographic fieldwork. And Naseem (chapter 18) has some observations from the other side, as a natural scientist. The high status that they report some scientists assume, and their dismissive attitudes towards indigenous knowledge, suggest the need for urgent re-education. This is one of the aims of this book. In the light of these comments, we have to ask ourselves some difficult questions. What percentage of internationally donated aid money can we justify going to relatively wealthy national scientists, legitimately to fund their research work (travel costs, laboratory expenses etc.), and what returns should we expect on the investment? These monies would support, to put them in perspective, a considerable number of desperately poor families, the target beneficiaries of aid agencies, and raise their standard of living above starvation. These comments illustrate the difficult issues that come up when we follow the dictate of indigenous knowledge research, as advocated here, and put our enquiries into wider socio-cultural context. But they are issues, however uncomfortable, that we should debate to advance the development research agenda. And the foreigner Bideshi researchers and administrators are caught up in the power plays too. They are also comfortably off, coming from wealthy nations. And they need in-country partners, who will only collaborate if the personal renumeration is right, and so collude in meeting their demands.

Starting from the apparently unexceptionable premise that indigenous knowledge and practices should inform development, we are led to question the very foundations of development. Who should be making decisions about the proper distribution of limited assistance and resources? International agencies contribute them and expect to maintain some control over their use; it would anger English tax payers and politicians to hear that funds are going to the wealthy, not poor people. But Bangladeshis understandably wish to have control over what happens in their own country. Again we have another contradiction, of the kind that politicians regularly wrangle over. Indigenous knowledge research cannot act as awkward commentator alone, it is caught up too. The outsider definition of anthropology given above raises important methodological issues regarding interference. Outsiders prying into others' lives relates to issues of power relations of the kind that have recently lead to a growing Asian critique of the Western driven notion of development. By what right do outsiders come and enquire into others' lives? Ahmed's reflections (chapter 23) bear on this question. It is one that indigenous knowledge research has to address, not only in Bangladesh but worldwide, because associated with development it implies, more so than academic anthropology, facilitating some interference in peoples' lives. Should this research be undertaken by invitation only, and if so, whose invitation (national or regional government, local community or headman)?

Asian philosophy and development

In response to these anomalies and conflicts an Asian reappraisal of development is evident, informed both by Eastern philosophy and world views (Dallmayr 1996*a*) and contemporary orientalist and postmodern debates (Said 1993). The Bengali interest in indigenous technical knowledge might further be interpreted as unwitting support of this critique. It focuses on quintessentially Bengali things, such as fishing nets and traps, the use of plough and ladder in rice cultivation, and so on, which may symbolise Asian lifestyle and values. These may serve as a rallying point to fend off undesireable aspects of development imposed interventions. It gives a political aspect to the assertion of identity. The association of Bangladeshi material culture with political identity is direct, parties regularly using ploughs (Jatio Party), boats (Awame League), ladders (minority parties), sickles (Communist Parties) rice (Bangladesh Nationalist Party), vendor's scales (Jamet Party) and so on, as readily recognisable symbols to illiterate peasants during campaigning and at elections.

We have a questioning of the Western notion of development. There are parallels with the ideas of cultural revival that featured in Asian and African nationalist struggles, and likewise they invite interpretation as symbolic discourse expressing anti-colonial, and more recently anti-development sentiments. While the recent power discourse in the West may inform this critique (which has attracted left wingers as the shortcomings of marxism have become evident — Escobar 1995; Fergusson 1994; Nabudere 1997; Nederveen Pieterse 1998), it is taking on a decidely Asian perspective. It is not advocating a return metaphorically or otherwise to the stone age, but creating space for the expression of Asian views, with their roots in an ancient philosophical tradition. The emergence of this critique further vindicates the indigenous knowledge movement's insistence on setting problems in cultural context, which includes historical context. In going beyond indigenous technical knowledge we have also to consider the social and intellectual history of Bengal. This includes centuries of written history and reflection, which indigenous knowledge research needs to access, with all its methodological implications (research to-date occurring exclusively through inter-views and oral history, as illustrated by the many contributions to this volume).

The commitment for which this Asian critique is calling has a moral and spiritual quality, a concern for social relationships and experiential reality, not only academic enquiry and debate. We should be participating in the world of which we are a part, not merely commenting on it. Advocates talk in terms of political commitment, as a manifestation of love and wish to transform reality, not as a quest for power. They view development as a monolithic imposition by the West on the Rest, the Western idea of knowledge being used to steamroller a uniform world (Kothari 1988; Sachs 1992; Hobart 1993; Mehmet 1995). It is about power. The occidental tradition of science and technology puts humans at the centre of creation and encourages us to use our knowledge to advance our power and domination over everything: nature, other humans, the universe. The Western modernist framework dominates the quest for knowledge, setting a narrowly utilitarian corrosive agenda motivated largely by materialistic objectives, assumptions and values, driven by capricious market forces. It crushes 'alternative traditions of thinking about knowledge, for instance, knowledge being concerned with understanding, love and selfless devotion to humanity. The modernist framework of knowledge alienates the man of knowledge from the wider social and cosmic reality' (Giri 1997:6).

But there is an alternative view. Asian authors talk of knowledge traditions, such as their own, which search for enlightenment and liberation, not control and domination. They are holistic and allow for pluralities of knowledge as opposed to 'annihilating universalism' (see Uphoff 1996a who contrasts Western 'and/or' thinking with Asian 'both and'concepts). The brief contribution by Lalon (chapter 9), an NGO worker involved with the health of the poor, gives an inkling of this tradition. These writers are mindful of philosophies that accept contradictions, indeed welcome them as part of the human condition, and look to pluralistic traditions that embrace these such as the Hindu pantheon with its many *avatar* manifestations of the single god. The cultural heritage of these writers makes them deeply unhappy with the Cartesian duality of subject and object that has until recently informed science. They argue for its dissolution, for us to realise that human beings and the world comprise part of a single universe. The goal is moral and ethical, to transcend the self for humanity, while not denying that knowledge contributes to empowerment (Das 1995). They cite the *bhakti* spiritual tradition of India where knowledge is sought to serve the world in a spirit of devotion.

A central characteristic of the Asian world view is the oneness of everything, its experience as a unity of mutually interrelated phenomena and events. In everyday life we are blind to this unity, necessarily dividing our experiences up, as in reductionist science, according to things and events in order that we can manage our daily lives and the world around us. The flaw is to mistake these intellectual and operational abstractions as fundamental aspects of reality. We need to conceive of these discriminations as relative within all-encompassing unity. According to this view, the distinctions that comprise opposites are relative, intellectual constructs that originate in thought. We cannot accomodate this relativity in our normal state of consciousness. The experience of reality beyond opposites requires freeing of the mind from the rigid divisions of conventional logic, allowing it to flow constantly and seamlessly. The *sadhu* transcend these abstractions in meditation to comprehend the unity of opposites, as Krishna says in the *Bhagavad Gita* to 'Be in truth eternal, beyond earthly opposites', a vivid experience. Life and death, hot and cold, happiness and despair, light and dark, male and female are extreme aspects of the same reality, not separate experiences, for one can only exist in contrast to the other. Revealing contradictions and accomodating them, as we have seen, features centrally in indigenous knowledge enquiries. We see how making space for others' perspectives, whether Muslim Bengalis or Hindus or whomever, can cast new light on problems. This should prove a major contribution of indigenous knowledge research to understanding, when released from narrow technical concerns and set in wider cultural context.

We also have here an inkling of the manner in which indigenous knowledge research, allowing a voice to other cultural traditions, may inform the redirection of

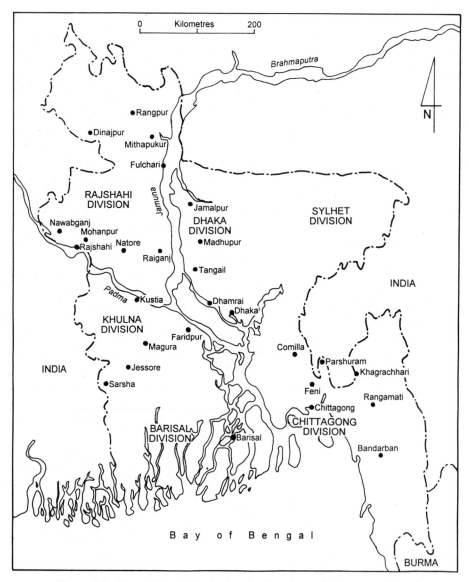

Figure 1.2 *Map of Bangladesh showing locations of places mentioned in this book*

development, as argued for in contemporary critiques. The complementarity and interdependence of opposites means that neither pole can achieve dominance — good cannot win over evil. Virtue is to achieve a dynamic tension between the poles, in their interplay (Bhaskar 1994). The balance of relations between the male and female poles of humanity serve as metaphors for the Asian critique of Western notions of development. In Eastern philosophical traditions there is a striving for a balance between female and male aspects, symbolised in androgynous Hindu art, depicting gods as on one side virile and on the other matronly and meeting in a serene union of both. This perspective is potentially subversive, for it is a short step to questioning the very assumptions of development, when thought to be manifestations of Western power. Other traditions of society and philosophies of life may disagree fundamentally about the propriety of development. The argument is that Western society, and hence development, over-emphasises the male, and hence rational thought, aggressive go-getting and competition, at the expense of the female, and intuitive wisdom, caring co-operation and gentleness. The occidental emphasis is sick, an unbalanced relationship between necessarily equally complementary opposites. The Eastern transcendental and Western scientific perspectives should complement one another, reflecting the rational and intuitive intellects. We cannot reduce one to the other, each leads to an entirely different comprehension of the world. Together they give a fuller and deeper understanding (Dallmayr 1996*b*). It is misguided to seek a synthesis, as one cannot be comprehended in the other. Instead the aim might be to seek a dynamic balance between rational analysis and mystic intuition, scientific enquiry and local wisdom. This is the objective of indigenous knowledge research in development. We should not strive to subsume local understanding into scientific analysis, but seek to opitimise the insights of both perspectives, aim for balance and synergy (Bhaskar 1986).

The message of the Asian critique is that we need to strive to get the balance right. There is a deeper reality behind the superficial appearance of day to day life. We are currently out of step. The rational scientific view that dominates our society and the development agenda is unhealthy, as manifest in the destruction and pollution of the natural environment, increasing social unrest and mindless violence, the emergence of strange new viruses and unhealthy living arrangements, both physical and social. The mechanistic and fragmented world view denies nature's complex harmony and wholeness at its peril. But to move towards a more dynamically balanced view will require an occidental socio-cultural revolution. It is to this that the oriental critique points. It indicates that the processes of development and globalisation should not be thought one way, an imposition of Western values on the rest, but a drawing on the combined strengths of different cultural traditions in this increasingly cosmopolitan world. This is the philosophy that informs the indigenous knowledge movement.

Conclusion

The centrality of contradictions and the resolution of opposites to Eastern philosophy puts these at the heart of Bengali identity. We are increasingly coming to realise that paradoxes characterise the development agenda too, as it seeks to facilitate participation and allow all voices to be heard, with focus groups, workshops and so on. These not only allow the expression of different stakeholder interests but also promote the accomodation of, sometimes conflicting and diametrically opposed views through equitable negotiation. Development is not a clear cut process as depicted in previous modernisation and dependency views, but a disparate and polytheistic one. We should perhaps be wrestling with the incorporation of the Asian perspective into development thinking, not only to ensure that the identity demands of millions of people are expressed but also to further the very notion of development, what it is and what it is trying to achieve. The need to face up to and try to resolve the tension inherent in the paradoxes that characterise development is clear in the movement to incorporate indigenous knowledge into development, which has an important contribution to make to this debate.

This introduction has argued that it is necessary to go beyond the narrow focus of 'indigenous technical knowledge' which currently dominates indigenous knowledge work in Bangladesh, to set local technology and resource management practices within wider socio-cultural context, to advance consideration of these in development programmes and better frame problems for enquiry. The comments on Asian philosophy intimate some of the implications. On the other hand, it is suggested that the emphasis on 'indigenous technical knowledge' is important for contributing to a needed sense of cultural identity and worth in the face of the development onslaught, and furthermore that it may lend support to the growing Asian critique of development, thus helping to advance our understanding of what development itself is all about. The argument is that we should both discourage and encourage work focussing on indigenous technical knowledge! Clearly we need to strive for some resolution, there is a call for the sort of balancing act central to Asian philosophy.

This volume is structured to reflect these intriguing tensions, and hopefully contribute something to their long-term accomodation in development programmes in Bangladesh. It introduces the field of indigenous knowledge research in development and current interest in it in Bangladesh, namely the indigenous technical knowledge focus, with a series of chapters that report on studies in this technological vein. The later contributions point the way beyond these technological studies by expanding on their definition of indigenous knowledge to encompass a more holistic approach with attendant methodological advances, looking to the future and the wider cultural contextualisng of indigenous knowledge research and the fuller integration of its potential into development.

Notes

1 An NGO based in the United Kingdom which represents the interests of tribal people worldwide.
2 While this paper emphasises the material side of identity, appropriate to current ideas about indigenous knowledge in Bangladesh, this is not to imply that these have some priority over other issues. Language, for example, has been a particularly emotive issue in defining Bangla identity, with the Language Movement and Ekushey martyrs through to the Independence War from Pakistan and Urdu domination.

Ackowledgements

I thank Sukanta Sen, on behalf of all participants, for acting as local organiser of the meeting from which this book originates, and Professor M.I. Zuberi for his support. For assistance with numerous editorial tasks, such as liasing locally with contributors, tracking down obscure references and so on, without which this volume would never have come into being, I thank VSO volunteers Ben Angell and Anna Miles, and Matt McLennan and Jane Stokoe who subsequently took over from them working in Dhaka with BARCIK helping to establish the indigenous knowledge network. I also thank my colleagues Julian Barr and Peter Dixon for their unfailing help throughout our work in Bangladesh. And as always, I thank my wife Jackie for her support in seeing this project through.

**PART 1   INDIGENOUS KNOWLEDGE AND
DEVELOPMENT ISSUES**

2 Indigenous Technical Knowledge: Unexplored Potential for Sustainable Development

Abdul Momen Miah

BANGLADESH IS A POOR and densely populated country with approximately 130 million on a land area of 147 570 sq. km. Thus land and other resources are limited. The majority of the population (86%) lives below the poverty line. The continuing population explosion exacerbates the rate of fragmentation of land holdings, resulting in increased numbers of small and marginal farmers and landless people. In 1973 the number of landless poor people comprised 29% of the population, today it has increased to 65% (Bangladesh Bureau of statistics 1998). The population explosion has created enormous social, economic, political and environmental problems. Today's poverty is the accumulated effect. The government, along with development agencies, has taken various steps to combat and alleviate poverty. For example, in agriculture and extension activities, it supports programmes seeking to increase production, to strengthen agricultural education, and to further research.

The country has made substantial progress towards achieving its goal of self-sufficiency in food production, made possible mainly as the result of using modern crops, agrochemicals, engineered irrigation and associated improved management practices. These new agricultural technologies in Bangladesh have been generated by various research organisations, and are transferred to the end users — usually the farmers — by extension agents. The increased agricultural output is essential for the alleviation of poverty as well as for national economic growth. The continuation and improvement of these intensive farming practices is considered necessary. However, continued use of high cost technology has aggravated the social imbalance of many farming communities. It has also resulted in increased pollution of the natural environment to the growing concern of those advocating sustainable agricultural development. Technological intervention in agriculture has exacerbated problems of sustainability (Farouk and Salam 1996). Yield declines are also occurring which are strongly associated with the length of time that intensive production has been practiced. A recent World Bank report found that the overall yield of rice has either stagnated or is in decline. According to several commentators, the possible causes of declining productivity include: nutrient imbalance due to improper use of inorganic fertilisers; concentration on high yielding modern crop varieties; increasing prevalence of multiple cropping; overuse of agrochemicals and inadequate use of organic manure. Policy makers, planners, researchers, educators, NGO activists and development donors are seeking ways to maintain the benefits of technological interventions on the one hand, while mitigating the resulting environmental degradation on the other. The issue of sustainable agricultural development is central.

'Sustainability' is a word that has different meanings for different people. It can be defined in two ways: either from a resource base focus emphasising conservation;

or from an output focus emphasising livelihood or development (Benbrook and Mallinckrodt 1994). "The resource base focus states that natural resources must not lose their capacity to produce, through depletion or pollution. The output focus states that productivity must not decrease" (Wilcock and English 1994). Resource base sustainability is linked to livelihood sustainability, although the relationship is not always clear. A pragmatic definition is given by Reijntjes *et al.* (1992): "... in the context of agriculture, sustainability basically refers to the capacity to remain productive while maintaining the resource base. The environment in a wider sense is uncertain and changing, and sustainability is the ability to survive that uncertainty. In an important sense, therefore, it is a preparation for the future, and it may never be possible to say that a system or community has become sustainable." Sustainability implies achieving satisfactory yields without threatening the environment and usually demands minimal use of external inputs. Firstly, high agricultural production needs to be maintained through the application of scientific technical knowledge, and secondly, the rate of environmental degradation needs to be minimised and kept within acceptable bounds. Increases in food production must be sustainable in the long term.

Efforts to achieve sustainable development in agriculture should take into account indigenous knowledge and technologies to reduce reliance on scientific technical knowledge. The potential of indigenous technical knowledge in the further development of agricultural production systems has recently been recognised (Sillitoe 1998*a*). It has tremendous potential for furthering sustainability. According to Warren (1991) "... indigenous knowledge is local knowledge — knowledge that is unique to a given culture or society. This knowledge is the information base for a society, it facilitates communication and decision making." Chowdhury *et al.* (1996) assert that "... indigenous people and farmers develop their location-specific knowledge and practices of agriculture, natural resource management, veterinary and human health care and many other subjects over centuries. This complex of knowledge, traditional beliefs and practices are generally known as indigenous or traditional knowledge." Indigenous technical knowledge comprises practices derived from past collective experience. It is the knowledge of people living in particular areas, which helps them to address life's problems. It is dynamic and changes through indigenous creativity and innovation, as well as through contact with other knowledge systems. When innovations are found appropriate to the local culture, they are incorporated into the main body of the knowledge system. If alterations and modifications prove non-sustainable they do not survive (Reijatjes *et al.* 1992). We may assume that most of the indigenous technical knowledge and practices of farmers are fundamentally sustainable. The dissemination of indigenous technical knowledge through extension is discussed by Sharland (1991) who states that "... the use of indigenous knowledge in extension therefore involves the recognition that indigenous knowledge is a combination of knowledge created indigenously, together with knowledge from outside. The outside knowledge is incorporated into the store of indigenous knowledge only if it is compatible and considered relevant by the traditional practitioners."

The existence of indigenous technical knowledge and its potential for development is still largely unexplored in Bangladesh. Few attempts have been made to document the indigenous technical knowledge heritage in different parts of the country (see Mallick, this volume). Chowdhury *et al.* (1996) identified two hundred examples of indigenous technical knowledge, practiced by both males and females of various farming tasks in crop production, fish culture, livestock and poultry management.

Islam (1996) cited one hundred examples of indigenous technical knowledge during a study conducted at Dinajpur. He found that farmers generally favoured the advance of indigenous technical knowledge in the development of agricultural production.

Innovations based on scientific technical knowledge have been widely adopted by resource-rich farmers but this has not been possible for resource-poor farmers, a larger segment of the rural population, who are dependent mostly on indigenous technical knowledge. Recently extension agencies have started to advocate the use of some selected indigenous technical knowledge by farmers to mitigate environmental degradation. The practices are many and examples include:

- the use of bamboo sticks or tree branches for insect control;
- the sprinkling of cattle urine or spreading of tobacco dust to control pests (nicotine is an effective insect repellent);
- the use of *neem* leaves with its active insecticide 'azadirachtin' and *Biskatali* leaves when storing seeds to deter insect attack;
- the laddering of standing wheat crops and pulling of ropes across rice/wheat fields early in the morning to moisten the soil with falling dew drops;
- the intercropping of garlic with potato;
- the use of ash in vegetable cultivation, which contains all essential minerals (in varying proportions) and adds to the water-holding capacity of the soil; and
- the application of poultry excreta to vegetable gardens to provide nitrates.

In ensuring that agricultural development is sustainable scientific technical knowledge should not be abandoned, but rather combined with appropriate indigenous technical knowledge. As Sillitoe (1998a: 225) points out, "The assumption is that our scientific tradition has something to contribute to the development process and that indigenous knowledge needs to be conveyed to scientists in such a way that they can appreciate its relevance." An example of this is provided by the National Agricultural Research System (NARS) in India, in collaboration with NGOs, who developed an integrated nutrient management system for crop production in Maharastra to increase and sustain crop productivity whilst also protecting the environment. The system was developed for resource-poor farmers who could not afford expensive agrochemicals in crop production. The system, a blend of scientifically generated technical knowledge with indigenous practices, is flexible in that it can adjust to agroclimatic changes as well as the variable socioeconomic conditions faced by farmers. We should aim to strengthen the potential of both scientific and indigenous technical knowledge by considering the following:

- we should encourage the identification, collection and documentation of indigenous technical knowledge before much of it is lost;
- research should be conducted to determine the performance potential of indigenous technical knowledge. Necessary modifications and improvements to indigenous technical knowledge should be made according to scientific findings and verified in different locations;
- a nation-wide awareness campaign should be instigated to warn people of the harmful consequences of injudicious use of scientific technical knowledge;
- the existing policies and strategies of extension agencies (governmental and NGOs) should be changed to emphasise sustainable issues, and the value of many centuries-old indigenous practices.

3 Towards an Understanding of Indigenous Knowledge

M. Millat-e-Mustafa

THIS CHAPTER PROVIDES a background to indigenous knowledge. It looks at various definitions and discusses how indigenous knowledge contrasts with scientific knowledge. The problems surrounding indigenous knowledge research are considered, notably the manner in which it varies between individuals. Indigenous knowledge is of local people, unique to their cultural heritage. It is increasingly recognised as a resource that should be mobilised to complement scientific knowledge, to promote appropriate plans and interventions for rural development programmes. The importance of involving farmers in the development process is now increasingly recognised by researchers and development professionals throughout the world in participatory approaches to development.

Indigenous knowledge is the knowledge held collectively by a defined community (Walker *et al.* 1991). The term 'indigenous' is synonymous with 'traditional' and 'local', differentiating this knowledge from that developed by formal science in institutions such as universities and government research centres. Warren and Cashman (1988) define indigenous knowledge as "... the sum of experience and knowledge of a given ethnic group that forms the basis for decision making in the face of familiar and unfamiliar problems and challenges".

Whilst distinguishing between indigenous and scientific knowledge is contentious, the principal difference according to Biggs and Clay (1981) is that "... the former concentrates on adaptation of knowledge and is less formal in both its social organisation and its research methods". Howes and Chambers (1980) suggest that "... scientific knowledge and indigenous knowledge may be contrasted and evaluated according to three criteria: as systems of classification, as systems of explanation and prediction and in terms of speed of accumulation". They go on to suggest that "... while indigenous knowledge and science are comparable with respect to the first criterion, science is generally superior with respect to the second and markedly so in respect to the third". Similarly, Walker *et al.* (1991) suggest that "... the differences between indigenous and scientific knowledge are not at a fundamental, conceptual level but in terms of formal structure, institutional framework, technical facility and ability and scale of perspective".

Attributes of indigenous knowledge — potentials and limitations

Indigenous knowledge is especially relevant to sustainable development planning. It is locally appropriate, having been tried and tested through time to meet the demands of local conditions, and it is fully integrated into a region's social institutions (Brokensha 1986). Indigenous knowledge can be said to be both dynamic and adaptive, these knowledge systems having often evolved over many centuries, accommodating to on-going environmental and social change. It is both flexible and conservative, for while allowing for innovation and experimentation, it also provides risk-minimising strategies which enable rural communities to survive through times of stress (Richards 1985).

The potential utility of indigenous knowledge in research and development contexts has been succinctly summarised by Walker *et al.* (1991): "... the understanding that indigenous people have developed can complement scientific understanding; indigenously developed techniques of investigation can complement scarce scientific manpower; understanding indigenous knowledge and incorporating it into the research and development process can avoid duplication of work; and, understanding indigenous knowledge can help in targeting problem oriented scientific research by providing a firm basis for formulating realistic research objectives and hypothesis".

The dependence of livelihoods in Bangladesh upon localised rural production ensures that indigenous knowledge is 'local' or community specific. This may limit its general applicability to other environments or social circumstances. It informs decisions, which are entirely rational within their own socioeconomic context, but if this context is subject to external pressures then the logic informing the decision making may be compromised. It is in conditions of relatively rapid social and environmental change that indigenous knowledge systems are liable to malfunction, because their coping mechanisms are no longer adequate to meet the changed circumstances. People seldom record their indigenous knowledge but transmit it largely by word of mouth from generation to generation. Once forgotten, it may be lost forever. We should not allow this to happen.

Researching indigenous knowledge

Researching indigenous knowledge from the perspective of the demands of formal science throws up a number of challenging issues. Firstly, indigenous knowledge is difficult to categorise since it is holistic in nature, not disciplinary like conventional science. It is specific in relation to place, having evolved in response to local conditions, yet it is diverse in content, with concepts that may combine agroecology with social relations of production (Fairhead 1991).

Secondly, indigenous knowledge systems have been most studied by social anthropologists who have immersed themselves in cultures other than their own in order to comprehend the knowledge and values of those societies (e.g. Conklin 1954; Gladwin 1970; Sillitoe 1998*a*). The immersion approach is arguably non-scientific, having no predetermined structure or theory, and it can result in the collection of large amounts of field data that are difficult to assess (see Barr and Sillitoe, this volume). Additionally, because anthropologists can become 'experts' in a way similar to the people they study, they may often have difficulty in communicating their experiences to others who do not know what they know (Chambers 1983). This is to the detriment of rural development, since the insights and wealth of knowledge gained through these experiences have remained locked up in jargon-surrounded anthropological discourse and have been of little practical relevance. They need to be made into a form accessible to rural development policy-makers (Sillitoe 1998*a*).

Thirdly, there is the danger that local knowledge may be interpreted in terms of formal scientific concepts, of agriculture and economics (Norgaard 1987). This is grossly distorting and what anthropologists call 'ethnocentrism'. This results in some researchers portraying local practices in terms of their own external perspective of technical expertise without having a sympathetic understanding of the cultural conditions that have informed their evolution.

Fourthly, informants may find it hard to give formal accounts of their knowledge and how they use it. The process of questioning the "knowledge provider" can interfere with his or her perception of what is being discussed "... we constrain understanding in reducing everything to words. People transfer much knowledge between generations by tradition learnt and communicated through practical experience and are not familiar with trying to express everything they know in words ... . Knowledge is passed on by informal experience and practical demonstration; more often shown than articulated, it is as much skill as concept." (Sillitoe 1998*a*: 229; see also Johnson and Johnson 1987). Much knowledge learnt through experience may be used without a conscious awareness of details (Hart 1986) and even conscious knowledge may not be expressed in terms of rules or procedures (Breuker and Wielinga 1987). This has implications not only for the elicitation process but also for the subsequent representation of the knowledge for use by others. Moreover the 'knowledge provider' may be unwilling to impart information because he or she recognises that holding knowledge gives power or status.

Fifthly, problems of communication are central to indigenous knowledge research, as they are to all cross-cultural work. The familiarity and skill with which words are used to express concepts and procedures will affect the status and quality of knowledge elicited through interview. Although people identified for interview may be 'experts', it is unlikely that they have previously been required to describe their knowledge and decision making procedures. They are not familiar with communicating them in this way.

Finally, the status assumed by the researcher when studying the community will influence the data collection process (see Alam, this volume; Ahmed, this volume). Attempts to reduce social and intellectual barriers and improve understanding will enhance cooperation and thus knowledge elicitation. If the researcher assumes the role of 'learner' informants are more likely to be responsive than if he presents himself as a 'scientist' or 'planner'.

The individual nature of knowledge

There are many variables affecting the type and degree of knowledge held by various members of a community, as well as their ability to communicate this knowledge to others. It is important for development workers and researchers to recognise that indigenous knowledge can vary greatly within a group. It may help them to identify those best informed to assist them in their work. The main variables are as follows:

- age affects an individual's life experience. We may expect that the older members of a community will be most knowledgeable about the history and development of the farming system, including past successes and failures;
- formal education affects the type of knowledge held and particularly the way in which people express information. Social factors influence access to and levels of educational attainment such as wealth and caste;
- gender affects the knowledge held by an individual, particularly where there is a sexual division of labour (see Stokoe, this volume). Gender also affects access to formal education.

- occupation informs the type of knowledge held by an individual. This becomes an issue where particular expertise needs to be understood, in the study of specialist topics, or to verify occupational knowledge gathered from the wider community.
- the environment affects what knowledge an individual has, much of which will be site-specific. Only the more mobile members of a community will have knowledge relating to different locales. Differences in ecological knowledge reflect different perceptions of factors that affect crop production such as climate, altitude, soil type etc. Factors relating to location, such as proximity to markets, may influence attitudes to, and knowledge of, particular crops and decisions regarding cultivation.

Conclusion

Indigenous knowledge is now recognised as an under-utilised resource in rural development. Scholars have pointed out that many technological solutions to problems in rural communities have failed because they did not take into account local knowledge and practice (Chambers *et al.* 1989). Brokensha *et al.* (1980) present several case studies that demonstrate how an understanding of indigenous knowledge of a given group could greatly enhance participatory and sustainable approaches to rural development. This should not mean that indigenous knowledge is superior to scientific knowledge. Understanding indigenous knowledge can help to determine whether or not external scientific alternatives are appropriate, and if so how they may be adapted, and how best to introduce them. It may be possible to adapt indigenous techniques to enhance their benefits. Such an approach may be particularly profitable since farmers may be more open to adaptations of a familiar method than to a completely new technique. It will be by comparing and integrating scientific and indigenous knowledge that the most appropriate solutions will be found for many development problems.

4 Indigenous Knowledge and Sustainability: On the Brink of Disaster or Revolution?

H. Zaman

BANGLADESH HAS DEVELOPED over millennia a knowledge base and agricultural technologies suitable for its subtropical climate. Subsistence focused farming developed with a mixed crop/livestock/fishery culture more or less minimised risk in a land where natural calamities are common. But due to various historical and contemporary factors the farming community has become the victim of social, economic and political injustices that diminish agricultural efficiency. As the population has increased so too has the pressure on land. A population of 120 million limits arable land to 0.33 ha. per family of five persons. Arable land has decreased and continues to decline, reinforcing a vicious circle of poverty and land degradation. Environmental degradation, including gene pool diminution and land erosion, is one result of continuous poverty. Impoverishment is pervasive in Bangladesh, with a mean per capita annual income of Tk. 11,192 in 1995-96 (~ £160) and an energy intake of 2266 Kcal. (Bangladesh Bureau of statistics 1997). Large amounts of foreign assistance, amounting to billions of dollars, have been made available during the last fifty years, but poor management and political instability has resulted in a failure to use it correctly to alleviate poverty. The cynical might conclude that our politicians, planners and administrators have become highly successful at making poverty a sustainable condition to ensure continuing supplies of such aid. These factors have increased instability in farming communities, undermining their indigenous knowledge, technologies, and their ability to cope.

Today 'sustainable' has become a catchword around the world, with particular concerns expressed about developing areas. The penetration of alien and modern high technology into agriculture and local industry has, in many cases, displaced traditional or indigenous technologies. Some of these modern technologies are high-input and expensive and as such are not well suited to the needs of poor local people. Partial adoption of these foreign technologies may adversely affect the local physical and social environment, harming people and their society.

There are a number of examples of farmers apparently successfully adopting high-input modern technology in agriculture only to revert later to their age-old practices because the profit margin is inadequate or the risk too high (Winkelmann 1976). In other words, subsistence low-input technology farming remains the basis of practice, notably where there is no favourable market. But it is questionable to suggest that this subsistence farming is 'sustainable'. There is disagreement as to whether indigenous technologies are sustainable or desirable. For example, the *Jhum* (Slash and Burn) type of farming is described by some as environmentally degrading and by others as positive in both physical and socioeconomic terms. Whatever the truth, people have abandoned this system as population pressure and deforestation undermined its basic principles. Again change has undermined local knowledge and practices.

The nature of agriculture in Bangladesh

The major factors associated with agriculture are land, climate, crops, domestic animals, fish, forest, human population, a society's structure and both local and foreign markets. It is no good seeking to improve one of these in isolation (e.g. breeding higher yielding crops); we need to take into account all of these factors when considering sustainable production (see Wennergren *et al.* 1984).

Bangladesh is a small sub-tropical country (143,998 sq. km.), although the influence of the Himalayan mountain system to the north on seasonal airflows results in a short period of temperate conditions from November to the end of February. The country receives abundant rain (200-300cm annually) with the monsoon, but the distribution is uneven. There are several large rivers draining through Bangladesh from India and Nepal into the Bay of Bengal, which flood much of the country during the monsoon season. The unpredictable climate makes agriculture risky. There is no modern or indigenous technology that can ensure food security for the average family, even with triple cropping. In the face of geographical uncertainties farmers have succeeded in evolving well-adapted crop varieties (e.g. deepwater rice) and appropriate soil fertility management strategies. They developed low external input technologies that minimised risk given their unpredictable climatic conditions. There has been hardly any effort, in either the public or private sectors, to develop and build on this agricultural tradition, facilitating market linkage. Farmers are forced, given their adverse physical and socioeconomic position, to cling on to their low-input based mixed farming, which assures a minimum food supply. But this minimum is insufficient to ensure food security for all the family, let alone provide a balanced daily diet.

Due to the vagaries of nature and the constant threat of flood, cyclones, 'norwesters', tornadoes and hailstorms, farmers find it safest to grow rice throughout most of the year. Historically, rice production was seasonal and the wealthy could engineer famines and earn enormous profits at the cost of human lives and misery. Few rice traders die during famines unlike many rice farmers. Bangladeshi farmers have learnt through bitter experience that a rice stock in the house assures freedom from hunger and starvation and also earns prestige. While agricultural scientists have promoted a revolution in rice culture — the so-called 'green revolution' of high yielding varieties (HYVs) — this has not eased the plight of the poor, and may even have exacerbated it with its high demand for expensive external inputs. The Bangladesh government and aid donors are trying to promote increased crop diversification to break this rice monopoly but progress is slow because they have been unable to ensure a fair price for crops. The current mixed farming does not depend on a diverse range of crops nor ensure maintenance of soil fertility. As long as rice remains people's preferred staple, progress is likely to be slow.

Endangered practices and sustainability

The ancient South Asian civilisations of Mohenjodaro and Ur perished when they fell out of balance with nature and became unsustainable. In these civilisations humans thought, as many do today, that they controlled nature. They failed to realise that in subjugating nature they over-exploited resources and jeopardised their survival. They evolved a fragile and ephemeral material and social security. We are in danger of repeating these errors and need to learn from our history. In 1929 the Royal Commission on Agriculture in India recorded that the sub-continent's soils had reached a serious state of degradation 100 years previously. Due to various

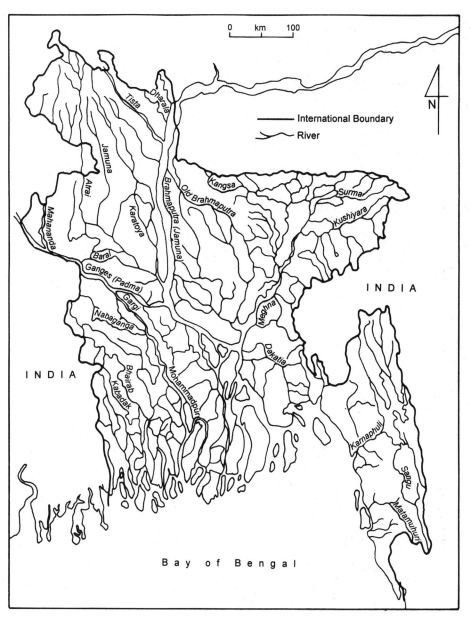

Figure 4.1 *Map of Bangladesh showing river system across delta (after Hussein 1992)*

socioeconomic and agroecological factors farmers have been forced to continue to follow practices that erode soils, deplete them of plant nutrients and barely sustain growth of crops. We all continue to exploit farmers: the intelligentsia, businessmen, administrators and politicians. This presents a long-term threat to everyone because we all depend on the same natural resources to feed us. We have much to learn from our indigenous knowledge heritage. Maintaining species either in sanctuaries, national parks or gene banks cannot restore nature's fragile ecological balance or the process of evolution in its proper sense. We are currently fighting a losing battle with gene pool erosion and increasingly endangered species. As soil fertility began to decrease farmers had no alternative but to select crop varieties that could stand the lower levels of nutrient availability; they culled out plant genes associated with higher soil fertility and yields. This caused 'gene erosion', and Bangladesh lost many of its higher yielding traditional crop varieties. The loss of rice varieties may be as high as 60% (Zaman 1993, 1997). Continuous selection of hardier lower yielding stock gave rise to today's local varieties. The malnourished condition of both Bangladeshi cattle and their owners illustrates that such a farming strategy undermines even the subsistence level of farming. In these systems domestic animals are reared as scavengers. The present day decline in crop yields and soil fertility in Bangladesh (Karim 1998) is a consequence of the neglect of balanced progress. Instead we have the so-called solutions of both micro and macro economic development. The relentless unilateral efforts of economists, planners and scientists have created a spiral of decline. We have bankrupt intellectual and technological interventions that have made poor farmers the scapegoats.

Crop production, traditionally for subsistence in Bangladesh, was controlled by the seasons. The summer crops were mainly rain-fed, grown using local technologies. However, introduced high-cost technologies, notably irrigation together with the use of fertilisers, pesticides and new varieties have overridden these seasonal constraints to a large extent. Nonetheless some operations, including tillage practices and post-harvest procedures, are still done using age-old techniques and technology. There is a mixture of traditional and modern technologies in the field of agriculture. For example few farmers follow the 'recommended' package of introduced technology in full, using only some urea, triple super phosphate, pesticides and partial irrigation. Otherwise they resort to traditional practices. This hybrid culture does not improve profits, neither is it a sound practice for the maintenance of fertile soil. Farmers have no control of markets and cannot earn reasonable returns. We may have to abandon these modified technologies to get back to a sustainable agricultural regime. The new technologies are beyond the reach of the poor, and no one is investigating the potential of the affordable old technologies for increasing crop production. Many old technologies, passed down to us by our ancestors, remain undocumented. The Bangladesh Academy of Agriculture is urgently trying to document existing local technologies (BAA 1997). This knowledge must not be lost for it is vital to the promotion of sustainable agriculture in the future.

Conclusion

In 1973 a book of agricultural statistics, published by the Ministry of Agriculture, recorded that land productivity was declining for nearly all major crops. This was in the early days of the introduction of high yielding varieties, when the per ha. yield of rice increased dramatically and was more than 6 tons. Yields have subsequently decreased and at present the mean HYV yield per ha. is 3.5 tons. Various investigators (Sobhan 1997; Planning Commission 1997) have discussed this worrying trend and conclude that it is the result of the following factors:

- Environmental degradation;
- Loss of soil fertility;
- Unfavourable/unpredictable weather conditions;

- Lack of efficient drainage during floods because of unplanned infrastructure (including roads and highways);
- Siltation of riverbeds accelerating flood;
- Farmers' apathy toward flood action plans;
- River water pollution;
- A scavenger livestock rearing system;
- Population pressure;
- Socioeconomic inequalities;
- Low levels of education;
- General disregard by society for the farming profession (which is seen by many as just one rung higher than begging);
- Farmers' inability to use complete technology packages;
- Lack of adequate and easily available credit for farmers;
- Governmental failure to provide adequate market opportunities for farmers, (for example, whenever the rice price increases the Government immediately announces "Open Market Sale" of rice at lower rates);
- Corruption at almost all levels of society and lack of law and order.

All of these factors contribute to some degree to the current instability of Bangladeshi agriculture and loss of indigenous knowledge. They have undermined the sustainability of local agricultural technologies. Action is urgently needed. The contemporary advocacy of participation, of which engagement with indigenous knowledge is one strand, is a step in the right direction but it is unlikely to take us far without considerable social changes.

Bangladesh can trace the start of the degradation and loss of its rich natural resources to the instigation of the caste system by the Aryan invaders, which placed farmers in a low social position. The subsequent Moghul invaders from the Middle East and later European colonial powers failed to rectify this social evil, instead silently supporting it. Although the national constitution does not support this social hierarchy, one can easily find those in the élite social classes residing in the wealthy Dhanmondi, Gulshan and Banani suburbs of Dhaka who tacitly do so. The so-called "Bangla" intelligentsia, supported by the Bangla Academy, coined the word "*chashi*" as a term of abuse for persons of low social status. Some noble-hearted Babus and Sahibs have put *chashi* either before or after their names and made themselves famous. Many Bengali poets have written poems depicting the poverty and helplessness of farmers and become famous too. Yet not one of these exalted persons eradicated the poverty of a single struggling farmer. During recent decades Governments and NGOs have become adept at using poverty to secure large amounts of foreign aid. Instead of alleviating poverty we have instituted it permanently into our society and economy. Only a social, economic and political revolution can rescue poor farmers from this vicious circle.

5 Development Disasters: The Role of Indigenous Knowledge and Practices

Mahfuzul Haque

THIS CHAPTER LOOKS at some of the development projects in Bangladesh and neighbouring countries, which have been turned into "development disasters" due to faulty planning and implementation. Most development projects in and around Bangladesh follow a typical "top-down" approach; that is, they are often implemented with little or no 'grass-roots' level participation. Rural people are typically treated as illiterate and ignorant, without scientific and technological know-how. They may be illiterate, but does this mean they have no worthwhile knowledge? For example: a farmer knows the quality of a soil without scientific tests; a farmer's wife knows how to conserve and store seeds; a fisherman knows where and when to fish; a boatman can give a weather forecast with more reliability than the Met Office; a young girl knows when a hen will lay an egg. Is this not knowledge? It is, and people at the grass-roots clearly receive a form of education and know more about their lives and livelihoods than we do. The projects discussed here include hydro-electricity and forestry projects, the Chittagong Hill Tracts re-settlement scheme, Flood Control Drainage and Irrigation (FCD/I) projects in South-west Bangladesh and shrimp cultivation in the south. The indigenous knowledge and practices of local people were ignored in developing many of these projects of national importance. Policy planners and executives need to be made aware of the adverse effects of these projects on the surrounding environment.

In general terms, "development" means progress, advancement, improvement etc. Development projects are generally designed to bring about a qualitative change in the lives of the people in a particular locality and country. However, when conceived without paying due attention to local people's knowledge, projects may turn into disasters. In Bangladesh and neighbouring countries we have experienced many such projects that failed to consider socioeconomic, ethnic and environmental issues (see Haque 1997). Perhaps the planning processes were faulty, the grass-roots beneficiaries not consulted, or maybe the implementation of the projects was poor.

Hydroelectricity projects

The construction of hydroelectric dams on rivers to store water for power generation is well-known for its adverse effects on the environment and forced population displacement. Those persons affected by the projects rarely receive any compensation. In India, a dam built under the Subarnarekha Multipurpose Project in Jharkhand, Bihar State submerged 120 villages and thousands of acres of agricultural land. About one lakh people, mostly tribal, were forced from their land and turned into "development refugees". In Maharastra State, Ms Medha Patkar, a firebrand activist, led a resistance group, *Narmada Banchao Andolon* (Save the Narmada) with the *adivasi* indigenous community. They protested against the construction of the massive Sardar Sarovar hydroelectric dam across the Narmada valley, and due to the local community's resistance the World Bank later abandoned the project.

The Kaptai hydroelectricity project on the Karnaphuli River in South-east Bangladesh submerged 250 sq. miles of land and displaced around 100,000 people, mostly Chakma sedentary rice farmers. The turbulence caused in the lake by the dam affected the normal growth of fish and caused soil erosion. Is it right for the country to incur such colossal socioeconomic damage to generate electricity? In 1976, in a memorandum to the late President Ziaur Rahman, the hillmen told of their grief: "the vast expanse of water captured by the dam provides a scene that impresses every visitor with its beauty. But could anybody have thought that the immense body of water is to some extent filled with tears of the local people? Through the cables of the electric line not only current flows but also the sighs of grief." The dam adversely affected the self-sufficiency of the tribal economy. Moreover, it failed to create job opportunities for the hill people, as envisaged. The government encouraged the tribal people to take up new occupations such as fishing or horticulture but the response was poor, mainly because of a lack of necessary skills and cultural shock. Such skills and knowledge are not part of their heritage (see Chowdhury *et al.* 1979).

Re-settlement in the Hills Tracts
During the implementation of the "Upland Settlement Project" in the Chittagong Hill Tracts some tribal people took up horticulture and some new cash crops such as rubber, building upon their *jhum* 'slash and burn' farming knowledge. The Chittagong hills settlement programme was an attempt by the government to change the population structure of the region. Around 375,000 people from the plains were resettled there between 1980 and 1982 and each family was given 2.5 acres of valley land or 5 acres of hill land. The plan was to create a "human wall" on the Indo-Bangladesh border to thwart any insurgency activities, isolating guerrillas from the neighbouring populations. According to the 1991 Census, non-tribal people now constitute just over half of the total population, whereas they were previously only 10%. The tribal people were unhappy with this invasion for it not only ignored their knowledge but also their rights. The settler communities faced armed resistance from *Shanti Bahini*, an armed tribal group. In 1986 the communities were placed in enclosed *Guchcha Gram* (cluster villages) for security reasons, receiving 85kg of wheat or rice per family per month. They became prisoners with ration cards. The accord of 2nd December 1997 between *Shanti Bahini* and the Bangladesh Government has not solved the land problem. The Hill Tracts are over populated; the 1991 Census showed population density to be at 85 per sq. km, the carrying capacity being 18-25 per sq. km. Only 2% of the land is suitable for rice cultivation, 21% for horticulture with the remainder under forest (Anti-Slavery Society 1984: 17). No attention has been paid to the traditional *jhum* system and its relation to the environment.

Forest development projects
Elsewhere forest dwellers have also become victims of government policies and development programmes. For example, the forest dwellers of Jharkhands in the Chotanagpur region of India used to collect honey, timber, silkworms, medicines and oils from their forests. It was a symbiotic relationship. Forest Acts have removed many of their rights and exotic teak and eucalyptus trees have replaced indigenous trees such

as *Saal, Mahua, Kendua* and *Kusum*. The Forest Department took charge and barred their access to the forests. In the Bihar, the forest dwellers, started the *Jangal Kato Andolon* 'movement to clear the forests'. Although the movement did not last long, it was the first protest by an indigenous community against a development project taken without their consent. In Uttarkhand, Uttra Pradesh in India, there was the Chipko movement in which local activists embraced the trees to protect them from felling. In the Madhupur Tract forest of Tangail district in Bangladesh, we witnessed large-scale deforestation by commercial loggers. The local forest dwellers, the Mandi people, had no traditional lease deeds over their ancestral lands, and were stripped of them. Some were forced to cede land to the dominant Bengali community. In the name of commerce, trees were felled and the Mandi people were dispossessed. Paresh Chandra Mree, a Mandi leader said, "... we are the children of the forest. We were born and brought up here. We want to die here. We are so accustomed to forest life and we cannot survive if we get evicted from the forests." Their resistance against the Forestry Department evicting them met with limited success (see Gain 1998*b*). Again, not only is local peoples' knowledge of sustainable forest use disregarded, but so are their rights.

Water logging in Beel Dakatia, Khulna

In the early sixties, the Water Development Board undertook a number of coastal embankment projects in South-west Bangladesh to protect the area from tidal surges, flooding and salinity. In the past, the natural tidal system played an important role in elevating the sunken *beel* lands. The local practice was to set up submersible embankments, which stored water during the post-monsoon period for irrigation. The establishment of large-scale flood control, drainage and irrigation (FCD/I) projects has resulted in the massive siltation of rivers. The projects were conceived to protect the area from salinity but due to inappropriate engineering, the sluice gates became clogged, riverbeds rose and failed to drain away the excess water. The resulting water logging brought many problems to the people of the area. In Beel Dakatia region it affected an area of 400 sq. miles and 10 lakh people. The Water Development Board has now undertaken another new project, the Khulna-Jessore Drainage and Rehabilitation Project (KJDRP), to correct some of the earlier mistakes. Local people are anxious that this will be another disaster, and when asked, say they do not support the project. They believe that if the rivers are allowed to take their own course the problems of prolonged water logging will be relieved, as this was the traditional practice. Experience has taught them that humans should not tamper with the rivers. Again, people at the grass-roots level have not been consulted during the conception and implementation of the project.

Narayanganj-Narsingdi Irrigation Project

The Narayanganj-Narsingdi Irrigation Project, situated a few kilometers from Bangladesh's capital, Dhaka, is another typical Water Development Board flood control, drainage and irrigation project. The project was commissioned in June 1994 with the following objectives:

- to turn the areas along the banks of the Sitalakhya into flood-free zones;
- to bring the area under intensive irrigation; and
- to drain off excess water to avoid water logging.

A tour of the area shows that these objectives have not been met. Parts of the area remain water logged due to faulty design. The local people were again not consulted during any phase of the project. This typical top-down approach has resulted in the local water-user groups refusing to take over management with the withdrawal of the Water Development Board. They regard it as ill-conceived and at odds with their local knowledge and practices regarding the management of floods.

Destructive shrimp cultivation

In the past one and a half decades shrimp ponds have destroyed a unique mangrove forest in Chokoria Sundarban, Cox's Bazar district, in Southeast Bangladesh. Shrimps, living in brackish water, need large saline ponds to survive. People lease and clear land for shrimp cultivation but this unplanned and unscientific commercial shrimp cultivation is taking its toll on the environment. Faulty fry collection is destructive of biodiversity, disease often attacks the shrimps and fish diversity is being increasingly threatened. Little or no regard is paid to traditional shrimp farming practices. Shrimp cultivation has also changed the social fabric of the area. In return for lease money, local landowners are ousted by outside commercial interests. Some poor rice farmers are forced to become fishermen or work as labourers and the resulting social clashes have been destructive. The local people should have been consulted before the introduction of this commercial product. They support designated areas for shrimp cultivation, building on traditional knowledge of their region and more environment-friendly 'sweet water' shrimp farming. They would have prevented today's problems.

Conclusion

Experience shows that failure to consult people at the grass-roots level results in many development projects becoming "development disasters". The question is are we planning for the people or with the people? We need to evolve a bottom-up planning process, one that recognises indigenous knowledge, experience and practices as a useful resource. We should place people at the centre of their own development. They should be involved in all stages of project planning, implementation and evaluation. Politicians, policy planners and implementers must be made aware of the adverse effects of projects that are planned without the full consideration of the population and local environment.

6 Investigating Indigenous Knowledge: A Review of the Bangladeshi Literature on Natural Resources

Dwijen Mallick

BANGLADESH POSSESSES a rich heritage of indigenous knowledge through which people try to manage their production systems on the floodplain, exploiting land, fisheries, livestock and forests, to earn their livelihoods. Their floodplain production systems are unique examples of agroecological systems at the land/water interface, supporting a high-density population (Barr *et al.* 1996*a*). But much of this knowledge has been lost with the 'modernisation' of agriculture and the rapid spread of new technology. This literature review focuses mainly on indigenous knowledge in relation to the natural resources of the floodplain of Bangladesh, including terrestrial and aquatic resources i.e. those exploited in agriculture, fisheries and forestry. It presents information on traditional farming systems, fishing and local environmental management practices and ideas from the resource user's perspective, particularly those of poor farmers and fishers.[1]

There is growing consensus among development practitioners and academics that due respect should be given to indigenous knowledge (IK) whilst planning and implementing development programmes, for different sectors such as agriculture, fisheries, forestry etc., and also for a country or region. Indigenous knowledge is understood here as the local and traditional knowledge used by rural people in all aspects of daily life including natural resource management, agriculture, fisheries, livestock raising, health practices and other activities relating to their livelihoods. There is increasing interest in the contribution indigenous knowledge has to make to sustainable resources management and agricultural development. The indigenous knowledge of a farming population living in a specific area is derived from people's past experiences; it is the knowledge handed down from previous generations together with that of the present generation.

Sillitoe *et al.* (1998) maintain that indigenous knowledge relates to any knowledge held collectively by a population, which informs understanding of the world. It may encompass knowledge of any kind/domain including that pertaining to sociocultural and natural processes. It is culturally relative, being informed by people's sociocultural tradition and history of which it is an integral part. Chambers expressed his interest in indigenous knowledge for rural development from the early 1980s (e.g. Chambers 1983). The main thrust to his argument is that farmers have an intricate and detailed knowledge of their environment from which they earn their livelihoods through experimentation and innovation. Such indigenous knowledge should not be viewed as a constraint, but as a positive resource for development and for social development in promoting participation and empowerment.

Since the 1980s, these has been a growing recognition that indigenous people have their own effective "science" and resource-use practices. Development practitioners can build upon this knowledge. To achieve this goal and improve productivity and sustainability of Bangladesh's agriculture, it is first necessary to understand indigenous knowledge and practices and then integrate this local knowledge with modern knowledge. A meaningful blending of indigenous knowledge and modern knowledge could ensure agricultural productivity and sustainability.

The importance of a literature search on indigenous knowledge

This literature search is an attempt to systematically document people's knowledge relating to their organisation of farming and fishing practices and associated activities to ensure their livelihoods. There is a serious lack of written material on indigenous knowledge and technologies in Bangladesh. Whilst searching the literature, few relevant articles, reports and papers were found. However a summary of the available literature demonstrates how people of the floodplain use their local knowledge in agriculture: to select crops, preserve seeds, manage soil fertility, control pests, manage home gardens and orchard production, to rear livestock and so on; and also in fishing, where small-scale production depends mainly on local fishing gear and associated crafts. In addition, indigenous knowledge plays an important role in rural health, weather forecasting and disaster management (e.g. floods, cyclone, droughts and riverbank erosion).

It is anticipated that the literature search will contribute to a conceptual understanding of floodplain production systems and livelihood strategies set in the context of the land/water interface ecosystem. The people of rural Bangladesh have developed different farming systems and techniques through generations of innovation and adaptation, which have been fine-tuned to the local environment, economy and sociocultural system. This study reveals that people of the floodplains have a rich store of local knowledge and associated practices, but unfortunately this knowledge base is not only poorly documented but is also fast disappearing.

Traditionally people used to live a relatively self-sufficient life in rural areas, growing the crops they needed, raising animals and collecting fuel and fodder within their own domain. But the 'modernisation' of agriculture and adoption of new technologies has resulted in dependency upon the outside world. The local heritage of knowledge is eroding. The changes brought about by the introduction of modern technologies during the last few decades have promoted environmental and socioeconomic instability on the floodplains undermining the integrity of natural resource systems. Small-scale farmers and other rural poor, who depend intimately on these natural resources for their livelihoods, have been the most adversely affected.

Once Bangladesh had more than six thousand varieties of local rice, but due to High Yield Varieties monoculture the local varieties have disappeared at an alarming rate and only 100 are presently estimated to remain (Khan 1998). It is assumed that the same applies to fisheries and forest resources. If anything, the local knowledge base is eroding faster than that of natural resources. The exploration and documentation of people's knowledge regarding natural resources and their management, farming systems and fisheries, has been too long delayed. The rationale behind this search was to contribute to furthering this work in earnest, by demonstrating the richness of the knowledge and the gap in our understanding of it and its potential for our country.

Search method

A checklist was drawn up listing the types of literature and information to be included in the survey and which sources should be explored to find them. A number of libraries were visited including those at the Bangladesh Institute of Development Studies (BIDS), the Asiatic Society of Bangladesh, some departmental libraries at Dhaka University (including Sociology, Anthropology and Bengali departments) and Dhaka Public Library. Relevant government departments were also visited (Agriculture, Fisheries, Environment) in addition to autonomous bodies including the Bangladesh Agricultural Research Council (BARC), the Bangla Academy and the libraries of some NGOs. Seeking information on indigenous knowledge, the literature search focused on accessible published works relating to livelihood strategies and the floodplain environment of Bangladesh.

The initial stages of the study were disappointing because almost nothing was found on indigenous technical knowledge in any of the libraries. However staff from the University of Durham advised me to start working with related materials which gave new direction to the study.[2] Some interesting articles on traditional aspects of farming systems including cropping patterns, seed preservation, pest control etc. were found. We also came across books and reports dealing with the coping strategies of local people following natural calamities such as floods, cyclones, drought and riverbank erosion. I discovered that some books on folklore contained relevant information on traditional agricultural practices, variations over time, the importance of water in local livelihood strategies and related cultural practices of rural peoples.

The present state of literature on indigenous knowledge

The Bangladesh Agricultural Research Council (BARC) undertook one of the earliest extensive works on indigenous technical knowledge in Bangladesh. The book entitled *Indigenous Agricultural Tools and Equipment of Bangladesh*, published in 1982, describes the various agricultural tools and traditional appliances that have been used and are still being used in many parts of the country. The book provides detailed descriptions of equipment including local names, size, mode of operation, and the materials from which each is made. More recently, Chowdhury *et al.* (1996) compiled one of the most extensive works on indigenous technical knowledge. In their nation-wide study they reported on knowledge relating to cropping, seed preservation, pest control and so on. Approximately two hundred different indigenous techniques and practices used in agriculture, fisheries and healthcare were documented.

In his thesis *Farmers' Use of Indigenous Technical Knowledge in the Context of Sustainable Agricultural Development*, Islam (1996) identifies a number of indigenous techniques that are still used in agriculture in the north-western part of the country, particularly in Dinajpur district. He explores the relationship between farmers' preferences for different indigenous technologies and the extent to which they are used. Of the indigenous techniques documented, 19% were used regularly and a further 46% were utilised only occasionally; the remaining 35% were rarely employed. It was also found that farmers' ages, family size, farm size and family income were correlated with their use of identified technologies. Furthermore, media exposure related positively to farmers' attitudes towards the use of indigenous technical knowledge.

In 1997 Bangladesh Academy of Agriculture (BAA) published a book entitled *Indigenous Technologies of Agriculture in Bangladesh* that includes information on

147 indigenous technologies used in agriculture. Practices relating to community production, harvest, post-harvest operation in crops, animals, forest and fisheries were documented. Efforts were also made to depict the background in which the technologies emerged and in which they are still being used today.

A study on Indigenous Technology for Watershed Management by a group of researchers identified 52 local technologies and practices (Sharma 1998). Most of the technologies are used for forest, water and soil conservation and intensive production systems. The tribal people residing in upland areas have employed such technologies to sustain their livelihoods for generations. The report contains descriptions of some of the tools used by upland people that differ in size, shape and function from those of the plainland people. But technologies are being transferred from the upland people to the plainland people. It was also suggested that technologies being used today should in many cases be refined, revitalised and improved to effectively contribute to watershed management and improve productivity of local resources.

Lewis *et al.* (1996) show that fish traders of Northwest Bangladesh have considerable local knowledge of fingerling collection; from producing to preserving and risk management, to travelling and trading the young fish. Researchers documented the network of fingerling trading and found that the silver seed (young fish) pass through many hands before reaching the final pond in which to be raised. Small traders are the distributors. These traders have to take care of the fingerlings and take risks while travelling by train, bus and on foot. In the process they use their indigenous knowledge. For example, fingerling traders always change the water in the *patil* (a container made of mud) before entering an area of anticipated sale. This makes the young fish appear healthier and stronger whilst also reducing the mortality rate among the fingerlings. The book effectively documents the fish trader's local knowledge and their behaviour, using participant observation as the primary research method. It provides a good understanding of the specific indigenous knowledge possessed by fish traders working within the functioning system of fish-culture.

Chadwick *et al.* (1998) provide a synthesis of previous works in the field of indigenous knowledge and techniques in a recent study entitled, "*Understanding Indigenous Knowledge: Its Role and Potential in Water Resources Management in Bangladesh*". The main aim of the study was to document indigenous knowledge relating to traditional water management practices from a regional perspective. It also reviews related issues, exploring the strengths and usefulness of indigenous knowledge for improved maintenance of local ecosystems as well as production systems.

In a pioneering early study Ahmed (1955) describes and illustrates the major fishing crafts and gear used by the fishing community in what was then East Pakistan. The *donga* used for shallow water fishing is described. The five major fishing boats are the *Balam Nauka, Chandi Nauka, Bachari Nauka, Bhesal Dingi* and *Kosha Nauka*. The crafts differ from district to district in shape, length, breadth, depth and other details but all share some common characteristics such as being lightly built and highly buoyant.

Tsai and Ali (1997) provide a valuable compilation containing information on different aspects of open water fish and fisheries in Bangladesh. This book deals with tropical floodplain fisheries, riparian rights and socioeconomic and policy issues pertaining to floodplain fisheries set against a historical perspective of organisations relating to inland fisheries in colonial Bengal.

Ullah (1996) in his study *Land, Livelihood and Change in Rural Bangladesh* documents aspects of the survival and livelihood strategies of small farmers in rural areas. He examines the dynamics of changes in land ownership patterns. Although not directly related to indigenous knowledge, this book is useful for gaining an understanding of the livelihood strategies of rural people.

In 1996 *Unnayar Bikalpa Nirdharani Gabeshana* (Policy Research for Development Alternative) published a booklet on *Nayakrishi Andjolon* (The New Agricultural Movement) describing a recent initiative by peasants to innovate using indigenous technology. Farmers draw on indigenous knowledge to grow crops in an environmentally-friendly sustainable way. The guiding principles of *Nayakrishi* are: to increase the use of compost fertilisers over chemical fertilisers; to encourage and enhance multicropping, intercropping and mixed cropping in place of High Yield Variety mono-culture; to promote agroforestry practices; and to facilitate the use of other local familiar methods of agriculture which are eco-friendly. *Unnayar Bikalpa Nirdharani Gabeshana* (UBINIG) also produced posters protesting against the indiscriminate use of agro-chemicals. The posters urge peasants to revive traditional farming practices. The Department of Agriculture has also produced some booklets highlighting integrated pest control methods that involve local knowledge.

There are a number of rhymes and proverbs in Bengali that refer to various aspects of rural life including cropping patterns, nature and climate, seasonal changes, vernacular housing, food habits and heath-promoting behaviour. Ahmed (1974) records many such rhymes that describe how people traditionally cultivated their land, their cropping patterns, how seeds were selected and preserved and how people responded to natural events. Shahed (1988) in *Bengal Society and Culture Reflected in Rhymes* describes how in Middle-Age Bengal an ideal homestead had a tank, trees and surrounding cultivated plants. Islam (1990) in *Folk Literature of Tangail Districts* describes the seasonal rhythm and variation in the pattern of rural life over twelve months known as *Baromashi*. It includes a depiction of how traditional cropping patterns change over the year.

Key findings

The available literature demonstrates that people of the floodplains have a rich store of local knowledge. The following summary of the findings of this literature search is presented under three broad sections: local knowledge pertaining to (1) farming systems; (2) fisheries and livestock; and (3) local environmental management. It also outlines potential uses of indigenous technical knowledge in development contexts.

Farming systems

The literature shows that people widely use local knowledge and practices in soil conservation and land management, seed preparation, pest control, crop rotation, irrigation and agroforestry. Local knowledge bases and techniques have evolved through time and are adapted according to population demands and socio-environmental changes. Knowledge and skills are transferred from generation to generation. Alim (1981) noted that in traditional society, farmers' sons received an agricultural education from their fathers and neighbours with whom they lived and worked in co-operation. Daughters also received an education from their mothers and other female relatives during the course of their everyday lives.

Soil conservation and land management: Alim (1981) reports that the major rivers of Bangladesh and their tributaries deposit enormous quantities of silt beyond the river basins and across the entire floodplain delta each year. If the flow of the rivers is obstructed or changed in any way soil fertility may decline. Local communities address the problem of soil conservation by digging drainage canals and building protective *bundhs* (temporary embankments). These *bundhs* also protect crops from damaging inundation. Farmers also plant *dhaincha* (a shrub) in erosion prone areas. Young plants are sometimes chopped up after serving their protective function and mixed into the soil to add organic matter.

People use logs and banana leaves, stems and roots to prevent soil erosion from rainwater. The logs act as barriers and banana is often planted in erosion-prone areas. Ash is used to improve soil structure and fertility in agriculture. This is practised by upland people in shifting cultivation and plains people in broadcast *aman* cultivation. Ash mixed into the soil helps to create humus, especially clay humus complex, provided that the clay content is high. This increases the nutrient and water holding capacity of the soil thus improving soil structure and quality.

Pest control: Farmers have used various traditional methods of pest control for generations. Alim (1981) reports that people throughout the country have developed different ways to destroy, or at least to control insects harmful to crops. The simplest and oldest method is to destroy them by hand; farmers pick off harmful insects and pull up diseased plants that nurture pests. These are frequently burned to reduce the chances of pests infesting nearby healthy plants. Many farmers use various natural repellents such as powdered *neem* leaf, tobacco *biskatali (Polygonun hydropiper)* and ash to protect seeds and plants from insect attack. For example, farmers in Gazipur and Rajshahi use *neem* leaf-powder mixed with water that is sprayed onto plants to repel insects from rice fields. Farmers in Gazipur have developed an innovative method for controlling caterpillar attacks on cabbage, cauliflower and *brinjal*, by digging a deep circular trench in the soil around the plants. When the caterpillars approach the plants they cannot reach them because of the trenches, "appear to get frightened" and move on. Householders protect seedlings and saplings of various fruit trees from grazing animals by applying liquid cow-dung to their stems. Potatoes are protected from tuber moth attack by covering them with layers of dry sand and rice husk. Farmers in Joydebpur push bamboo sticks or small branches into their rice fields to attract insect-eating birds to their paddies (Chowdhury *et al.* 1996). Water from *hookahs* (a type of water pipe) is sprinkled onto plants to repel the 'rice bug'. Farmers of Sunamganj control pests by making a thick 'rope' from paddy straw soaked in kerosene, which is then dragged over paddy fields several times. They say the odour of kerosene repels insects. Also in this region women mix ash with kerosene and spread it over the leaves of vegetables to control aphid infestation. Such practices lessen the need to use chemical pesticides.

Seed preservation: Farmers regularly use earthen pots and pitchers to store wheat, chickpea and paddy seed. In Sunamganj and other areas rhizomes of ginger and turmeric and tubers of garlic are spread thinly on bamboo trays and covered with clean dry sand. Farmers preserve bottle gourd seeds by keeping them sun-dried inside the fruit (see also Shah and Nuri, this volume). Selected gourds are kept on the vine and when the season is over they are exposed to strong sunlight for thorough drying. When the inner pulp dries up completely the seeds rattle inside when the shell is shaken. The gourds, with seeds inside, are stored in a dry corner of the house. At sowing time a small cut is made in the upper part of the fruit and the seeds shaken out. In this way germination capacity is fully retained (Islam 1996).

Cropping patterns: Farmers have experimented over time with growing crops in many combinations in mixed cropping adapting to soil conditions, land type and climatic variation in different regions. Cropping systems particularly adapted to rainfall regimes are continuing in areas of the country where irrigation is not available. The practice of mixed cropping helps to conserve soil fertility whilst also maintaining biodiversity in the ecosystem. Chowdhury (1996) reports that farmers in different regions follow various techniques of multiple cropping strategies according to local socio-environmental conditions. For example:

- relaying potato with pointed gourd, sweet gourd or pepper;
- intercropping potato and bitter gourd or leafy vegetables;
- intercropping vegetables like cauliflower, cabbage, tomato, *brinjal* etc. with sugarcane.

Farmers may cultivate a range of crops on the same plot of land in different seasons (Alim 1981). In the past, instead of only two rice crops as today (*boro* and *aman*), many rice varieties and jute were cultivated in the *kharip* (summer and rainy season) and pulses, oil seeds, root crops, wheat, barley, tobacco and many other vegetables in the *rabi* (winter season). Farmers scatter seeds of jute after one or two showers in April and May. The jute is harvested after 3 to 4 months and then *amon* rice is planted during the monsoon. The *amon* rice is harvested in November-December and then pulses, oil seed, millet, and vegetables are cultivated in the almost rain-free winter season.

Chowdhury (1996) reported that farmers of central Bangladesh, particularly in Narayanganj, traditionally practice effective relay cropping sequences; seedling and seeds of pointed gourd, sweet gourd, bitter gourd, water melon and musk melon are planted in the potato field during November and December before the potato harvest. After the harvesting of these vegetables and fruits, local *aman* rice seeds are sown. This practice reduces the time for land preparation and allows maximum usage of land. Farmers also practice intercropping, raising ridges over the potato crop and sowing wheat seeds of the *kanchan* variety and sometimes, *napasak* and *lalsak* into the furrows. Cauliflower, cabbage, tomato and red amaranth are also grown as short-term intercrops in sugarcane fields.

Irrigation: Hassan (1996) reports that rainwater harvesting is important to supplement water supplies for both domestic and agricultural purposes during dry periods, due to it being technically, economically and ecologically sound. Rural people intercept and collect rainwater in two ways: roof catchment and ground catchment. Reasonably pure water can be collected from house roofs made of corrugated galvanised iron sheets. Such water is used mainly for domestic purposes and for irrigating homestead gardens. Rainwater collected in ground catchments such as ponds and canals is used for agriculture.

Farmers use different kinds of local tools and equipment for small-scale irrigation. A book entitled *Indigenous Agricultural Tools and Equipment of Bangladesh* (BARC 1982) reported that the Swing basket is a common traditional device for irrigating water in rural areas. This is a simple device triangular in shape and generally made of a bamboo woven sheet fastened with sticks. (Today plain iron sheets are sometimes used instead). Two people are required to operate it. Another example of irrigation equipment used extensively by farmers to lift water from ditches and canals is the *done*, made mainly of wood. Its shape is like a channel section a few feet in length with one end slightly curved and closed. The appliance is fitted to bamboo cross bars with a long bamboo pole which works as a fulcrum. A counter weight is added to facilitate the working of the *done* with minimum exertion (BARC 1982).

Ali (1997) reported that local people of Munshiganj, Comilla and Rajshahi districts use mulch to conserve soil moisture for potato cultivation. After planting seed tubers the farmers cover the fields with rice straw or water hyacinth and allow the plants to grow until they reach a stage of first earthing up. This practice helps conserve the soil moisture and reduces irrigation for potato cultivation.

Sharma (1998) found that farmers and tribal people in upland areas employ many techniques to save water for farming and other income-generating activities. One of the age-old techniques for conserving rainwater is to build a small embankment across a canal or stream with an earth dyke (often 5m wide and 2.5 to 3.5m deep) to create a reservoir. The catchment of the reservoir is often 80-90 ha. In the dry season the water is used for irrigating the lower and nearby agricultural fields. Aquaculture and duckling rearing is practiced along with small irrigation. This indigenous technique enhances efficiency of water use and helps maintain availability of water throughout the year.

The cropping systems practiced until very recently in many parts of the country depended upon natural rainfall (Alim 1981). After one or two showers in the months of March and April, rice and jute seeds were sown. These crops were harvested after 3-4 months during the monsoon. *Amon* was then transplanted in the months of July and August, sometimes sown with *aus* rice as a mixed crop. After the rice harvest, pulses, oilseed, millet and different kinds of vegetables were grown as the monsoon water receded. Good rainfall meant good crops but with little rainfall crops suffered, resulting in famine. In areas of scanty rainfall people would use rainwater stored in tanks and canals to irrigate crops.

During the dry season farmers pull a rope across the rice field early in the morning so that the drops of dew accumulated on the leaves during the nightfall moisten the soil. Raw cow-dung is diluted in water and sprinkled in paddy fields during the dry season thereby increasing the water retaining capacity of the soil (Chowdhury 1996).

Agroforestry: fuel and fodder: Agroforestry in Bangladesh, particularly surrounding the homestead, plays a vital role in providing fuel, fodder, fruits and timber for rural households. People grow trees to protect their houses from severe winds, storms, erosion etc. Homesteads generally have a range of trees and bamboos, although these are recently decreasing due to population growth and endemic poverty, stripping regions of natural resources.

People also cultivate trees and shrubs around the borders of their farmland to mark the boundary, maintain it after floodwaters recede, and to provide fuel and fruit. The trees trap ground water and help alleviate the effects of drought. Traditionally farmers followed a range of agroforestry practices around the country (Chowdhury *et al.* 1993). They cultivated a wide variety of trees around their homesteads and fields. In Tangail as many as 52 different species have been identified around the homestead. The needs and preferences of the family, together with local environmental factors, determine the selection of tree species. Trees and shrubs also produce nutritious fodder for livestock; for example, the leaves of jackfruit trees, provide an abundant supply of valuable feed for livestock during times of scarcity.

Sharma (1998) reported that in home-gardens fruit trees are preferred to timber and forest trees. More multipurpose trees are raised in the homestead. The land around the dwelling houses and huts is more intensively used for cultivating, for example, vegetables, fruits and betel nuts. Raising bamboo and other bushes protects the slopes around the homesteads. Such agroforestry practices ensure increased productivity as well as conservation of the soil.

Fisheries and livestock

Fisheries: Fish contributes a substantial amount of protein to the Bangladeshi diet, and about 10% of rural people live by fishing. The major fish resources include rivers, and perennial waterbodies (*haors, baors, beels*) on the floodplains. People continue to catch fish using traditional fishing crafts and techniques, developed over generations. People fish with their hands, spears, traps and nets. All the technologies used in the fishing sector are mostly indigenous and to date no modern fishing technology has entered into the arena of inland fishing in Bangladesh.

Alam *et al.* (1997) provide a valuable overview of the indigenous fishing technologies utilised in Bangladesh, including insights into management strategies associated with different waterbodies. A total of 51 types of fishing gear are reported. Gears used change with the seasons, according to flood conditions, target species and size of fish (Tsai and Ali 1997). Ahmed (1955) describes the principal fishing crafts and gears used by what was then the East Pakistani fishing community. All are locally made. Fishing boats depend on rowing, punting and sculling, the current and sometimes sails for propulsion. Fishers use comparatively big boats for fishing in large rivers and open waterbodies and small ones for fishing on narrow and shallow waterbodies like canals and *beels* (Jansen *et al.* 1989). Many different kinds of nets are used (see also Islam *et al.*, this volume).

Indigenous knowledge features in many spheres of aquaculture (Chadwick *et al.* 1998; Lewis *et al.* 1993; Lewis *et al.* 1996). This concerns two broad categories: production and trade. Production knowledge relates to the best locations, times and means of collecting wild hatchlings and how to handle them (i.e., correct temperature, most suitable feed etc.). It also concerns pond maintenance, feeding of fish, harvesting and treating disease. Trade concerns the sale and transport of eggs, fry and fingerlings, and later the harvested fish via formal and informal networks of fish traders and merchants. In many areas fish are dried, salted or fermented as a means of preservation.

In Lalmonirhat farmers frequently grind up the intestines of livestock (cattle, goats and poultry) to use as feed for fish in ponds. In Joydebpur fish are fed on termite eggs; carp sp., particularly *rui, katla* and *thai saputi,* are particularly fond of these. A common practice is the application of lime to ponds and *pagar* (small ponds lacking strong embankments) to clear unclean water. Many people add fragments of banana plant pseudostems to ponds to clear algal growth on the water's surface.

In Sunamganj rice husk is the preferred fish feed. After cleaning poultry runs, the droppings are fed to fish. Further fish cultivation techniques include:

- putting cow-dung into ponds instead of chemical fertilisers to increase fish production;
- stirring up the bottom of the pond by dragging a fishing net across it to increase food availability;
- putting lime, banana plants or *neem* tree branches into the water to prevent fish diseases; and
- spreading kerosene over aquatic weeds to destroy them (Chowdhury 1996).

Muniruddin (1997) found that many fish farmers place and fix a number of bamboo-tops and branches of trees in the middle of the pond where fish are raised. Whilst swimming the fish rub their bodies against the sticks and branches. It is thought that this rubbing of the body stimulates and enhances growth. Fish farmers also grow water lilies in ponds as they believe that the broad leaf of the lily provides shade and helps to keep the pond water relatively cool. This is congenial for the growth of fish.

Livestock rearing: Livestock supplies a considerable proportion of protein to people's diets. Archaeological evidence shows that people have raised goats and cattle for thousands of years. They not only eat the meat and drink the milk of cattle but also use the animals as draught power for ploughing the land. Livestock and poultry also produce manure and fuel for farmers. People collect snails from crop fields, break the shells and cut the flesh into small pieces to feed to young ducklings. This quality protein promotes rapid growth in the ducklings (Chowdhury 1996).

Farmers have a range of indigenous veterinary practices to treat different animal diseases (see Bandyopandhy and Shah 1998; Chowdhury *et al.* 1996). For example farmers in Tangail feed leafy branches of fresh *Lantana camara* to cattle to cure gas formation and poor digestion. They also use juice extracts of s*hati (Cercuma amada)* leaves, raw turmeric and ginger to treat this condition. Warm boiled rice mixed with paddy husk is often fed to cattle to remedy poor digestion. An ointment called *dade* made from *motihari* tobacco and *pathar chun* is applied to cure infected sores on the haunches of draft animals. Two types of medicine are used to treat cattle affected by a disease that causes the throat to swell so that they cannot swallow food; one is applied externally, the other administered orally. The medicine, used externally, is made with the stalks of aroids cut into pieces, mashed and mixed together with mud spilled by crabs. This is heated with water in an earthen pot and then smeared onto the swollen throat 3 or 4 times daily. The oral remedy is made by crushing *neem* leaves and bitter gourd leaves together (1:1 ratio) and stirred into water with a few drops of mustard oil. This is then heated and the liquid fed to affected cows whilst inserting wild aroid leaf stalks into the throat to clear the passageway. When hens develop the habit of sitting in the same place after they have finished laying eggs, their next ovulation is delayed. To prevent this hens are dipped into water several times and a long feather picked from the tail inserted into the nostrils. This irritates the bird and 'cures' it of inactivity (Chowdhury *et al.* 1996).

Nayakrishi

As mentioned above, *Unnayar Birkalpa Nirdharani Gabeshana* (UBINIG), a policy research organisation for alternative development, has established an innovative project known as *Nayakrishi* (meaning 'New Agriculture') to revive traditional farming practices in three rural areas: Tangail, Pabna and Cox's Bazar. It is a peasant initiative motivated and organised by UBINIG that aims to produce healthy food, an unpolluted environment and a better life for rural people. The principal aims of *Nayakrishi* are to increase the use of organic fertilisers instead of chemical fertilisers and to increase multicropping, intercropping and mixed cropping in place of High Yield Variety monoculture. The movement also encourages agroforestry and other eco-friendly local aspects of agriculture (see UBINIG 1996).

The initiative is gaining in popularity among poor farmers. This was seen in an assembly of peasants in Tangail (February 1998) supporting mixed cropping, and the use of organic fertilisers. Mrs Sameda Yasmeen, a representative of the *Nayakrishi* peasant group said, "We cultivate vegetables and fruit trees in the homesteads. We do not use chemical fertilisers and pesticides, rather we apply composed manure prepared by ourselves" (Baral 1998).

Local environmental management

Flood and weather forecasting: The people of Bangladesh depend on their local knowledge to cope with the extremes of the country's climate such as flooding, cyclones, drought etc. Many believe that floods are a blessing as well as a curse. Rural people are faced with floods every year and are accustomed to living with them. Although usually moderate, floods are sometimes devastating and people have developed a range of coping strategies (e.g. Schmuck 1996). Floods are divided into two types: *Borsha* (normal flooding due to monsoon rain) and *Bonna* (abnormal flood due to heavy rainfall and up-stream flow). People say that *Borsha* is necessary for agriculture and fisheries and view it as good for rural livelihoods, but *Bonna* is seen as harmful. Ullah (1991) and Huq and Das (1989) list a number of local strategies devised to help people cope with natural disasters like floods. When floodwaters begin to rise people move food and essential goods to safer places well above the water level. Children are often sent to nearby public buildings. Communities help each other, adopting common strategies to overcome their difficulties. In this way collective action is taken, providing a source of strength and a guiding principle for survival during crisis. People take shelter on comparatively high land and also move cattle onto the nearest roads, embankments etc. During severe floods, as in 1988 and 1998, people construct *macha* (platforms of bamboo) when the floodwater covers the floor of their home. They sleep and store their important material goods on top of these. The platforms are raised as the water level rises. Cereals and seeds are stored and preserved in large earthen pots known as *chari* during flooding and heavy rain. When the flood level drops the land is quickly prepared for early short-term crops. Farmers take seedlings nurtured on higher land and plant them as the water recedes on lower land.

Signs of impending rain include: thick clouds and lightening in the north-east combined with the moon having a 'halo'; streaks of lightening in the east with a rainbow in the west and high winds from the north; north-westerly and southerly winds; and ants building mounds. No rain is signalled by: a wind from the south-west; the frequent formation of a halo around the sun and moon; a rainbow in the east with the occurrence of clouds followed by the sky remaining clear at night; and the sun 'hiding behind the clouds'. Ahmed *et al.* (1996) discovered some folklore sayings and rhymes about the weather and occurrence of rain. One rhyme states that if the weather remains very dry in the month of *Chaitra* (March to April), storms and thunder will follow in the month of *Baishakh* (April to May). Another claims that if the sky remains clear in the month of *Jaishta* (May to June), there will be heavy rain during the monsoon.

Riverbank erosion: The displacement of population due to erosion is a common phenomenon in Bangladesh. About one million people are directly affected by riverbank erosion every year. People's perceptions and awareness of erosion plays a profound role in their preparation and adjustment, particularly for those living in high-risk areas. These people adopt indigenous strategies to cope. An investigation of indigenous adjustment strategies to riverbank erosion hazards (Mamun 1996) concluded that inhabitants of the floodplain are reluctant to take measures to control or intervene directly, which would often prove futile. Instead, they tend to adopt reduction of loss strategies through investment in moveable assets and insurance through the maintenance of social ties and group coherence. Many argue that the Government could better serve the population by redirecting resources towards the reinforcement of indigenous adjustment strategies.

Drought management: Drought occurs on the floodplain during the pre-monsoon period of low rainfall when evaporation losses are high and soil moisture is greatly decreased. This hampers crop production. Farmers prepare their land early to combat this problem as they know that young plants need reasonable topsoil moisture levels to survive and once established the plant-roots can explore the soil for moisture. Crops differ in their demand for water and farmers are aware of those that are more drought-tolerant. For example, farmers in many areas of the floodplain grow *aus* rice from seed in preference to transplanted *aus* because it requires less moisture (Brammer 1997). Another technique is to ladder fields of local *aus* rice and wheat when the seedlings are between 15 to 20 days old as this increases yield (Islam 1996). A local variety of *brinjal* with thorns on the stem and leaves that allow minimal water loss through transpiration is favoured in the dry season. Farmers heap extra soil around the plant stems to reduce evaporative water loss.

Rural health practices: Many people in rural Bangladesh depend on local medicinal plants and practices (see Begum *et al.*, this volume; Rahman *et al.*, this volume). The following are a few examples to give the reader some idea of this pharmacopoeia. *Telakucha* (*Coccinea cordifolia*) is a wild herb found in the backyard 'jungle' around many rural homesteads. It keeps the body cool and free from skin diseases. Women gather and cook the leaves with other leafy vegetables and either small or dried fish or mixed with a boiled mash of *lata* fish. People apply the fresh leaf extract to their foreheads as a cure for headache. Dried leaves are stored in tin containers for frying and making a mash eaten with rice. When heated slightly, the leaves aid problems associated with blood-sugar levels. In Tangail region, diabetics consume five to six leaves daily after lunch. Fresh *tulshi* (*Ocimum americanum*) leaf extract is popular as a cure for the common cold. Mothers who are breast-feeding, unless sick or incapable, eat certain foods to increase milk production such as black cumin mash with warm rice, curry made of catfish and bottle gourd and rice made with milk. During the winter mothers frequently massage their babies with mustard oil mixed with camphor or garlic and lay them in the gentle sunlight to cure coughs and aches. They mix burnt, powdered *sohaga* with pure honey and apply to babies' tongues to cure fungal thrush. In many areas of the country, women regularly serve *thankuni* (*Centella asiatica*) runner leaf mash as a lunch time meal as this is an effective preventative against digestive problems. It also helps to maintain a healthy appetite in people of all ages. Women follow many local health and household hygiene practices. They also follow a number of traditional methods of water purification, as they are aware that water taken from tanks and wells is often contaminated with bacteria, silt and floating solid particles (Chadwick *et al.* 1998). They filter water through a filtering cloth and also boil it thus destroying micro-organisms.

Conclusion

This review indicates that Bangladesh possesses a rich heritage of indigenous knowledge, though much has been lost during the 'modernisation' of agriculture. Rural people continue to maintain many practices, beliefs and traditions. Agriculture

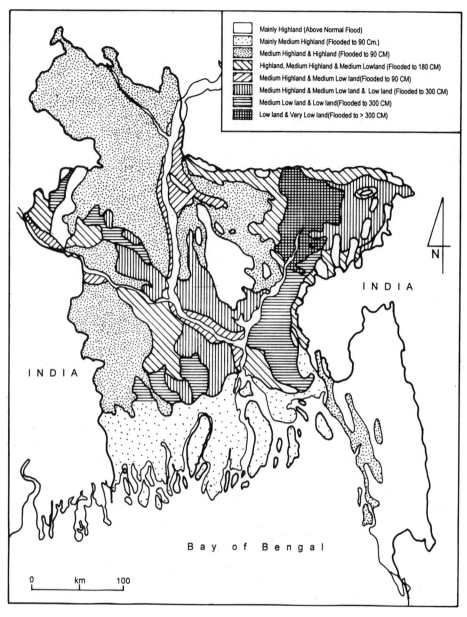

Figure 6.1 *Map of Bangladesh showing extent of flooding during monsoon (after Brammer 1996)*

remains the main occupation for the majority of the population and technologies that have been practiced for thousands of years continue to be utilised. Indigenous agricultural technologies are characterised by long-term risk-minimising strategies within the farmer's control. These ensure survival even during times of natural disaster such as floods, droughts, cyclones and tornadoes. They can help withstand market fluctuations, a regular occurrence in Bangladesh.

The literature documents how people of the floodplains draw on their local agricultural knowledge in selecting crops, preserving seeds, conserving soil, controlling pests, maintaining orchards, and so on. This knowledge is also employed for livestock rearing practices, veterinary medicine and small-scale fishing with indigenous fishing gear and locally constructed boats. Furthermore local knowledge is important for environmental management and rural healthcare.

In order to feed a growing population, modern agricultural technologies (including High Yield Variety seed, chemical fertiliser and pesticides and tube-well irrigation technology) have been widely adopted in recent decades and have increased crop yields many times over. But the extensive introduction of High Yield Varieties and associated agricultural technology promoted by top-down development strategies and programmes, has destroyed many local agricultural practices and the corresponding knowledge base that was fine-tuned with local ecological systems. It is time to capture and document properly the indigenous knowledge that our ancestors have developed over countless generations. The different ways in which people earn their livelihoods through farming, fisheries and other activities, need to be recorded urgently in order to prevent total loss. The *Unnayar Birkalpa Nirdharani Gabeshana* (mentioned earlier) has taken encouraging steps to revive traditional farming practices. Further action research is required to this end.

Notes

1 This chapter is part of a literature review and annotated bibliography for a project investigating "Indigenous knowledge and Natural Resources Research in the Floodplain Production System in Bangladesh". The purpose is to contribute to a more comprehensive understanding of local agricultural and environmental knowledge in relation to the floodplain production systems and rural livelihood strategies in Bangladesh. The study, undertaken by the University of Durham in association with the Bangladesh Centre for Advanced Studies (BCAS), was funded by the Department for International Development, UK.

2 My thanks to Peter Dixon and Paul Sillitoe.

**PART 2   INDIGENOUS KNOWLEDGE AND
AGROFORESTRY**

7 Use of Indigenous Knowledge in the Sustainable Development of Bangladeshi Farm Forestry

M. A. Quddus

IN THE ABSENCE OF SUFFICIENT NATURAL FORESTS, more than 50% of timber, 85% of fuelwood and 90% of bamboo used in Bangladesh comes from trees and shrubs grown by people on their farms, predominantly around their homesteads. This is known as "farm forestry". The homestead plots also provide most of the fruit and vegetables produced and consumed by the country, and contain many medicinal and other under-utilised plants. Unfortunately, due to increasing population pressure and the consequent over-exploitation, these homestead resources are becoming increasingly depleted. This includes the disappearance of many native species of plants, particularly ones that are lesser-known and under-utilised. Many native species are already extinct and many others are under threat. Although the government and NGOs are now quite active in tree planting campaigns, little has been done to restore and conserve the biodiversity of homestead woodlands.

Foresters and agriculturists lack sufficient knowledge of the ecology of the native species of plants to manage them effectively. The rural population's indigenous knowledge should be used in the design and launch of research and development programmes to restore and conserve the biodiversity of these wooded areas and to augment their productivity. This chapter describes some of the indigenous farm forestry knowledge and practices of Bangladeshi farmers and indicates the scope of utilising these to promote sustainable development. It also highlights policy and programme interventions that are needed to achieve this end. The suggested interventions include: identification and documentation of indigenous knowledge, launching indigenous knowledge-based research and development activities, and the training of research and development workers in related research techniques. It emphasises the need for the establishment of a data bank and a network of indigenous knowledge workers for effective research and development.

Bangladesh has only 2.19 million of its total 14.4 million ha. of land (i.e. 15.2% of total area) under state-owned forest. Furthermore, due to over-exploitation and poor management, the state forests have been depleted to such an extent that their actual tree cover is not more than 6-7%. These forests produced less than 50% of timber and 15% of fuelwood used in Bangladesh in the years 1986-87 with the remainder coming from farm woodlands (Bhuiyan 1994). The total area of homestead woodlands is about 0.27 million ha., approximately one-eleventh of the state forest area, yet it produces about four times more in terms of total volume of wood. Aside from timber and fuelwood, the homestead forests supply about 90% of all bamboo (Bhuiyan 1994) and almost all of the tree fruits consumed in the country. The traditional homestead forests of Bangladesh are not only highly productive, they are rich in species diversity.

Abedin and Quddus (1990*b*) recorded 49 different tree species in the homesteads of a village in Tangail district, central Bangladesh, and 34 species in the homesteads of a village in Ishurdi in the northwest. There were many other cultivated and naturally occurring herbs and shrubs in addition to these trees.

Bangladesh currently has a population of more than 120 million. Due to increasing population pressure and consequent over-exploitation, homestead woodlands are being depleted at an estimated annual rate of 10% (Bhuiyan 1994). As a result the gap between the demand and supply for various tree products is increasing. In the face of an acute shortage of fuelwood, people burn cow dung and crop residues, reducing the recycling of organic matter to the soil. This consequently affects productivity and the sustainability of crop cultivation. Bhuiyan (1994) estimates that 34% of the cow dung and 38% of the crop residues produced in the country in 1986-87 was used as domestic fuel. A silent but perhaps more insidious consequence of the depletion of homestead woodlands is the loss of biodiversity.

To combat this crisis, the government and many NGOs in Bangladesh are attempting to increase tree planting in rural areas, including farmers' home gardens, through motivational campaigns, training on nursery techniques, and other extension support. The campaigns have increased awareness, but diversity continues to decline because the species that farmers are now planting are those available from local nurseries where the range is substantially less than that of the traditional home gardens. Nurserymen generally receive training from a government agency or NGO in techniques applicable to common species but not for the lesser-known or rare species. In fact, there is a lack of knowledge among concerned professionals about the ecology, adaptation, and complex interactions on homestead wood plots and appropriate propagation techniques, production strategies and management practices for the numerous native plant species found there. Neither the forestry curriculum in the country or abroad, nor the vocational training facilities of the government and NGOs provide the opportunity to learn about them.

There is much to learn from indigenous knowledge systems. These may help to initiate and guide efforts to restore and conserve the biodiversity of homestead wooded holdings and to augment the overall productivity of the farm forestry sector in Bangladesh. There is considerable evidence that farmers in poorer countries have developed improved and sustainable farming practices grounded in their own knowledge and experience using locally available resources with little assistance from development workers (Haverkort 1991). Indigenous knowledge of forestry includes the farmers' understanding of the ecology, management and utilisation of various herbs, shrubs and trees in their home gardens and the practices and technologies they follow based on their knowledge, trials and experiences.

Indigenous forestry knowledge of Bangladeshi farmers

The efficient production and rich biodiversity of homestead wooded areas, which have evolved and been maintained by farmers without external inputs, are testament to their rich heritage of indigenous knowledge regarding the ecology, management and utilisation of the numerous plant species that grow there. The principal aspects of indigenous farm forestry knowledge of Bangladeshi farmers are as follows:

- farmers have an intimate knowledge of the major species of various herbs, shrubs and trees growing in their homesteads, crop fields and other places around their villages. Many of these are not known to professional foresters or agricultural scientists. A few elderly or especially interested people in any locality know the rare or minor species, and can readily identify them, locally and elsewhere. These knowledgeable farmers can assist professionals in the identification of minor and rare species, helping to trigger conservation programmes for such species;

- local people have detailed knowledge of the ecological adaptability of different species; for example what kind of niche and microclimate species favour — dry or swampy land, in open places or in shade, and so on. Farmers have developed multi-storey home gardens that are highly productive and biologically diverse based on this knowledge;
- farmers are knowledgeable about reproductive biology and cultivation techniques; for example the best mode of propagation, and the flowering and fruiting time of the different herbs, shrubs and trees occurring in their villages. They also have a heritage of cultivation practices for various plants, including seed preservation, seed treatment, planting time and method, vegetative propagation techniques etc. Much of this is not known to professionals, especially where the minor native species are concerned;
- farmers know various uses for the different parts of various herbs, shrubs and trees. They are well informed about the relative qualities of different species for similar uses and the relative timber, fuelwood, and fodder values of different trees. Some farmers also know special uses (e.g. medicinal) of some herbs, shrubs and trees that are unknown to others, including professional foresters and agriculturists;
- the people of Bangladesh have traditional knowledge and skills regarding the efficient processing of plant products. Some of these practices are widespread while others are restricted to particular areas or known only to a few people within a village. For example, lac culture and manufacture of shellac occurs only in the district of Chapai Nawabganj. On the other hand, preparation of herbal medicines, the making of bamboo baskets, and so on are known throughout the country, although sometimes only a few people in a village are knowledgeable.

Indigenous farm forestry practices and farmers' innovations

The farmers of Bangladesh have evolved a sophisticated range of farm forestry practices that form the basis of their indigenous knowledge, and which are subject to constant updating through trials, observation and experiences. To give the reader some appreciation of the extent and sophistication of this knowledge, the following list gives a sample of some of these practices and innovations. Firstly, some indigenous farm forestry practices and innovations relating to agroforestry and tree management:

- knowledge of preferred vegetative propagation techniques for different tree species e.g., stem cuttings for *sajina*;
- application of soil mulch in bamboo groves in the spring (March-April) to induce regeneration and vigorous growth of young bamboo shoots;
- application of water hyacinth and other mulching materials at the base of coconut and other trees during the dry season to conserve soil moisture;
- the technology of lac culture on Indian plum (*Zizyphus nummularia*) trees in Nawabganj district (Hussain *et al.* 1991);
- cropland agroforestry practices of the High Ganges Floodplain region include the deliberate retention of naturally growing *babla* (*Acacia nilotica*), date palm

(*Phoenix sylvestris*), palmyra palm (*Borassus flabellifer*) and *khair (Acacia catechu)*. These trees are maintained in sparse stands through thinning operations (Abedin *et al.* 1988);

- some farmers also plant mango (*Mangifera indica*), jackfruit (*Artocarpus heterophyllus*) and *sissoo (Dalbergia sissoo)* trees, regularly spacing them around their crop fields (Abedin *et al.* 1988; Aktar *et al.* 1992; Quddus 1996);
- in the Madhupur Tract, farmers plant jackfruit trees along the boundaries of their fields (Quddus 1996).

The multi-storey homestead agroforestry system found throughout Bangladesh features the cultivation of shade tolerant crops under trees in orchards. The species combination varies between locations. Some examples are:

- cultivation of taro (*Colocasia* spp.) and ginger (*Zingiber officinale*) under *sil koroi (Albizia procera)* trees in the Chittagong Hill Tract District (NAWG 1996);
- cultivation of turmeric (*Curcuma longa*) and ginger under bamboo (*Bambusa* spp.) and coconut (*Cocos nucifera*) trees in Barisal (NAWG 1996);
- cultivation of turmeric and ginger as under-storey crops on mahogany (*Swietenia mahogani*) plantations in Madhupur (NAWG 1996).

Some climbing vegetables are cultivated to climb up trees. Again species' combinations vary throughout the country. Some examples include:

- country bean (*Dolichos lablab*) grown on *sajina (Moringa oleifera)* trees in many parts of Bangladesh (NAWG 1996);
- black pepper (*Piper nigrum*) and betel leaf (*Piper betel*) grown on mahogany trees in raised plantations in Madhupur (NAWG 1996);
- yam (*Dioscorea* spp.) grown on different trees in farmers' homesteads, most commonly on non-fruit and light-crowned trees (Alamgir 1997).

Secondly, some indigenous farm forestry practices and innovations relating to pest management technologies:

- the use of dried *neem* leaves to protect stored grains from insect infestation (Rana 1997; see also Lalon, this volume);
- application of ashes to tree seedlings and vegetables to control insects;
- the use of *gabion* (a bamboo enclosure with four sides but no ceiling) to protect planted tree seedlings from goat and cattle;
- the use of cow dung solution to control damage of tree seedlings and saplings by goat and cattle;
- the use of *kaktarua* (scarecrows) and the beating of tins (as drums) to protect mature fruits in orchards (mango, litchi, banana etc.) from damage by birds;
- seasoning of bamboo by submerging in water for several days before use in construction work to prevent shrinkage and insect infestation;
- protection of bamboo poles and rafts from insect attack by coating them in coaltar or bitumen.

Thirdly, some indigenous farm forestry practices and innovations relating to processing and utilisation of tree products:

- use of timber to make furniture, wheels for carts, agricultural implements, toys and handicrafts;

- use of bamboo and cane to make furniture and handicrafts;
- use of palmyra palm leaves to make hand fans;
- use of the midribs of coconut leaves to make brooms;
- manufacture of molasses from datepalm and palmyra palm juices;
- manufacture of tannin from *khair* tree bark;
- lac processing to manufacture shellac by Nawabganj farmers (Hussain *et al.* 1991);
- preparation of herbal medicines by *kabiraj* (herbal doctors);
- preparation of pickles from different fruits, e.g., mango, jujube, Indian olive (*Eliocarpus longifolia*) and lemon (*Citrus lemon*).

It is important to note that these indigenous know-hows and practices are not static. Farmers continuously experiment to improve on them. For example, the Village Farm Forestry Project (VFFP) has found some innovative farmers planning and trying alternative tree propagation and management techniques quite different from standard practices (Quddus *et al.* 1998). Some examples are:

- propagation of eucalyptus (*Eucalyptus camaldulensis*) using stem cuttings in Magura district (VFFP 1997);
- propagation of *chambal* (*Albizia richardiana*) through root cuttings in Jessore district (VFFP 1998*a*);
- control of an epidemic disease affecting *sissoo* trees by using diesel and kerosene in Kushtia district (VFFP 1988*b*);
- control of insect infestation in tree seedlings in a nursery by applying extracts of *bishkatali* (*Polygonum hydropiper*) leaves in Dinajpur district (VFFP 1988*c*).

Identification and documentation of such farmers' experiments and innovations may save a great deal of time for researchers and hasten the development of appropriate technological interventions.

Indigenous knowledge and sustainable farm forestry development

There is much scope for utilising indigenous knowledge for the sustainable development of farm forestry in Bangladesh (Mathias 1994). Only some of the possibilities are explored here. There has been little documentation of the occurrence, distribution, biology, use and management of many native plant species that are cultivated or maintained by rural people in different parts of the country. Agricultural and forestry students acquire no knowledge of them in their training which limits their ability to experiment and encourage the potential of these native species in their work. If farm forestry indigenous knowledge is taken seriously and documented, foresters and agriculturists can learn from it and apply any insights in their professional activities.

Indigenous knowledge has an important role to play in our efforts to restore and conserve the biodiversity of village forests in Bangladesh. Immediate steps must be taken to conserve threatened species and to restore species diversity in rural home gardens. We should identify experienced rural persons who know about the ecology and management of the lesser-known and fast disappearing species and document their knowledge. This knowledge could then be disseminated among others through participatory development programmes. The best practices of farmers could also be disseminated among other farmers to augment productivity, helping them to improve the yield and quality of their woodlands. One area of farm forestry that could benefit from the wider dissemination of indigenous knowledge is the development and promotion of intercropping practices on wooded plots of land. For example, the establishment of small areas of *sissoo*, mahogany, eucalyptus, *goda neem* (*Melia azaderach*) and other fast-growing species is an increasingly popular land-use practice in Bangladesh, and although indigenous knowledge exists about many crop species that are suitable for growing under the shade of trees, no under-storey crops are cultivated.

Indigenous knowledge also offers scope for broadening technological options available to social forestry projects. Today, fast growing exotic species are widely used in social forestry projects along roadsides, on embankments, in encroached forests and on other public and communal lands, which are intended to increase resources available to the poor. Indigenous knowledge may suggest appropriate native species and management practices for these forestry programmes which might have advantages such as product diversification, pest control, easier marketing, etc.

Indigenous knowledge may further the development of cottage industries. Farmers' knowledge and skills in making handicrafts and using tree products in other activities may be converted into more lucrative commercial activities. This could build on recent precedents, such as taking the traditional handicraft skills of rural women in Bangladesh and turning them into export-oriented cottage industries, such as *Nakshi Kantha* (embroidered quilt) making by some NGOs. Similar ventures may be initiated for traditional handicrafts using raw materials from trees that show potential for further development as either export or domestic market oriented cottage industries.

Some rural people possess knowledge about the medicinal value of plants, their processing and application as herbal medicines (see Begum, Haq and Naber, this volume; Zuberi, this volume). Integrated efforts are needed to promote the production of these medicinal plants and the processing of herbal medicines from them, possibly on a commercial scale. We need scientific research to identify the biochemically active ingredients of these plants with a view to further refining the technology to enable large-scale production of herbal medicines.

Policies and programme interventions

We need to start programmes of research to identify and document indigenous farm forestry knowledge and practices, particularly those that are unique to a community or held by a few people but have potential for use in other areas. The research and development organisations dealing with farm forestry, social forestry, agroforestry and farming systems in Bangladesh are in a position to take the initiative. The major areas demanding urgent indigenous knowledge documentation are:

- the occurrence, ecological adaptation, biology, management and use of lesser-known native plants (herbs, shrubs and trees);
- the management and manipulation of trees to obtain higher yields, better tree forms, more effective pest control, etc.;
- the processing and use of homestead woodland plant products, alternative uses and opportunities to increase value.

Participatory Rural Appraisal (PRA) could be an efficient means of data collection (Abedin and Haque 1991). Some indigenous knowledge data could be collected during field visits by scientists or by asking extension staff. This can be achieved by inter-viewing individuals in the area, depending on costs and time. The case study method is valuable for documentation. A team of two scientists, one with a biological and the other a social science (preferably anthropological) background would be ideal for indigenous knowledge investigations. The selection of reliable informants is the key to successful indigenous knowledge identification and documentation. The gender of those who hold the indigenous knowledge under investigation may be critical, men and women frequently specialising in different domains (see Stokoe, this volume). Innovative farmer workshops could be devised for further authentication (Abedin and Haque 1991).

Further research is needed to advance on indigenous knowledge and develop more useful technology, to further improve on farmers' traditional practices. Ideally such research and development activities should be planned and conducted with the active participation of farmers so that they can evaluate the alternatives for themselves and adopt the best one(s). In fact, farmers have their own research methods, which we should strive to promote. Research and development organisations should be a catalyst for the technological development process by supplying additional information to increase the options for testing and shorten the research time. Researcher-managed on-farm trials and even on-station trials can be undertaken simultaneously when appropriate, to incorporate basic agronomic research procedures such as replication avoidance. Laboratory based research may be undertaken to establish the science underlying indigenous or farmer-innovated practices.

If entrepreneurial confidence and skills are fostered among those involved, some local farm forestry indigenous knowledge practices may be transformed into commercial activities from cottage industries. These may include the manufacturing of shellac from lac insects, making wooden tools and toys, the preparation of herbal medicines, etc. Development organisations, government and NGOs, may promote entrepreneurship helping individuals and communities to prepare projects to secure bank loans where needed. Co-operatives may be encouraged where activities are difficult for individuals to carry out alone. Research and development organisations could help communities to create formal organisations and plan and implement projects based on indigenous knowledge.

The protection of intellectual property rights should be accorded priority. Indigenous knowledge and practices with the potential for commercial use should be considered the intellectual property of the individuals or communities. We should take steps to ensure that property rights should be protected legally. Citation of the names of innovators when documenting indigenous knowledge may be one way of accrediting intellectual property. The entrepreneurial farmer or community may be prompted and assisted to register their patent and trademark so that they can take legal action for unauthorised exploitation of their knowledge and innovations.

The identification and documentation of farm forestry indigenous knowledge needs knowledge and skills in appropriate research methodologies. If such skills do not exist among the research and development staff of organisations, training should be arranged for them (e.g. in participatory methodologies, anthropological techniques, social survey procedures, etc.).

Several government agencies and NGOs are now involved in the development of the farm forestry sector; some are also marginally involved in indigenous knowledge related activities. The experiences and findings of these organisations should be exchanged to avoid unnecessary duplication and efforts should be made to integrate their work. A network for organisations interested in indigenous knowledge research and its potential for development should be supported. We already have umbrella organisations such as the Bangladesh Agricultural Research Council (BARC) and the Bangladesh Resource Centre for Indigenous Knowledge (BARCIK; see Sen *et al.*, this volume). But they need adequate funding. Interested individuals from various organisations should support one another through a network. The indigenous knowledge network should develop and maintain a database to provide an information storage and retrieval service. It should facilitate networking between organisations, establish a central information service, and serve as a venue for activities of common interest, such as training in indigenous knowledge research methodology.

Conclusion

Research into indigenous knowledge of homestead woodlands should not be undertaken as an isolated or occasional activity; research and development organisations have often limited themselves to piecemeal studies, identifying and documenting isolated knowledge and practices but rarely looking beyond them. Rather, the goal should be to make use of indigenous knowledge to further the sustainable development of rural communities and conservation of their environments. We should strive to identify and document indigenous knowledge and local practices, undertake research to validate and develop them, and work to integrate them into the mainstream development process (Figure 7.1). There is a need here for an umbrella organisation to promote research and the utilisation of indigenous knowledge in various areas of rural development, including farm forestry. We should promote awareness, interest and motivation for indigenous knowledge research in both government and non-government organisations who routinely use a top-down and not a grass roots approach in their development programmes.

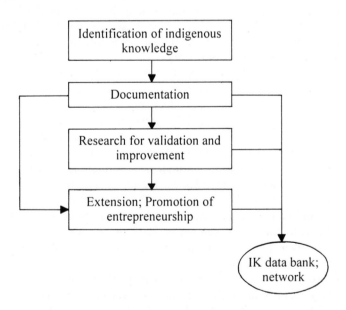

Figure 7.1 *Framework of indigenous knowledge-based research and development programme*

8 Tree Pathology and Bangladeshi Agroforestry Practices

Mohammad Abdur Rahman

APPROXIMATELY 9% OF BANGLADESH'S land is under forest. The forest areas are principally in the Sundarbans (mangrove forest), Chittagong, the Chittagong Hill Tracts and Sylhet (hill forest), Dhaka-Mymensingh (sal forest) and as village wood lots in some of the 68,000 villages scattered across the country.

Bangladesh's continuing population growth, and corresponding shortage of timber and fuelwood, is a major concern for the present and the foreseeable future. Recent research has revealed that nearly 70% of timber and 90% of fuelwood comes from villages. A huge gap exists between supply and demand of fuelwood, timber and other forest products. This has resulted in over exploitation of both state forests and village homesteads. Over exploitation of cultivable land has depleted soil fertility in much of the country. Scarcity of fuelwood has resulted in the burning of cow dung and crop residues. This too has contributed to the depleted fertility of the land.

Agroforestry is thought to be an appropriate strategy for sustainable increases in land productivity under both forest and crops. It can help satisfy people's need for fuelwood, timber and food, whilst at the same time protecting the environment and generating income opportunities (Magno 1986; Singh 1987; Dalmacio 1989). Agroforestry strengthens the economic security of poor people by diversifying their sources of income and staggering harvesting times. Agroforestry around forestland acts as a kind of 'social fencing' which protects the forest resources (Abedin and Quddus 1990*a*).

Indigenous agroforestry practices in Bangladesh include shifting cultivation of the *jhum* 'slash and burn' variety in hill forests and mixed cultivation of perennial trees and annual vegetable crops in homesteads. Additionally *Phoenix sylvestris, Acacia nilotic,* and *A. catechu* are grown on higher areas of the Gangetic flood plain, along with *Artocarpus heterophyllus* and *Mangifera indica*, which have been cultivated for centuries. Recently in the districts of Chuadanga, Meherpur and Kushtia there has been a trend towards planting *Dalbergia sissoo* trees on agricultural land. This is especially true of richer farmers. Some farmers have begun establishing plantations of *A. heterophyllus* and *P. sylvestris.* Also the planting of *A. heterophyllus* on plot boundaries has become popular in the last 15 years, especially in the Madhupur tract (Abedin and Quddus 1990*a*). In Dinajpur a number of fast growing trees are cultivated including *Eucalyptus camaldulensis, Acacia auriculiformis, A. mangium, Cassia siamea, Albizia procera* and *Dalbergia sissoo.*

Researchers from the Bangladesh Forest Research Institute have been investigating the following tree species:

* Long rotation: *Dalbergia sissoo, Eucalyptus camaldulensis, A. lebbek, Azadirachta indica, Mangifera indica and Artocarpus heterophyllus.*

- Medium rotation: *Bambusa* spp. and *Zizyphus jujuba.*
- Short rotation: *Leucaena leucocephala* and *Sesbania sesban.*

On-going research at The Bangladesh Agriculture Research Institute includes assessing multi-purpose tree species for plot boundary plantation in the High Barind Tract. The agroforestry systems promoted by the Government, NGOs and by the farmers themselves on the floodplain can be broadly categorised as follows:

- homestead agroforestry;
- agroforestry on private agricultural land;
- agroforestry in the denuded and encroached-upon public forests; and
- strip-side agroforestry.

Pathological considerations

A serious problem facing the indigenous cultivation of trees is disease. This paper reviews knowledge pertaining to some pathological conditions that affect commonly cultivated tree species and their treatment. Pathological aspects of the trees most commonly used in agroforestry systems are as follows:

Dalbergia sissoo: a large deciduous tree with a loose spreading crown that demands strong sunlight. The principle diseases affecting the tree are:

Wilt disease: A systemic disease that manifests itself during the rainy period *borosha* (July to September). Symptoms include yellowing and death of leaves in acropetal succession. Eventually the entire tree turns yellow. In the later stages of the disease the leaves drop off and the branches become increasingly bare. Affected trees die within a few months. It is likely that the disease is caused by a *Fusarium* sp. The wilting of the tree is most common on plantations with hard soils and inadequate drainage. Many local farmers appear to understand that if *Dalbergia sissoo* is grown on raised sites with lighter textured soils and adequate soil moisture where drainage is good, trees tend to grow free of this disease.

Root rot: Ganoderma lucidum causes root rot in *sissoo* trees of advanced age. The affected trees exhibit a 'stag-headed' appearance, which they may maintain for a number of years before eventually dying. The fungus is spread by root to root contact and therefore spreads most rapidly in plantations. The fungus commonly produces a sporophore at the base of dead trees. Indigenous techniques for combating the disease include digging trenches around affected trees, raising mixed plantations and removing the stumps of dead trees.

Eucalyptus camaldulensis: A number of diseases affect this quick-growing tree. They include:

Damping off: This disease is a fungal rot that causes seedlings to collapse at the collar area of the plant. It is usually *Pytthium* sp., *Fusarium* sp., or *Rhizoctonia solani* that cause damping off. Indigenous techniques to avoid outbreaks include ensuring good soil drainage and avoidance of particular organic manures. Maintaining a soil pH between 5 and 6, and the application of 2% forman/copper oxychloride/Dithane M45 as a soil drench may also be useful.

Pink disease: This disease is caused by the aptly named *Corticium salmonicolor.* Pink disease causes mortality to major branches accompanied by an invasion of the stem cambium by the pathogen with resultant girdling. In severe cases this may affect the whole crown but rarely kills the tree completely. The disease is first apparent when gum is exuded from stems or young branches. This is followed by the growth of white silky threads on the surface of the bark. As the bark dies the superficial growth dries up and pink masses of sterile mycelium appear as either pustules or crusts. The pustules may form in lines along cracks in the bark, whereas the crusts coalesce separately on the underside of branches. The disease is readily identifiable at this early, sterile stage but subsequent developments are important for the dissemination of the fungus. Indigenous control measures seem to centre on the excision and destruction of infected branches. Treatment of infected areas by fungicides (such as Bordeaux mixture) is also recommended.

Gummosis: Symptoms of this disease include swelling and splitting of the bark, which often exudes a shining golden viscous liquid. In severe cases bark may die varyingly on the main bole, exposing the wood from beneath. If the girdling is partial, the affected trees continue to live; but if complete or nearly so, the plant parts above this region usually die. Bakshi (1976) theorised that gummosis represents a reaction to a wound. With this in mind, plants should be protected from injury where possible thus minimising the risk of gummosis. Species should be planted on suitable sites to avoid damage.

Mildew: A powdery mildew caused by *Oidium eucalypti* can occur on *E. camaldulensis*. The main symptom is whitish, powdery patches on leaves. These spread and are later associated with leaf distortion and necrosis, which leads to leaf cast. Airborne condida are produced on the infected leaves. A spray of a sulphur-based fungicide, an introduced practice, helps to control the spread of the disease.

Acacia auriculiformis: This is an important fast growing species that has been widely planted in Bangladesh, primarily for biomass production. The principal diseases of this tree species include:

Powdery mildew: Up to 50-70% of *Acacia auriculiformis* seedlings may be affected by this condition caused by *Oidium* spp. Although the disease does not cause plant mortality it does affect seedling development. To control powdery mildew, elemental sulphur (dust) or 0.2% MANOB can be applied every other week.

Leaf spot: On nursery seedlings and saplings of *Acacia auriculiformis* small dark brown lesions may form on the foliage. These later coalesce into large dark brown to black necrotic areas. This condition is caused by the *Colletotrichum* state of *Glomerella cingulata*.

Artocarpus heterophyllus: The 'jackfruit' tree is a multi-purpose tree species and is widely planted in agroforestry systems in Bangladesh. Two new diseases of this tree are 'dieback' and 'canker', first recorded in a plantation at Dulhahazza in Chittagong during 1978 and 1979.

Dieback: The first visible symptom of dieback is a change in leaf colour from green to pale green, then light yellow, through to reddish-yellow. The older leaves fall off first followed by younger ones. This may occur on small branches, on one or more of the major branches, or on most of the crown. After the leaves fall off the branches die. Initially the small young branches die followed by the older ones. The transition zone of healthy and dead wood of a dying branch is brown in colour. The older, dead branches dry up and turn greyish white. Dieback in jackfruit trees can cause severe damage but so far no control measures, indigenous or scientific, have been discovered. Further study is required, especially considering the extent of loss due to this disease and the economic potential of the jackfruit tree as a multipurpose tree species (Rahman *et al.* 1987; Rahman 1997*a*, 1997*b*).

Canker: Canker on jackfruit trees starts as a blackening of the bark, generally at the bases of small, dead branches. The dead area gradually expands followed by a light brown discoloration and the death of sapwood underneath. As the tree increases in girth the canker-affected portion fails to show any new growth and a depression usually develops. On the bark of the dead area small, rounded, reddish-yellow fruit bodies of *Nectria haematococca* develop profusely during the monsoon. Again, we have no treatment.

Bambusa spp: Bamboo in village groves is an important resource for villagers. A large proportion of the total supply of bamboo in Bangladesh comes from these groves.

Bamboo blight: Bamboo blight is the principal disease causing severe mortality of young culms in recent years and is most severe in the greater Rajshahi, Chittagong, Comilla and Sylhet districts (in decreasing order of occurrence). *Bambusa balcooa* and *B. vulgaris* are the most severely affected bamboo species. So far, there are no grounds to suggest that cultural practices encourage the disease. Traditionally bamboo blight has been controlled by local methods such as the removal of blighted culms, burning debris in-situ in clumps in *chaitra* to *baishak* (April), adding new soil to culms before the onset of the monsoon in *baishak* (April to May). More recently this has been replaced by the application of the fungicide Dithane 45 as a soil drench (Rahman 1987*a*, 1987*b*, 1988; see also Rahman 1978; Rahman and Khisa 1981; Boa and Rahman 1983, 1987). It should be noted that the simpler cultural practices were in common usage before the popularising of western techniques. This valuable indigenous knowledge is rarely called upon today. These traditional indigenous techniques are effective and the author strongly advocates their use.

Gmelina arborea: The *gamar* tree is often damaged by root rot or leaf spot.

Root rot: A moderately severe root rot of *gamar* seedlings in the nurseries of the Pulpwood Plantation Division, Kaptai occurred in 1978. *Fusarium solani* was found to be the pathogen. The problem has also been noted in strip-side plantations in north Bengal. Control of the disease is achieved by the application of Granosan M applied as a soil drench on dying and apparently healthy seedlings (Rahman *et al.* 1982; Rahman and Alam 1994).

Leaf spot: The most common foliage disease of *gamar* is *Colletotrichum* leaf spot. Initially small pinhead spots surrounded by light yellow haloes appear on mature leaves. Under high humidity, a favourable condition to the fungus, the spots enlarge. Severely affected leaves turn yellow and fall off. Isolation and pathogenicity tests confirm the presence of *Collectotrichum gloeosporioides*. This can be controlled by the application of an industrially produced copper fungicide such as copper oxychloride every week for about three weeks.

Mistletoe: Infestations of mistletoe, an angiospermic parasite, have been found to be most severe on *gamar*, teak and *malakana koroi* (*Paraserianthes falcataria*). These parasitic bushes have green foliage and small branches in rather dense clusters and are seen to grow on various parts of the crown of affected trees. The parasite is quite distinct from the host foliage. Mistletoe produces its own flowers and fruits. It absorbs water and nutrients from the host plant by way of inserting an extensive system of sinker roots into the xylem of the host. This hampers the growth of the host. As the parasite grows it engulfs the host branch and ultimately kills this part of the tree. The greater the shade and thicker the canopy cover, the less likely *gamar* will be affected by mistletoe. It is difficult to control.

***Melia azedarach*:** This tree species can be severely affected by both collar rot and heart rot.

Collar rot: Nurseries of *Melia azedarach* seedlings are sometimes affected by collar rot after a period of heavy rain. Infection occurs directly at the base of the main stem causing a rapid wilt of foliage and the subsequent death of the infected seedlings. Surviving seedlings produce new growth below the dead region. Mortality is not high but the high infection rate makes this disease problematic. Water logging must be avoided to reduce the severity of any damage. Application of 2% formalin as a soil drench may also limit damage.

Heart rot: Heart rot of twelve to fourteen year old *Melia azedarach* plantations has been reported. The pathogen is a *Phellinus* sp. The degraded logs can only be used for hardboard chips instead of veneer. Dieback caused by *Graphium* sp. also occurs. Indigenous knowledge of the problem suggests that avoidance of wet sites and selection of resistant varieties is beneficial. Heart rot affected trees should not be allowed to over mature because this serves to encourage the spread of the disease.

***Calamus guruba*:** Known locally as '*jali bet*' this species is particularly susceptible to leaf spot.

Leaf spot: This disease, first noticeable as light brown spots on leaves, is caused by the fungus *Guignardia calami*. The spots on the leaves gradually enlarge and coalesce to form dead areas. Foliage lower down in the tree can be severely affected. Outbreaks of leaf spot have been recorded on *jali bet* in nurseries at BFRI campus, Hazarikhil, among other places. The disease can be controlled by the application of the fungicide Dithane M 45 (50g in 16 litres of water) sprayed onto the foliage of the seedlings until they are soaked. Generally 2-3 weekly applications are enough to control the disease if it is diagnosed early (Rahman 1997*a*, 1997*b*).

***Anthocecephalus cadamba*:** Known locally as '*kadam*', this species can be severely affected by 'dieback'.

Dieback: In December 1987 a severe case of dieback in seedlings of *kadam* occurred in Rajshahi and a number of other nurseries under the Pulpwood Plantation Division, Kaptai. The disease began with the rotting of a certain amount of foliage. The rotting areas quickly coalesced to form a larger necrotic area that killed both young and old leaves. Since affected seedlings exhibited healthy roots it was concluded that infection was foliage-based. The fungus *Rhizoctonia solani* was found to be the cause of dieback. A specific control measure has not yet been devised for this disease but it seems likely that the application of a fungicide such as copper oxychloride in the early stages of the disease would be effective.

Conclusion

There are a range of diseases affecting commonly cultivated trees in Bangladesh and only a limited range of indigenous control measures. The control of tree pathogens is a promising area for the combination of scientific research with indigenous knowledge of forestry. Local agroforestry practices are effective but control of diseases could substantially increase production of trees, which is sorely needed. Demand for fuel, biomass, timber and so on is increasing relentlessly.

9 In Praise of the Indigenous *Neem* Tree

L. Mohammed Lalon

THE INHABITANTS OF BANGLADESH have known about the *Neem* tree since time immemorial. From the dawn of civilisation in South Asia people from all walks of life have depended on *Neem* for its beneficial qualities. Historical documents tell that the early settlers of Bengal thought of *Neem* as a life saving tree, depending on it for many purposes. They used it to combat various diseases, in addition to using it in routine household tasks. During the early period it served as an all-purpose drug. The *Neem* tree was respected by Hindu and other indigenous communities. Indeed it became an object of worship.

Knowledge about *Neem* is therefore ancient. The oldest known texts on South Asian medicine provide information on it. In the traditional *Ayurveda* system of Indian medicine *Neem* plays a central role. There is also mention of *Neem* in the rural communities in the region. Subsequently, during the middle ages, the *Unani* system of medicine continued to recognise the beneficial effects of *Neem* in preventing and curing different diseases. In recent times *Neem* has created something of a sensation as a wonder tree; scientists from different disciplines recognise its many values. It has been discovered as a source of natural wealth for all humankind. It has many uses in addition to its traditional role as a medicine. For example, people use it as a contraceptive and also to control insects; being natural it does not have the undesirable effects of biocides.

The potential for *Neem* in Bangladesh

At present there is little scientific research on *Neem* in Bangladesh and few commercial uses have been developed for day to day life. Indeed use of *Neem* is on its way to extinction in parts of Bangladesh. Neither individuals nor any institution is preserving this traditional natural resource. We should take appropriate measures now to protect existing *Neem* trees and encourage plantations throughout the country. We should declare *Neem* a national asset of Bangladesh and encourage its many uses. The government should play a pioneering role in achieving these objectives by starting a social movement to promote awareness and motivate people to relearn about *Neem* and its uses. The entire tree is useful. The following are among the multifarious uses of *Neem*:

Leaves: These are effective against skin diseases and scabies in particular. The leaf extract is traditionally used in Bangladesh for bathing chicken pox patients. The extract also controls crop pests and insects. Tea prepared from the leaves is effective in preventing fever. Fried leaves serve as a de-worming agent.

Fruits: A favourite food of domestic fowl, meeting their nutritional needs. Oil extracted from *Neem* seeds has various traditional uses: treating skin diseases, controlling lice and curing certain diseases in domestic animals. It also has commercial industrial uses, being used in the preparation of soap, shampoo, pesticides and a medicinal drug.

Neem *Cake*: This is used by betel leaf cultivators to prevent viral infections. It can also be used to protect crops from insect pests; spread on the land it has no harmful effects on crops or nature.

***Bark*:** An important ingredient in some drugs and medicine.

***Wood*:** Toothpicks and toothbrushes made from new growth have long been used in rural areas. *Neem* wood is in demand for making furniture and particularly doors and windows because it is so resistant to all sorts of pests.

***Honey*:** *Neem* flower honey is considered very high quality.

Neem also has a role in conserving the environment of our planet by reducing erosion, desertification and excessive temperatures. We at Rajshahi Niskrity NGO intend to start a social movement to help *Neem* to help us, now that we understand its many varied uses above other trees to the benefit of humankind. In addition to its traditional role in pest control and its wonderful capacity to heal, it can also help us to control the excessive growth of our population with its contraceptive properties. We cannot afford to lose this natural resource and associated indigenous knowledge. We must act now to preserve them.

PART 3   INDIGENOUS KNOWLEDGE AND PLANT RESOURCES

10 Indigenous Knowledge of Plant Use in a Hill Tracts Tribal Community and Its Role in Sustainable Development

M. A Rahman, Aditi Khisa, S. B. Uddin and C. C. Wilcock

IN BANGLADESH there are about nineteen major tribes of which fourteen live in the Hill Tracts districts (Chakma 1992, 1993). They include the following tribal groups: *Chakma, Marma, Murong, Tripura, Thanchumga, Chack, Bhome, Pangkhoa, Kheyang, Rheyang, Rhakhain, Lushai* and *Kuki*. The lifestyle, culture and language differ between each tribe (Rahman 1997c). These tribal communities remain dependent on the natural resources available in the forests of their hilly region for their livelihoods. They have a long historical association with the area and a rich cultural heritage distinct from the dominant Bengali population. In Bengali they are called *Pahari*. The tribes make extensive use of the biological resources of their homeland, including many wild plants. We have yet to fully document their vast store of knowledge, which together with associated indigenous practices is being lost, day by day with the advance of development and modernisation. For example the establishment of community health services in the hill areas is resulting in people discarding traditional herbal cures.

This chapter presents the results of an investigation conducted under a Biodiversity Link Project between Chittagong and Aberdeen (U.K.) universities in the Rangamati, Khagrachhari and Bandarban districts. We worked with the *Chakma* tribe, focusing on tribal knowledge and practices regarding the use of wild vascular plants, thirty-four of which were used in the treatment of diseases. We conducted an ethnobotanical survey among these tribal hill people to explore and document their indigenous knowledge of wild plants, particularly as sources of medicine but also as food and for other products. The tribal and scientific names and traditional uses of forty plant species are listed in Table 10.1.

Table 10.1: Catalogue of *Chakma* plants

A. **Medicinal uses**

Chakma name	Specific name	Family/Colln.no	Uses
1 *Bhuti tida*	*Hedyotis corymbosa*	Rubiaceae/L654	Leaf extract is used to alleviate abdominal pains
2 *Kuduk junjuni*	*Crotalaria verrucosa*	Papilionaceae/L1314	Leaf extract is applied to soothe skin allergies
3 *Udul pata*	*Sterculia villosa*	Sterculariaceae/L2742	Water extract of petioles is given with sugar as a treatment for rheumatism

(Contd.)

(Continued)

Chakma name	Specific name	Family/Colln.no	Uses
4 *Bhutta ladi*	*Dioscorea pentaphyla*	Dioscoreaceae/ L1542.A	Paste of the plant, when mixed with oil, is used to treat rheumatic diseases
5 *Aash mul gach*	*Vitex* sp.	Verbenaceae/L656.B	A paste prepared from the bark is used in the treatment of jaundice
6 *Khona gach*	*Oroxylum indicum*	Bignoniaceae	Extract is taken as a cure for jaundice. Young shoots and fruit are considered foodstuffs
7 *Ga urbo*	*Vitis* sp.	Vitaceae	Bark extract is used in a cure for jaundice. Fruit is eaten
8 *Aada thora*	*Buddleja asiatica*	Buddlejaceae/ L659.A	Paste prepared from leaves is applied to the forehead during fever
9 *Fessya gach*	*Hoya parasitica*	Asclepiadaceae/ L667.B	Leaf extract and paste are used to alleviate fever and body pains
10 *Dumurjja*	*Derris robusta*	Leguminosae/ L2473.C	Broken or wounded limbs are treated with slightly warmed leaves of these plants to reduce pain and aid healing
11 *Kuruar gach*	*Mallotus philippinensis*	Euphorbiaceae/ L2473.A	–
12 *Monriccha*	*Grewia laevigata*	Tiliaceae/ L2473.B	–
13 *Jharabbya hogoiya*	*Thevetia palmate*	Araliaceae/ L669.A	Paste prepared from roots is applied to child's penis when swollen and painful
14 *Bangori bhanga*	*Phyllanthus* sp.	Euphorbiaceae/ L1744	Leaf extract is used to treat snakebites and allergies
15 *Tengbhang gach*	*Ficus* sp.	Moraceae/ L2470	Paste prepared from roots and fruits is applied to snakebites
16 *Kura tethoi*	*Maesa ramentacea*	Myrsinaceae	Fruits are eaten. Leaf juice is given to children with symptoms of diarrhoea
17 *Shinguri phul gach*	*Nyctanthes arbortristis*	Oleaceae/ L664.B	Stem extract is taken against dysentery
18 *Asam ludi*	*Mikania micrantha*	Compositae/ L2342	Leaf extract is used to stop bleeding
19 *Ketaki*	*Mallotus roxburghii*	Euphorbiaceae/ L1554	The crushed roots of *Ketaki* and *Amaranthus spinosus* are taken with water to stop bleeding through nose and mouth
20 *Bhuth shan*	*Piper longum*	Piperaceae/ L671.A	Stem extract with hot water is given to children to treat mumps
21 *Bilai lengur*	*Uraria* sp.	Leguminosae/ L662.A	Root extract is taken to treat epilepsy
22 *Cheodhima*	*Rhynchotechum ellipticum*	Gesnariaceae/L1560	Leaf extract alleviates coughs in children
23 *Kala sona*	*Eclipta alba*	Compositae/ L1741	Paste prepared from leaves is applied to boils
24 *Koba rashun*	*Crinum asiaticum*	Amaryllidaceae/ L663	Paste prepared from roots is applied to boils

(Continued)

	Chakma name	Specific name	Family/Colln.no	Uses
25	Kobabena	Morinda angustifolia	Rubiaceae/ L2466	Stem/root extract is taken with hot water to treat some urinary diseases
26	Keta boitta shak	Cardiospermum helicacacum	Sapindaceae/ L1547	A hot water extract of whole plant is given to treat chicken pox
27	Kam gach	Nauclea sessilifolia	Rubiaceae/ L1546	Paste prepared from leaves is used for the treatment of fungal or bacterial infections between toes
28	Khar tedoi	Begonia roxburgiana	Begoniaceae/ L669.B	Stem extract is used against abnormal conditions of the tongue in children
29	Chonga dana	Hyptis suaveolens	Labiatae/ L2329	Seed extract is taken for the remedy of urinary complications
30	Deldi pata/ Del ladi	Thunbergia grandiflora	Acanthaceae/ L658.A	Watered down sap of the stem is used to treat eye diseases
31	Hajjang ludhi	Vitis sp.	Vitaceae/ L1713.A	Leaf extract is applied as a remedy for eczema
32	Hoti gach	Leea sp.	Leeaceae/ L672.B	Warm paste, prepared from leaves, is applied to painful joints
33	Jungailya shak	Sarcochlamys pulcherrima	Urticacea/ L1174	A paste prepared from the leaves is used for the treatment of boils and blisters on the lips
B.	**Foods**			
34	Bigal biji	Solanum torvum	Solanaceae/L1815	Fruits and seeds are eaten
35	But batta shak	Commelina diffusa	Commelinaceae/ L1803	Leaves and stems are eaten
36	Dutta ludi	Euphorbia sp.	Euphorbiaceae/ L1179	After childbirth mother is given cooked leaves to increase lactation
37	Kekrak shak	Alternanthera sessilis	Amaranthaceae/ L1208	Vegetable foodstuff
C.	**Commercial uses**			
38	Chakkogach	Acacia farnesia	Leguminosae/ L2815	Bark extract is used as a light brown dye
39	Ful jumuri gach	Anogeissus acuminata	Combretaceae/ L2816	Bark extract is used as a brown coloured dye
D.	**Religious use**			
40	Khila tak	Entada phaseoloides	Leguminosae	A water-based extract of the seeds is sprayed on individuals to purify them after having witnessed the cremation of a dead body

There is a rich wealth of knowledge and associated practices regarding the indigenous exploitation of plant resources, unique to tribal communities and unknown to the wider Bengali community. It is imperative that this knowledge is investigated and documented. The knowledge may have potential industrial applications, leading to pharmacological developments that could help many people across the world. But care will be needed to protect indigenous intellectual property rights (Quddus, this volume), especially in view of the gross violations of Hill Tract people's rights until recently by repressive Bangladeshi governments.

Acknowledgement

This research, conducted under a Link Project, was funded by the Department for International Development (U.K.) and managed by the British Council (Dhaka) for which the authors are most grateful.

11 Wild Vegetables: A Valuable Natural Resource for the Rural Poor

Jane Stokoe

"Kachu-ghechu kheye bechey achi."

THIS IS A SAYING FREQUENTLY used by the rural poor in Bangladesh who own no land and survive on a very low income. The phrase, which refers to the collection and use of wild plant foods (which I will herefoth term 'vegetables'), means "hardly surviving on" and indicates an extreme lack of money and low social status. In the eyes of many Bengalis, these people are outcasts in society.

Despite a growing body of literature relating to development issues in rural Bangladesh, most of the research by both Bengali and Western natural resource scientists has tended to centre on rice, crop and cultured (i.e. pond aquaculture) fish production (e.g. Biswas and Mandal 1993; Mandal and Dutta 1995; Shah 1995; Ali 1997; Tsai and Ali 1997; ITDG n.d.; Gain 1998*a*). Such studies have often failed to recognise that for a growing number of rural people, research of this kind can be of little help since the poorest of the poor (the socioeconomic group most in need of help from development projects) are landless and have limited access to these resources. In addition to day labouring, rickshaw pulling and so on, these people are often dependent upon the daily collection of wild vegetables for their family's survival. That is, their food security is dependent upon food bought in the *hat* or market and/or supplemented with wild vegetables.

During the summer of 1997 I conducted field research in two rural villages: Ujankhalshi (Rajshahi District) and Agcharan (Tangail District). My objective was to examine the livelihoods of women in the homestead environment[1] paying particular attention to local woman's indigenous knowledge. During this time, the significance of wild vegetables for the daily survival of the landless poor became increasingly apparent. My informants were predominantly women from a range of socioeconomic backgrounds (defined in terms of wealth, status, and religion) and of different age classes. I collected preliminary data on the seasonality, whereabouts and usage of a variety of wild plant foods (Table 11.1). Previous research by natural scientists, often trained in botany, has not focused on wild vegetables, but rather on the biodiversity of plant life in general (e.g. Khan 1994). As far as I can ascertain no research has focused solely on wild vegetables from an anthropological perspective, i.e. to explore how these foods relate to people and their livelihoods and paying particular attention to the indigenous knowledge pertaining to this resource. This neglected area of study clearly requires further examination.

Collection of wild vegetables

A family's socioeconomic status determines how often and the reasons why wild vegetables are collected. For the very poor, these foods comprise an essential part of

Table 11.1:　Preliminary data on some types of wild plant foods collected by rural people in Bangladesh

Bengali name and/or local name (LN)[a]	English translation and/or description of plant	Locality	Seasonal availability: Bengali months[b] (with English translations)	If domesticated	Usage
Bathuashak[c]	Not known (leafy green plant)	Village[d]	Magh-Chaitra (January-April)	No (?)	Food
Dhep (LN Agcharan)	Not known (a type of shaluk [seed] found inside the bud of a lotus-type aquatic flower)	Waterbodies (e.g. beels and ponds)	Not known	No	Food. Seeds are dried and then puffed on hot coals, stored, and eaten as a snack either loose or mixed with gurr (molasses/ brown sugar) into a round cake
Fen (or Fenkhoto or Fenkachu)	Not known (thin leaves)	Village, esp. by ponds, low lying ditches and dug pits	All year	Sometimes	Food
Gadha puia	Not known	Village	Baishak (April-May)	No (?)	Food
Ghechu[e]	Not known (a type of tuber)	Grows under water in paddy fields (needs monsoon water to grow)	Not known	No (?)	Food
Gima	Not known	Village, grows naturally in the homestead	Not known	Rarely	Food
Kacha kola	Green Banana	Village	All year	Yes	Food and Medicine, e.g. eaten during pregnancy; used to alleviate stomach upsets
Kachushak & Katchulataf (or khotoshak & khotolata)	Not known (a type of tuber, Aram and/or Taro? with green, leafy shoots)	Village and field (widely available)	Sravan-Kartik (July-November)	Rarely	Food and Medicine, e.g. eaten during pregnancy for high iron content; root used to cure dysentery

(Contd.)

(Continued)

Bengali name and/or local name (LN)[a]	English translation and/or description of plant	Locality	Seasonal availability: Bengali months[b] (with English translations)	If domesticated	Usage
Katakhura or Motmoti (LN's Ujankhalshi)	Not known (a type of Amaranth with spines. Botanical name: *Amaranthus spinosis*)	Village and field (widely available)	*Jaishtha-Ashar* (May-June) or *Sravan-Bhadra* (July-September)[g]	Not known	Food and Medicine. Mixed with leaves of *panboti* (LN Ujankhalshi; unknown plant) to cure thrush. Used to treat dysentery and tonsillitis; also used as a diuretic (pregnant women use it to reduce swelling in ankles)
Kulmigach[h] or Kulmishak	Not known (a tree, type of *Ipomea* ?)	Edge of *beel*[i] (widely available)	*Jaishtha-Kartik* (September-November)	No (impossible, tree is reliant on water body for growth)	Food, 2 types: 1. used as animal food; 2. used as a vegetable and as fuel
Lail (LN Ujankhalshi) Mukhi (LN Agcharan)	Not known (a type of tuber, Aram ?)	Village and field	All year	Yes	Food and Medicine, e.g. root used to cure dysentery; eaten during pregnancy (high in iron)
Lota or Loti	Stem of Aram	Village and field, esp. fallow land, ditches, dried canal beds (widely available)	All year	Yes	Food and Medicine, e.g. eaten during pregnancy (high in iron)
Mankuchur-pata	Not known (A type of Aram)	Village and field	All year	No (?)	Food and Medicine, e.g. root used to cure dysentery; eaten during pregnancy (high in iron)
Nata (LN Ujankhalshi)	Not known (similar to Amaranth)	Village and field	*Magh-Falgoon* (January-March)	Not known	Food
Pipularpata	Not known (similar shaped leaf to betel leaf but smaller and hot tasting like *morich* [chilli])	Village	All year	No (?)	Food

(Contd.)

(Continued)

Bengali name and/or local name (LN)[a]	English translation and/or description of plant	Locality	Seasonal availability: Bengali months[b] (with English translations)	If domesticated	Usage
Puchupar	Not known	Village	Not known	Not known	Food
Sanchishak (LN Helencha, Ujankhalshi & Agcharan)	Not known (an aquatic weed; a type of Ipomea)	Village and field, esp. on banks of beel and homestead	Chaitra-Sravan (March-August)	Yes	Food
Shapla 2 types: 1. Rocoto 2. Shada	Lotus 2 types: 1. Blood red 2. White. All is eaten, the flower head, seed & stem. The seed ('shaluk') is found just behind the flower head beneath the water level	Waterbodies (e.g. beels and ponds)	Bhadra-Aswin (end of monsoon; September-October)	No	Food
Thankuchir-pata (means stomach problems)	Not known (A type of Aram?)	Village and field	All year	Rarely	Food and Medicine, e.g. root used to cure dysentery; eaten during pregnancy (high in iron)
Thankuny	Not known (possibly the same plant as Thankuchir-pata?)	Not known	Not known	Not known	Food

Notes: [a]*Naming wild vegetables*: It is difficult to identify a standard name across Bangladesh for many wild vegetables as many only grow in certain parts of the country and hence only have a local name. Also in many instances it is not possible to establish a homogeneous spelling when translating from Bengali into English, probably because the translation is from another language comprising of a different phonetic script. For the Western researcher this can be confusing because the same person may give different spellings in English on different occasions. Consequently a plant may be recorded as two different plants.

[b]See also Figure 11.1.

[c]'Shak' means 'leaf' and/or vegetable. Generally, town people take 'shak' to mean a 'cooked vegetable' whereas rural people take 'shak' to mean 'leaf'.

[d]'Village' broadly refers to all areas in the near vicinity of where people live and includes homestead areas, local pathways, jongla scrub, ponds and ditches. Unless stated, availability is unknown.

^eThis wild vegetable, which is always boiled, although not very tasty is well known to be nutritionally rich. '*Ghechu*' is commonly fed to pigs, which are thought to be dirty, ferocious creatures (according to Islam). Therefore any persons eating *ghechu* are known to be very poor and unable to afford oil or spices with which to cook. For this reason *ghechu* is boiled on its own and eaten purely to get rid of the feelings of hunger.

^f'*Lata*' means 'stem'.

^gThere was differing opinions as to when this plant was available; this may be due to regional variations in availability.

^h'*Gach*' means 'tree'. *Kulmigach* is referred to as both a 'tree' and a 'plant'.

ⁱ'*Beel*' refers to a body of water rather like a lake, which increases and decreases in size in accordance with the seasons.

^jMy informants told me that these two names refer to the same plant. However a botanist told me that '*sanchishak*' and '*helencha*', whilst similar are not the same and that rural people are aware of this difference. Perhaps the villagers thought that it would be too difficult to explain any differences and subsequently grouped these two plants as one. Interestingly however, the villagers readily distinguished between other very similar plants, and *all* of the villagers that I spoke to told me that these two names referred to the same plant.

their daily diet. This is particularly true for families who own no land, have a meagre or no homestead garden and little money to purchase meat, fish and vegetables from the local *hat* 'market'. For much of the year wild vegetables effectively substitute for meat and fish, although poor families are often less dependent upon them during the main fishing season (the Bengali months of *Ashar* until *Kartik*, see Figure 11.1). The poor *must* collect daily out of necessity unlike wealthier families (i.e. land owners) who *choose* to gather wild vegetables perhaps once or twice a week as they consider these foods rich in both nutrition and taste. Evidence suggests that the poor have a greater knowledge of and about the different wild vegetables than do wealthier people as a result of their need to access them throughout the year. In this sense the indigenous knowledge relating to this resource is to some extent structured by wealth (see below).

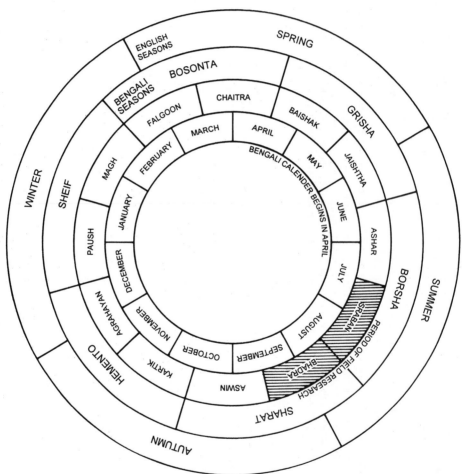

Figure 11.1 *Bengali calendar*

Indigenous knowledge of wild vegetables in Bangladesh is also structured by gender roles. For example, the strict practice of *purdah* (literally 'veil') in accord with the Koranic injunction, which keeps women in seclusion to guard their modesty and purity, is not widely practiced in Bangladesh.[2] Indeed, for the rural poor the costs involved in observing this ideal are simply too high; economic necessity forces landless families to abandon this practice. My research indicates that it is invariably women, and to a lesser extent children, who are primarily responsible for the collection of wild vegetables. This valuable resource is collected from *ashi pashi* 'near and far': from along roadsides, village pathways and riverbanks; from around ponds and *beels*; and from fallow land, woodland, *jongla* scrub and field peripheries. Some species such as *kachushak* grow naturally in and around homestead areas (Table 11.1). If no wild vegetables are available in the immediate vicinity poor women, free from the constraints of *purdah,* may travel far to collect them. By contrast wealthier women, who are often more restricted to the confines of the homestead and nearby area, may send a child or servant to search further afield. However, this distinction between wealthy and poor (and its effects on female mobility), whilst apparent, is by no means a hard and fast rule. For example, one wealthy lady told me that although women are not supposed to leave the homestead, they sometimes do and will collect any wild plant foods that they find.[3] If a husband asks "where did you get the *kulmishak* ?" (a type of wild vegetable), the wife may reply "oh, so and so brought me some this morning," or, "I sent so and so to collect some earlier today." In summary, whilst very poor women are predominantly involved in the collection of wild vegetables, wealthier women sometimes will collect this resource, but for the most part social implications serve to sanction their participation in this activity.

Knowledge of wild vegetables

Indigenous knowledge is difficult to define (Sillitoe 1998*b*; Sillitoe, chapter 19). Unlike much scientific knowledge it is not fixed or standardised. Nor is it homogenous; whilst some knowledge is shared by a community, often it is specific to particular individuals or groups in a society (Marsden 1994). For example, factors such as age, gender, status, wealth, religious orientation, experience and occupation will influence the body of knowledge held by an individual. Although men, women and children consume wild vegetables, their collection is for the most part a female pursuit, as indicated above. Consequently women are generally more informed about this natural resource than are men. The body of knowledge surrounding wild vegetables includes information concerning their nutritional and medicinal properties, preparation, seasonality and whereabouts. This knowledge is acquired from a number of sources: *kaviraj, piranee,*[4] family and village elders, doctors, health centres and so on. The interviews I conducted with informants revealed an age and wealth related difference in knowledge about wild vegetables. The older generation learnt about the benefits from family and village elders. By contrast, younger people, particularly from wealthier families apparently gained their knowledge primarily from local doctors rather than a family source. At first sight the latter's claim seems curious given that their parents and grandparents are undoubtedly willing to pass on such information as *their* parents and grandparents had done to them. The relatively recent introduction of Western medicine into rural Bangladesh however, has resulted in a general shift in people's perception of health care. It would appear that the younger generations increasingly have more faith in the wonders of the modern doctor than they do in traditional herbal practitioners (i.e. *kaviraj, piranee,* family and village elders) whom they often regard as outdated and immersed in superstition. It takes the authority of the doctor to convince them of the benefits of including wild vegetables in their daily diet. However, for the poorest of the poor, those most reliant on wild vegetables, a visit to the doctor is often impossible and consequently knowledge of this resource is largely acquired through word of mouth, particularly from mother or mother-in-law to daughter or daughter-in-law. In addition, individuals may obtain knowledge from media sources (such as T.V. and radio) and through involvement in training initiatives set up by Non Government Organisations (NGOs).

Decline in the incidence of wild vegetables

The majority of my female informants agreed that wild vegetables have become increasingly scarce in recent years. Women from poor households have to travel greater distances in order to find sufficient amounts of wild vegetables to feed their families.[5] The additional time involved is frequently at the expense of other equally necessary daily activities such as fuel collection. If women are unable to provide enough food to feed their family each day, many will face mental and/or physical abuse from their husband. The considerable pressures experienced by poor landless women in trying to sustain their families may have been intensified by the increasingly patchy nature of wild plant foods in rural Bangladesh. The women put forward a number of reasons for this apparent decline: population growth; a decrease in the amount of uncultivated land; heightened awareness of the nutritional and medicinal value of wild vegetables and perhaps most importantly the fact that they represent a free food source under increasing demand. Interestingly, most of the men I spoke to reported that wild vegetables were abundant and readily available everywhere. Recent scientific research and public consultation however has pointed to a general decline in the biodiversity of plant life in rural Bangladesh (NEMAP 1995; Zuberi, this volume; see also Gain 1998*b*) supporting the opinion of most women, that wild vegetables are increasingly in short supply. This suggests that either men are unaware of the true situation concerning the scarcity of wild vegetables because they are not primarily involved in their collection; or they dogmatically maintain this position in the face of counter-evidence for other reasons, whatever these may be.

   The above supports the point that women are more involved with wild vegetable collection than are men and further demonstrates that indigenous knowledge is gender-structured. It is also influenced by age. Generally speaking, older people (i.e. those with grandchildren) were more inclined to consider wild vegetables a dwindling resource, than were younger informants (i.e. those with no children or very young children). This probably reflects the greater time span against which the older generation can measure any decline. Furthermore, many women from relatively wealthy families who do not *depend* upon wild vegetables, also appeared largely unaware that these foods may increasingly be in short supply. Poor landless women, by comparison, were clearly more aware of this possibility. This is understandable if we consider the latter's dependency and hence greater involvement in the collection of wild vegetables. Thus, taken together older women from poor families were most likely to view wild vegetables as an essential but declining resource.

Domestication of wild vegetables

In response to diminished supplies, many women have begun to cultivate wild vegetables within the homestead in addition to the *shaks* or leafy plants (especially varieties of *Aram*) that grow naturally here (Table 11.1). There is a noticeable overlap between plants that are truly *wild* and those that have been *domesticated*, thus illustrating the emergence of 'new' indigenous knowledge practices in response to a changing environment. When asked whether they distinguish between notions of domesticated and wild, many people associate the former with hard work and money, whereas the latter is seen as 'free' in terms of financial cost and labour to produce. For these reasons, many families consider wild vegetables a preferable resource. On the other hand, for poor families who depend upon wild vegetables for their survival, the domestication of these plant foods can be seen as a response to the increasingly less available and unpredictable supply of this valuable resource in the wild (cf. IDS 1989 for Kenya). However, in rural Bangladesh, the poorest of families (often those of fishermen and day-labourers) typically inhabit marginal areas within the village where the land may be prone to flooding and subsidence and the soil is less fertile and where land for homestead gardens is very constrained. Consequently the domestication of wild vegetables may not be an option for some families even though this would be preferred given the loss of wild habitat for these plants to farmland.

The innovative establishment of *communal* gardens in an attempt to localise plant resources is taking place in a few villages. Apparently, the ideology behind this development is to empower the rural poor by giving them the incentive to take responsibility and hence control over growing their own food and medicinal plants. In practice however, this may not always be the case. The running of these gardens, at least in Rajshahi, seemed to be primarily co-ordinated by men in positions of power (seeking to further their status within the village) and not by the very poor.[6] Indeed because of the hierarchical nature of Bengali society, women from the poorest families (or women with no family at all) were perhaps inhibited from participating in these collective projects. This situation serves to highlight the often desperate plight of the rural poor and in particular of women.

Discussion

For many families in rural Bangladesh, wild vegetables comprise a significant part of their diet. Indeed for the very poor they are an essential resource often collected daily. To date there has been little or no research conducted on the incidence and use of wild vegetables in Bangladesh. As the population increases at an alarming rate (Bangladesh Bureau of Statistics 1995), so too do the numbers of landless poor dependent upon this resource. If we wish to improve the livelihoods of the rural poor it is crucial that this neglected area of study be accorded attention equal to that of rice and fish research.

As mentioned above, it is a widely held belief that wild vegetables are becoming increasingly scarce. The present lack of research means that it is difficult to establish the rate of decline and in turn predict the consequences of these ecological changes for those people reliant upon this resource. Attention needs to focus on issues relating to the long-term conservation of wild plant foods in order to prevent further depletion and ecological degradation. However in a developing country such as Bangladesh, with an ever-growing demand for land this objective will not easily be realised. New coping strategies must be devised.

Intensified efforts to promote domestication of wild vegetables could alleviate scarcity by relieving pressure on natural supplies, thereby giving wild areas time to rejuvenate, and in turn reduce time spent searching for such foods out of necessity.[7]

However, not all wild plant foods lend themselves easily to domestication, as many require specific ecological conditions for growth. For example, the *shapla* or lotus, grows exclusively on waterbodies. Moreover, domestication in response to dwindling local supplies is an option only for those fortunate enough to own a homestead garden with sufficient fertile soil and the rural poor generally do not have access to this resource. Perhaps development projects should explore the potential for commercial cultivation utilising *khas* or state land such as roadsides and *dosha jaiga* or communal land, thereby giving access to those who do not have the opportunity to grow their own plant foods. However, it may prove difficult, for local 'political' reasons, to ensure that such areas remain easily accessible to the very poor (Brokensha 1998). The many issues relating to domestication of wild vegetables represent an important future area of research.

My research has shown that knowledge pertaining to this resource is structured according to gender, wealth, status and age. Such sociological considerations cannot be ignored in any indigenous knowledge related research and development endeavour. This also suggests that the role of the anthropologist or social scientist, armed with the methodological tools needed to extract such information, is central (Sillitoe 1998*a*). In the case of wild vegetable research in rural Bangladesh, where access to women's knowledge and activities is largely impossible for male researchers to attain, the benefits of employing female social scientists are clear. The exclusion of the anthropologist from development projects will often compromise the validity of the data obtained thereby jeopardising the long-term success of any enterprise. A multidisciplinary, participatory approach linking indigenous and Western perspectives operating at the 'grass-roots' level may be a fruitful way forward in this area.

Notes

1 The rural people of Bangladesh live in what is known as a '*bari*' or homestead, commonly situated on *vita* or man-made land raised above the flood level. The homestead refers to the *ghor* 'house' or 'shelter' and adjoining houseyard occupied by a family. Homesteads come in a variety of shapes and sizes depending primarily upon the socioeconomic status of the family. They will typically have four to six separate houses (each inhabited by an average of five to six family members) surrounding an *uthan* 'houseyard'.

2 *Purdah* (or *parda*) is a social and religious ideal in rural Bangladesh. Strict practice means that a woman stays within the *bari* 'family compound' and is never seen by any males but those within her immediate family. Ideally, the woman is free from any menial work, which instead will be done by domestic servants. In reality however, only a small proportion of families are able to afford this ideal (see White 1992).

3 It is clear that Bangladeshi women regularly leave the confines of the homestead, but as White (1992:78) points out "... notions of 'inside' and 'outside' are open to complex manipulation." The social implications of the relative freedom of poor rural women to move around differed between the two villages where I conducted field research. The conservative attitudes of people living in Ujankhalshi, an all-Muslim village, means that the wealthier sector are particularly scathing of women whose economic circumstances forces them to disregard *purdah*. Such criticism was less apparent in Agcharan where people were generally more liberal-minded.

Even relatively wealthy people (for the most part Muslims) were more relaxed in their adherence to the values of *purdah* when compared to their Ujankhalshi counterparts. (This may partly be explained by Agcharan's closer proximity to Dhaka, the capital city). Consequently poor women (mainly Hindus) were able to enjoy relative independence free from disdain whereas in Ujankhalshi they were more likely to view their freedom as a curse.

4 *Kaviraj* and *piranee* refer to male and female herbal practitioners respectively.

5 When out collecting it may not be possible to find sufficient amounts of just one wild vegetable and so a variety of wild plant foods '*lata pata*' will be collected. This variety may be collected by choice, even if sufficient amounts of one wild plant food can be found, in order to obtain a wider range of nutrients and a tastier meal.

6 Brokensha (1998:236) comments that instead of reaching the poor, the benefits of development projects are often captured by wealthy rural people, usually men, "... no matter what safeguards are put in place."

7 It is important to note however, that for many women collection is not necessarily an unpleasant task, but may represent a welcome break in the day and a chance to socialise with family and friends.

Acknowledgements

I received funding from the Department for International Development (DFID) for which I am grateful. I have received much support and guidance from my supervisor, Paul Sillitoe and his colleague Peter Dixon. I would like to thank Mahbub 'Pial' Alam for his help and hospitality in Bangladesh and continued friendship here in England. In particular I would like to thank Matt McLennan for valuable editorial comments and assistance in the preparation of this paper.

12 Local Vegetable Seed Storage Methods and Women's Participation in Development

Wajed A. Shah and Salina Jahan Nuri

INDIGENOUS KNOWLEDGE has only recently been given due importance in the development of new technology and in rural development. Today it is recognised as complementary to scientific knowledge in development (Millet-e-Mustafa 1998). The adoption of innovated technology is generally not sustainable without the incorporation of local knowledge. Thus indigenous knowledge needs to be understood and adopted in agriculture and natural resources management for sustainable development (Zuberi 1998). This article is a brief analysis of how people use their local knowledge in vegetable seed preservation, and the extent and nature of women's participation.

Annual vegetable production in Bangladesh satisfies only about one-quarter of the total domestic demand (Shah *et al*. 1991). One of the primary requirements in expanding vegetable production is the supply of seeds and there is a need to assess vegetable seed storage at the farm level. Secondary information about farm-level vegetable seed storage methods and practices is scarce, as few studies have been made. In Bangladesh vegetable seed is supplied by the Bangladesh Agriculture Development Corporation (BADC), the Directorate of Agricultural Extension (DAE), private importers, farmers and small traders. The BADC and DAE supply annually about 15 and 5 metric tons of seed respectively and private importers about 150 metric tons. The remaining 830 metric tons of vegetable seeds are met at the farm level. The supply of seeds through national institutions satisfies only about one-fifth of the total demand. Production and supply of vegetable seeds at the farm level is crucial in meeting the vegetable seed requirement of the nation (see Samiruddin 1989; Mannan *et al*. 1990).

The question arises as to whether indigenous methods of seed preservation at the farm level are effective. Do they maintain viability and vigour of vegetable seed from harvest to next planting? This study was undertaken to survey preservation methods, the technology used and the extent of vegetable seed storage in different farm households. Since rural women in Bangladesh play a significant role in various operations in farming systems (Shah *et al*. 1991), an assessment of women's participation in vegetable seed storage technology at the farm level was also undertaken.

Methodology

Four villages around the Farming Systems Research Site in Kalikapur Thana, Ishurdi in Pabna district, were selected for study: Kalikapur, Dikshail, Degreepara and Azampur. Farmers were grouped into five categories: landless, marginal, small, medium and large farms. Twenty persons from each category were drawn using a proportionate sampling method making a total of 100 respondents. A female enumerator interviewed female respondents using a structured and semi-structured questionnaire. Data for this study was collected from January to May 1992 and case studies were carried out in subsequent years on seed storage methods. A small quantity of different vegetable seeds was collected from the respondents. Germination tests on seeds were carried out at the Seed Testing Laboratory, Department of Agricultural Extension in Ishurdi to determine their quality.

Results and discussion

The majority of female respondents preserved seeds of leafy vegetables such as *data, lalsak*, and Indian spinach (Table 12.1). Approximately 20% 'seldom' or 'never' preserved seeds. Up to one quarter of the households may run out of leafy vegetable seeds each year, otherwise they meet their need by collecting seeds from available sources. The leafy vegetables *batisak* and *kalmisak* were recently introduced to farmers through field trials. None of the respondents stored the seeds of these vegetables. Housewives did not like to grow *kalmisak* and *batisak* or similar leafy vegetables in their homestead (Shah *et al.* 1989).

Table 12.1:   Extent of seed storage of leafy vegetables in rural households

Name of vegetable	Extent of storage (%)		
	Never	Seldom	Always
Data	11	11	78
Lalsak	16	10	74
Batisak	100	0	0
Kalmisak	100	0	0
Indian spinach	3	18	79

Female respondents cultivated two types of beans: country beans and yard-long beans. Whilst 78% always stored country bean seeds, only 27% preserved yard-long bean seeds (Table 12.2). It appears that yard-long bean seeds are both less popular and less available than country bean seeds. If the extension programme plans to expand the cultivation of such beans, there is a need to increase the supply of seeds. Several types

Table 12.2:   Extent of seed storage of beans, gourd and other vegetables

Name of vegetable	Extent of storage (%)		
	Never	Seldom	Always
Country bean	10	12	78
Yard-long bean	56	17	27
Wax gourd	0	24	76
Bottle gourd	0	16	84
Snake gourd	79	9	12
Ridge gourd	18	12	70
Sponge gourd	12	0	88
Bitter gourd	46	31	23
Cucumber	52	25	23
Pumpkin	7	12	81
Brinjal	68	11	21
Lady's finger	62	10	28
Radish	98	0	2

of gourds were grown. The majority of respondents preserved seeds of wax gourd (76%), bottle gourd (84%), ridge gourd (70%), and sponge gourd (88%). Almost 80% of respondents reported that they 'never' stored seeds of snake gourd and 46% 'never' stored seeds of bitter gourd. Rural women grow pumpkin and 81% of them 'always' preserved these seeds. A majority of women reported that they 'never' preserved seeds of cucumber (52%), *brinjal* (68%), lady's finger (62%), and radish (98%). There is a need to motivate women and farmers to preserve the seeds of these vegetables.

Indigenous seed storage methods

Large quantities of seeds can be stored using 'bulk', 'flat ambient' and 'conditional' methods. 'Bulk' storage refers to the mass storage of seeds, such as when a farmer stores rice seeds. 'Flat ambient' storage differs from bulk storage in that seeds are cleaned, bagged and stored in a building or wire house rather than a bin. The 'conditional' method prolongs the viability of seeds through control of humidity and temperature within the storage room. This can be achieved by air cooling, by installing moisture vapour proof packaging or by dehumidification (Islam and Rahman 1989; see also Toole 1958). These technological methods of vegetable seed storage are not those followed by rural women, who rely on their age-old experience of seed preservation.

Female respondents followed three different indigenous methods of seed storage (Table 12.3). Most women preserved vegetable seeds in bottles. A few used polythene bags. The seeds of the country bean, ridge gourd and sponge gourds they preserved inside the dried fruits, a method based on traditional practices. Seed storage in bottles or polythene bags may be considered a conditional method in that such methods offer a degree of protection from environmental effects such as moisture, temperature and insect/pest infestation.

Table 12.3: Indigenous methods of vegetable seed storage

Name of vegetable	Seed storage method (%)[a]		
	In bottle	Within fruit	Polythene bag
Data	92	0	8
Lalsak	83	0	17
Batisak	0	0	0
Kalmisak	0	0	0
Country bean	5	92	3
Yard-long bean	100	0	0
Wax gourd	99	0	1
Bottle gourd	99	0	1
Snake gourd	100	0	0
Ridge gourd	3	97	0
Sponge gourd	1	99	0
Bitter gourd	100	0	0
Pumpkin	98	0	2
Cucumber	100	0	0
Brinjal	91	0	9
Lady's finger	94	0	6
Radish	100	0	0

Note: [a]Percent estimated from Table 12.1.

Quality of seed stored

Seed stored by indigenous methods was tested for quality in the laboratory. The test results were rated 'good', 'fair' and 'poor' (Table 12.4). Seeds usually deteriorate through irreversible physical, biochemical and physiological changes; seeds that do not germinate are likely to be dead. The results showed that out of 18 types of vegetable seed stored in different households, only three (*data, lalsak,* and snake gourd) rated 'good'. The germination of leafy vegetable seeds was considerably better than other types. The preserved seeds of yard-long beans, wax gourd, cucumber and radish were found to be of 'fair' quality. The seeds of the other nine vegetables preserved in the households did not germinate well and were considered 'poor' quality.

Women's participation in vegetable seed storage

Almost one-fifth of female respondents had no involvement in seed storage before marriage. Women from large farms had the least involvement. 38% of the respondents participated 'sometimes' and 43% 'always' in seed storage. More than 50% of women in small farms were 'always' involved in seed storage activities before marriage (Table 12.5).

All female respondents reported that after marriage, despite other activities in and outside their home, they were involved in some work on vegetable seed storage and management: 82% of respondents 'always' participated, and 18% 'sometimes' participated in such activities for all farm types (Table 12.6).

Table 12.4:   Germination test scores of different vegetable seed

Name of vegetable	No. of seeds tested	Percent germinated	Qualitative score[a]
Data	500	79	good
Lalsak	361	72	good
Batisak	na	na	na
Kalmisak	na	na	na
Indian spinach	200	26	poor
Country bean	144	46	poor
Yard-long bean	23	52	fair
Wax gourd	34	52	fair
Bottle gourd	40	50	poor
Snake gourd	13	100	good
Ridge gourd	106	11	poor
Sponge gourd	121	48	poor
Bitter gourd	16	33	poor
Pumpkin	88	32	poor
Cucumber	100	65	fair
Brinjal	220	5	poor
Lady's finger	160	46	poor
Radish	200	55	fair

Note: [a]Poor = less than 50% germination; fair = 50-70% germination; good = more than 70%; na = data not available.

Table 12.5: **Women's participation in vegetable seed storage before marriage**

Farm Category	Women's Participation in vegetable Seed Storage Before Marriage (%)		
	Never	Sometimes	Always
Landless	20	45	35
Marginal	10	45	45
Small	25	20	55
Medium	10	45	45
Large	30	35	35
All Farms	19	38	43

Table 12.6: **Women's participation in vegetable seed storage after marriage**

Farm Category	Women's Participation in Seed Storage After Marriage (%)		
	Never	Sometimes	Always
Landless	0	20	80
Marginal	0	15	85
Small	0	20	80
Medium	0	20	80
Large	0	15	85
All Farms	0	18	82

Women's participation in seed storage activities was higher than that of other family members (Table 12.7). Men and children had relatively less involvement, regardless of farm category. The children of large farms participated to a greater extent than did the children of other farm types. The joint participation of husband and wife was 21% in all farms taken together, with landless farms showing the lowest rate. Participation rates for marginal, small and medium farms were similar. The majority of rural women recognised the need for training in vegetable seed storage and management. Only 12% of respondents felt no need for such training.

Table 12.7: **Participation in vegetable seed storage (%)**

Farm Category	Children	Husband & wife	Women only
Landless	15	15	70
Marginal	10	25	65
Small	15	20	65
Medium	15	25	60
Large	30	20	50
All Farms	17	21	62

Conclusions

The supply of vegetable seed from government and private agencies satisfies only about one-fifth of the total requirement in Bangladesh. Seed stored at the farm level is the country's major source for vegetable production. In traditional farming systems, women play a significant role in vegetable seed storage and management. This study found that rural women usually store leafy vegetable seeds, although seeds of *batisak* and *kalmisak* are not preserved. Country bean seeds are frequently stored while yard-long bean seeds are seldom stored. The majority of women store seeds of wax, bottle, ridge, and sponge gourd and seldom those of snake and bitter gourd. Few women preserve seeds of cucumber, *brinjal*, lady's finger and radish. Seeds are preserved using three indigenous methods: storage in bottles, in polythene bags, and within the fruit. Germination tests revealed the majority of stored seed to be of 'poor' quality except that of *data*, *lalsak* and snake gourd. The study also found that married women participate in vegetable seed storage and management more than unmarried women do. In all farm categories rates of participation were higher for women than other family members. The majority of female respondents recognised the need for storage and management training. The study highlighted some of the potential constraints of indigenous seed storage at the farm level and demonstrated that the majority of vegetable seeds were stored using indigenous methods.

13 Medicinal Plants for the Survival of Rural People

N. Begum, M. F. Haq and K. Naher

OVER THE COURSE OF CENTURIES, rural people such as farmers and others have developed location-specific knowledge and practices for natural resources management, human and animal health care and many other fields. This knowledge is generally transmitted by word of mouth and forms the basis of people's decision making (Mathias 1994). It is also dynamic and changes in relation to the physical and social environment. This acquired knowledge features in all spheres of rural peoples' daily life. The agricultural production system of Bangladesh for example relies heavily upon indigenous practices. People also continue to depend heavily on local knowledge of the medicinal properties of plants and other available resources. Rural people living in small farming communities have to depend on local medicinal plants as they cannot afford medicines or to be visited by doctors. Moreover, medical facilities provided by the Government are so poor that even urban people do not have proper access to them.

Bangladesh is one of the poorest countries of the developing world. The country suffers from an annual food deficit and requires assistance from various aid giving countries to feed its population. The Government subsidises food production. The nutritional and health status of many people is dire. Due to its poor economy, the nation has inadequate basic facilities. Many people cannot imagine medical facilities being available for them, even in urban areas. In rural locations, few people have access to medical services because of their economic poverty combined with a shortage of trained medicinal practitioners in villages. Only one graduate medical practitioner is available for every 4,955 persons in the country (Bangladesh Bureau of Statistics 1995). Modern treatment is so expensive that only the rich can afford it. Local medicinal plants continue to be of great importance to rural people (see also Rahman *et al.*, this volume). For centuries village women have been doctoring common ailments with locally available herbs and shrubs found around their homesteads, or in fields and jungles.

This chapter reports on an investigation into the health beliefs and medicinal practices of local people, with a view to documenting the use of indigenous methods of treatment. It stands on the premise that indigenous knowledge should be valued, as it comprises a wide range of accumulated experience about natural resources essential for peoples' health and well-being, supplying them with much-needed medicines, not to mention food. The study observed that almost 100% of village households use locally available medicinal plants to treat common diseases. In all villages studied, one or two women have expertise in the use of medicinal plants and give their services free of charge. Many herbs and shrubs grown in and around the village are selected to treat patients, sometimes with astonishing results. Though not all plant species were available in all locations, certain species were particularly common and used by people everywhere.

Method of study

The use of medicinal plants by rural people in Bangladesh was studied using participatory rural appraisal (PRA) techniques in eighteen villages located in eighteen different thanas representing eighteen agroecological zones (AEZ). The study was undertaken by a multidisciplinary team of research and extension personnel from the Department of Agricultural Extension in collaboration with two National Research Organisations: the Bangladesh Agricultural Research Institute and the Bangladesh Rice Research Institute. The research on indigenous knowledge of medicinal plants was a subsidiary study. The project's main objective was to research sustainable farming systems, giving particular emphasis to the cultivation of cereals (rice, wheat, maize and barley) by employing irrigation technologies to increase production. The survey was undertaken in 1996-97 in a collaborative programme between the Department of Agricultural Extension and the Thana Cereal Technology Transfer and Identification (TCTTI) Project. We surveyed a total of fifty-three thanas to meet the project's objectives. Information on indigenous medicinal practices was collected from eighteen of the thanas during PRA exercises (Table 13.1.), allowing people to present the information themselves, as they thought fit. The participants comprised a group consisting of twenty men and twenty women from farming families, selected by stratified sampling from four land-holding categories. The four categories of farm holding were marginal = < 0.20ha., small = < 1.0ha., medium = < 3.0 ha., and large = > 3.0ha. The forty persons selected represented the ratios of these four categories in the village population.

Table 13.1:   Thanas involved in Participatory Rural Appraisal studies for indigenous medicinal knowledge practices by rural people

Name of Thana	Name of District	Agroecological zone
1. Mithapukur	Rangpur	3,27
2. Fulchari	Gaibandha	3
3. Natore sadar	Natore	5,11
4. Raiganj	Serajganj	4,25
5. Sarsha	Jessore	11
6. Faridpur sadar	Faridpur	10,12
7. Ghatail	Tangail	8,9,28
8. Melandah	Jamalpur	7,8,9
9. Dhamrai	Dhaka	8,28
10. Comilla Sadar	Comilla	19,22,29
11. Feni Sadar	Feni	18,19,23,29
12. Parsuram	Feni	23,29
13. Palash	Narsingdi	9,28
14. Nagorpur	Tangail	8,27
15. Madarganj	Jamalpur	7,8,9
16. Chowgacha	Jessore	11
17. Mohonpur	Rajshahi	11,25
18. Khansama	Dinajpur	1,3

We observed that women largely collect and prepare medicinal plants. Hence women, particularly the more experienced, were asked to collect samples, and then present them to the group (by arranging them on the floor), and to name and describe the preparation and use of the medicinal plants. The information was checked by all other participants. These observations support the contention that women have pioneered plant domestication and agriculture since the arrival of civilisation (Childe 1971), and that close attention needs to be paid to gender issues relating to plant use (Stokoe, this volume).

Major findings of the study

We identified ninety-three species of plants during the study as having medicinal value for rural people (Table 13.2). The majority were herbs and shrubs, with a few derived from trees. People identified the plants by their local names, so some species may have been repeated since names can vary between locations. People, mostly women, collect samples from the backyards of their homesteads, fallow lands, along field boundaries, around *beels*, along riverbanks, roadsides, and from copses and forests. We found only four or five shrubs growing in homesteads as ornamental plants and two or three species cultivated as spices in homestead gardens or fields. Three species were grown in homestead gardens for their edible fruit: wood apple, guava, and blackberry.

Table 13.2:   List of indigenous medicinal plants with their uses
              (Scientific names of plant species are from Huq 1986)

Catalogue of Medicinal Plants			
Local and scientific name	Thana location number (re. Table 13.1)	Medicinal parts and methods of use	Where available
1. *Arahar, Cajanas cajan*	4,7,11,12, 15,16,18	Leaves: together with the leaves of *swarnalata* mashed with 125 ml water. Used to treat jaundice.	Grown along crop field boundaries or in homesteads.
2. *Arjun, Terminalia arjuna*	7,11,15	Bark: soaked under water overnight. The water is given to patients suffering from jaundice, blood dysentery, heart disease (*Madarganj*).	Grows naturally in the forest.
3. *Almish* plant	10	Leaves: juice used for the treatment of amoebic dysentery.	Found around homesteads.
4. *Akanda, Calotropis procera*	10,18	Leaves: very effective if leaves are warmed and placed on wounds and fractures. Leaf juice is also used for curing coughs and colds and combating a low temperature (*Khansama*).	Found to grow around homesteads and on riverbanks.
5. *Aho-nondil*	5	Lower parts of young leaves: leaf paste used for quick drying of wounds.	Available in homesteads and bushland.
6. *Alaicha, Amomum aromaticum*	14	Leaves: juice used as a remedy for fever and to increase appetite.	Aquatic plant - grows in ponds and *beels*.
7. *Amrull, Oxalis corniculata*	8	Leaves: mashed with water and taken by patients suffering from dysentery.	Found around homesteads, ponds and fields.

(Contd.)

(Continued)

Catalogue of Medicinal Plants

Local and scientific name	Thana location number (re. Table 13.1)	Medicinal parts and methods of use	Where available
8. *Arash*	17	Leaves: mashed leaves, if applied to the forehead after warming, can cure colds. Especially effective for children.	No information.
9. *Ataswri*	17	Twig: used as a toothbrush and can cure pyorrhoea. The tender leaf sap is used to increase appetite.	Grows on roadsides, jungle and fallow lands.
10. *Alo kumari*	5	Leaves: juice used to reduce coughing.	No information.
11. *Aishada*	5	Leaves: half cup of juice of aishada mixed with one and a half cups of milk can control diarrhoea.	Found in jungle.
12. *Adamoni/Aguni*	8	Leaves: for indigestion the patient is advised to take this leaf with rice.	No information.
13. *Akh, Saccharum officinalis*	8	Root: half a cup of root juice, if taken before breakfast for 7 days, is very effective against liquirria.	Cultivated as field crop.
14. *Ashuti*	8	Leaves: mashed leaves mixed with salt are applied to forehead to control headache.	Found in jungle.
15. *Basak, Adhatoda vasica*	6,13	Leaves: juice of *tulshi* and *basak* leaves with *talmisri* used to cure coughs.	Found growing in backyards of homesteads, around *beels* and riversides.
16. *Bhanga lata, Anona reticulata*	6	Leaves: leaf juice is mixed with molasses and used to treat dysentery in people of all ages but especially children.	No information.
17. *Bel, Aegle mermelos*	14	Leaves and fruits: leaf juice used as a remedy for coughs and colds. Fruit juice is used to treat dysentery and constipation.	In backyard of homesteads or in forest.
18. *Bhamot*	15	Internodes: used for chicken pox.	Grown in homesteads.
19. *Bakcha*	5	Leaves: juice used for controlling coughs.	Found in homesteads and forest.
20. *Boita*	7	Leaves: juice used for controlling loose bowel movement in children.	Grown in bushland or backyards of homesteads.
21. *Bish katali, Polyponum hydropiper*	7	Leaves: juice used to coagulate blood if leg or hands injured.	Grown in the backyard of homesteads.
22. *Betel nut, Areca catechu*	16	Leaves: if mashed and applied to wounds prevents bleeding.	No information.
23. *Bash, Bambusa* spp.	8	Flower: used to alleviate labour pains and for easy delivery.	Found cultivated in the backyard of homesteads and on fallow land.
24. *Bat boila*	3	Used to treat amoebic dysentery.	Usually found on river banks.
25. *Bahat*	7	Leaves: treats tongue problems in children.	Found in bushland.

(Contd.)

(Continued)

Catalogue of Medicinal Plants

Local and scientific name	Thana location number (re. Table 13.1)	Medicinal parts and methods of use	Where available
26. *Chitki, Phyllanthus reticulatus*	4,13	Leaves: juice of green leaves used to cure dysentery and infant diarrhoea.	Grown around the homestead especially along old fences.
27. *Chirkuti*	3	Leaves: juice used to cure infant diarrhoea.	No information.
28. China rose, *Hibiscus rosa chinensis*	7	Used for cooling the scalp.	Found in homestead gardens as ornamental plants.
29. *Danda kalash, Leucas aspera*	4,14	Leaves: juice used to treat coughs and colds in children.	Grows beside roads and around homesteads.
30. *Durba, Cyanodon dactylon*	4,8,10, 14,15,16	Helps to coagulate blood. Root juice is used to treat problems associated with women (*Matherganj*).	Grows beside the road and around crop fields.
31. *Dolon, Hidychium crronarium*	3	Used as treatment for colds.	No information.
32. *Dhutura, Datura fastusa*	18	Leaves: juice used for scabies and chicken pox.	Found in jungle.
33. *Dheki sak, Ceratopteris thalictroides*	5	Leaves are fed to lactating mothers.	Grows on fallow land and around ponds.
34. *Daud*	15	Leaves: juice used to soothe skin irritation. The leaf is crushed on the palm and applied onto eczema 3-4 times daily; within 7 days the eczema is cured.	Found around homestead boundaries
35. *Dhol manik, Ipomoea fistulosa*	15	Leaves: juice used to treat dysentery.	Found around homestead boundaries and in jungle.
36. *Dhol kalash*	10	Leaves: paste, when applied to forehead reduces pain.	Found on footpaths and along riverbanks.
37. *Dom kalash*	7	Leaves: used for improving digestion and to increase appetite.	Grows in fields.
38. *Germanilata, Eupatorium odoratum*	5	Leaves: juice used for birth control.	Found in jungle and by the side of ponds.
39. Garlic, *Allium sativum*	10	Extract from garlic is used for amoebic dysentery.	Grown in homesteads and fields as a spice.
40. *Gella, Entada phaseoloides*	17	Spiny tender stem: eaten as a vegetable to cure skin disease.	Grown with dry land *rabi* crops. An annual weed.
41. *Gulal, Diospypos toposia*	7	Leaves: used to make curry with soft or half-rotten fish so that it tastes fresh.	Grown in homestead backyards.
42. Guava, *Psidium guajava*	17	Juice of tender leaves: cure for dysentery; 1 tablespoonful for a child and 2-3 tablespoonfuls three times a day for adults.	Grown in home gardens as edible fruit.
43. *Ganda badal, Paederia factida*	7	Leaves: juice used to increase appetite and as a remedy for stomach difficulties.	Grown around homesteads.
44. *Hotik jila*	10	Bark: extract used for gynaecological problems.	Grows on riverbanks and roadsides.

(Contd.)

(Continued)

Catalogue of Medicinal Plants

Local and scientific name	Thana location number (re. Table 13.1)	Medicinal parts and methods of use	Where available
45. *Himsagar, Kalanchae spatulata*	16	Leaves: juice used to cure indigestion.	No information.
46. *Harjora, Buetteneria pilosa*	3	Treatment for broken bones.	Found growing in bushland.
47. *Jasmin, Jasminum auriculatum*	5	Leaves: juice used to treat fever and chesty coughs.	Grown in homesteads as ornamental plants.
48. *Jam, Eugenia jambolana*	5,14	Bark: juice used to treat stomach pain.	Grown in homesteads, forest.
49. *Kharajora, Eugenia* sp.	14	Leaves: juice used to remedy scalp problems. Also effective for blood pressure.	Found growing in homesteads and bushland.
50. *Kota kare*	15	Root: used for treating wounds.	No information.
51. *Kemti kalokewcha*	10	Used as medicine for measles.	Found in homesteads, road-sides and fields.
52. *Kamranga, Stereosperonum chelonioides*	10	Fruit: juice used for amoebic dysentery and colds.	Grown in homestead gardens, forest.
53. *Kadam, Anthocephalus chinensis*	10	Leaves: used for arthritis.	Grows on roadsides, riverbanks and in forests.
54. *Kata khura, Amaranthus spinosus*	17	Root: eaten with betel leaf can cure *sutika*.	Found around ponds, on fallow land, roadsides and forests.
55. *Kuti pana, Spirodela polyrhiza*	7	Small green leaves: used for combating low temperature in infants.	Found around ponds, on fallow land, field boundaries, roadsides and forests.
56. *Kangra* grass, *Setaria italiac*	16	Runner: the stem of *kangra* grass prevents blockages when put in the ear.	Found in homestead backyards and in jungle.
57. *Kalo kachu, Colocasia nymphaefolio*	8	Leaves: juice used to control headache.	Found in homesteads and jungle.
58. *Kanchoti, Styrax serruletum.*	3	Oral medicine used with coconut oil.	Found growing in bushland.
59. *Kalo Dhutura, Datura starmonium*	17	Leaves: mashed leaves applied after heating to alleviate pain.	Found in jungle, on roadsides and around ponds.
60. *Lal pata, Aerva sanguinolenta*	13	Used to stop bleeding from minor cuts.	No information.
61. *Lebu, Citrus aurantifolia*	15	Roots: used for healing wounds.	Found in homestead backyards, bushland and jungle.
62. Marygold, *Tagetes patula*	4,13,14,15	Leaves: juice used to stop bleeding from wounds.	Grown as ornamental plant in homegardens.
63. *Mon matal dal, Oroxylum indicum*	15	Branches: boiled with water, used to treat jaundice.	Grows in bushland, jungle, on roadside.
64. *Mouthal*	7	Leaves: used to alleviate stomach pain.	Grows in bushland and jungle.

(Contd.)

(Continued)

Catalogue of Medicinal Plants

Local and scientific name	Thana location number (re. Table 13.1)	Medicinal parts and methods of use	Where available
65. *Michri dana*, *Scoparia dulcies*	7	Leaves and root: juice used as treatment for dysentery and stomach pain.	Grows in bushland and jungle.
66. *Misti madhu*, *Glycyrrhiza glabra*	8	Leaves: paste mixed with salt used for stomach pain.	Found on fallow lands.
67. *Mukta borry*, *Acalypha indica*	8	Leaves: juice used to cure acute skin diseases.	Found on roadsides and in jungle.
68. *Mochani*	3	Leaves: juice used as cure for colds.	No information.
69. *Neem*, *Azadirachta indica*	6,7,11,13, 14,18	Leaves: used for seed storage. Mashed leaves used to treat fungal infections.	Grows in jungle and on roadsides.
70. *Okajuli*	13	Leaves: juice taken with sugar to stop skin irritations.	No information.
71. *Pipul pata*, *Piper sylvanticum*	7,14,18	Leaves: used to make curry with half-rotten fish to make it taste fresh.	Grows in bushland and homestead backyards.
72. *Pathar kuchi*, *Bryophyllum* sp.	14	Leaf: juice used for stomach trouble. Leaf extract is also helpful in the removal of stones from the kidney or prostate gland.	Found around homesteads.
73. Potato, *Solanum tubersum*	13	Tuber: paste used to treat skin burns.	Field crop.
74. *Panbilash*, *Piper betel*	5,15,17	Fresh leaves: used to improve the flavour of *pan* (Betel leaf).	Grown around homesteads.
75. Pineapple, *Ananas cosmosus*	6,10	Juice of soft leaf is taken with sugar to control worms in children. Also used by women for gynaecological problems (*Comilla Sadar*).	Cultivated as horticultural crop.
76. Prickly herb, *Chiscira* sp.	5	Root: juice used to control lecurrhia in women.	Grows in jungle.
77. Papaya, *Carica papaya*	5,16	Milky juice of green papaya: mixed with *loppipop* to control jaundice. Also taken with *batasah* (*Saret*) to cure liver pain.	Grows around homesteads and in jungle.
78. Red *shapla*, *Nymphaea nouchal*	7	Flowers: mixed with *rakta chandan* for lowering blood pressure.	Found in ponds and *beel*.
79. *Sishsu*, *Dalbargia sissoo*	11	Leaves: juice used to cure dysentery.	Grows in forest and on roadsides.
80. *Swarnalata*, *Cuscuta reflexa*	10,11,13	Leaves of *Swarnalata* and *arhar* mashed together with 125 ml of water, taken as medicine for jaundice. Leaf juice also used to remove hookworm in children in Narsingdi and by women for gynaecological diseases in Comilla district.	Grows with or near to *ber* and *mehendi* (henna).
81. *Sajna*, *Maringa aliefera*	10	Bark: used to treat colds and coughs. Green leaves are eaten for the treatment of blood pressure.	Grows around homesteads and in forest.

(Contd.)

(Continued)

Catalogue of Medicinal Plants

Local and scientific name	Thana location number (re. Table 13.1)	Medicinal parts and methods of use	Where available
82. *Shada akanda, Calotropis procera*	7	Leaf: juice to treat colds, coughs and low temperatures.	Grows in ponds, ditches, and on muddy roads.
83. *Thankuni, Centella asiatica*	4,5,10,14	Runner: used for dysentery and gynaecological diseases (*Raiganj*).	Found along homestead boundaries, roadsides, and on cultivated land.
84. *Tulshi, Ocinum americanum*	4,6,10,14, 15,16	Leaf: juice used with honey to treat colds. It prevents eczema and other skin diseases when mixed with red salts (*Chowgacha*).	Found in homestead gardens and around ponds.
85. Turmeric, *Curcuma domestica*	6,10	Paste made from spice with *neem* tree used to cure skin disease and worms in children.	Cultivated as a spice in fields and around homesteads.
86. *Tita neem, Azadirachta indica*	17	Twigs: used as toothbrush can cure pyorrhoea. Leaf also cures skin diseases.	No information.
87. *Uchey, Momordica charantia*	14	Leaves: juice used to prevent chicken pox.	Cultivated in homestead gardens.
88. *Venna*	3	Immature fruit can cure rheumatic pain.	No information.
89. *Vat, Clerodendrum viscosum*	3	Leaves: juice used as medicine for worms and fever.	Found in dense bush/forest.
90. *Vamot*	15	Leaves: extract used for measles.	No information.
91. *Vati*	9,17	Leaves: juice used to treat fever and reduce body temperature.	No information.
92. *Ziga, Lannea coromandecica*	3	Bark: extract with sugar is used to treat dysentery.	No information.

Irrespective of land-holding category, all villagers usually used medicinal plants as the only treatment for disease. They reported thirty-nine different diseases that could be treated with local medicines. For example, jaundice is a prevalent disease and affects people of all ages. The most commonly used plant to control it is *Cajanas cajan* together with the bark of the *arjun* tree. We were surprised to find that villagers also use local plants to control conditions such as high blood pressure and arthritis. Women aged above 30 years suffer particularly from various diseases, evidencing symptoms of iron deficiency, liquirria, *sutika* and so on, and rely on some eight species of plants to control them and other problems specific to women, notably gynaecological ones. Almost all rural children suffer worm infestation, a problem throughout the year. Four plant species were used as specifics to control them.

People use selected parts of plants for medicinal purposes. In about 80% of species it is the leaves that have medicinal value. Juice extracted from fresh leaves is used as medicine to treat several diseases. The roots, bark and wood of some plants have medicinal value too and the whole plant is used with several herbal species. People usually collect material used to prepare medicines just before use. After collection, they mash or soak the plant material in water to extract the juice, which patients usually take in the morning before breakfast (on an empty stomach). In all the villages one or two women know how to prepare remedies, and do so for their relatives and neighbours free of cost.

Rural people depend on indigenous medicinal plants for several reasons. The main ones are poverty, lack of availability of medicinal services in rural areas, and poor communications. They have no alternative but to use indigenous remedies. This is not all bad. In ill-informed hands modern medicines can adversely affect health. We need to devote more resources to understanding indigenous usage of medicinal plants given their importance to poor people in coping with healthcare problems. Thus, we conducted our study with the aim of furthering understanding and awareness of existing indigenous healthcare practices. And we present the results of our survey (Table 13.2) to highlight the importance of contemporary indigenous practices in Bangladesh.

14 Indigenous Medicinal Plant Use, Sustainability and Biodiversity: Learning from the Grameen Bank Experience

M. I. Zuberi

ACCORDING TO THE WORLD HEALTH ORGANISATION more than 80% of people, mostly in less-developed countries, depend on traditional herbal medicine for their primary healthcare needs. Neglected over the last century, the village poor in Bangladesh rely on a traditional medicinal system, known as the *kaviraji* system, for primary healthcare. In the past, the plants needed were collected from local forests and fallow lands, but with extensive deforestation and over-utilisation, wild populations of these plant species are disappearing fast. Moreover, with the domination of the modern allopathic medical system and the continued neglect of the herbal system, traditional practitioners are vanishing. Thus the indigenous knowledge associated with this system is eroding fast.

Bangladesh, situated in the fertile alluvial delta of the Ganges-Brahmaputra-Meghna River system and having a sub-tropical, monsoon climate, has a very rich biodiversity, much of which has already been destroyed by over-exploitation and deforestation. In spite of this, there remains a wide diversity of plant species. In the late 1980s the Government of Bangladesh, realising the risks of rapid biodiversity destruction, directed that all development projects must be cleared by the newly formed Ministry of Environment to assess their probable negative impacts on the environment. Bangladesh also signed, ratified and accessed more than two dozen international conventions, treatises and protocols relating to environmental conservation, including the Biodiversity Convention. Though development projects have environment impact assessments, most of these report little or no expected negative impact on natural resources or on the livelihoods of local people. The reverse invariably proves to be the case. The non-participatory approach adopted in development has been disastrous: without local people's input it is difficult to see how one can fully assess the impact of interventions on their lives.

The Ministry of Environment and Forests has been trying to formulate the National Environment Management Action Plan to set out a policy framework. Another attempt by the same Ministry is the National Conservation Strategy, which also awaits final approval. Recent recommendations for regional collaboration for the conservation of cultivated and wild plant diversity are still being formulated. Several NGOs, including *Gono Sasthya Kendra*, have been trying to conserve traditional plants following conventional methods e.g., by collecting and growing them in herbal gardens. However, very little has been done to assess the present state of medicinal plant species in Bangladesh. There is no list of threatened plants, though there are many candidates. The necessity of a detailed field survey at the national level, which would designate 'Red List' threatened species, has been indicated but never followed up.

Even today many villages throughout Bangladesh plan, co-ordinate and run their everyday activities according to a nature-based production system and the indigenous knowledge relating to its manipulation. Decisions relating to livelihood activities such as land preparation, seed sowing, tree planting, crop harvesting or animal care are made taking into account the influence of particular days, stars and the moon, according to traditional knowledge passed down from generation to generation.

A base line survey supported by the International Development Research Centre (Canada) of about 200 villages in North-western Bangladesh found that virtually every village had a herbal practitioner. A total of 461 folk medicine practitioners including 19 women were recognised giving an average of 2.23 herbals per village. In another pilot survey of ten villages of Southern Bangladesh, more than 30% of those suffering from poor health reported using herbal medicine. Of the 150 medical practitioners in these villages, 38% were herbals (Zuberi, unpublished). According to a 1978 World Health Organisation report, there are over 5000 registered and more than 3000 unregistered traditional medical practitioners in Bangladesh. Another International Development Research Centre survey indicated far more herbals operating in Bangladesh than this (Zuberi, unpublished). Of these herbals, only 540 are institutionally qualified; the remainder are folk medicine practitioners dependent entirely on indigenous knowledge.

Folk medicine in Bangladesh is a diverse tradition, which is ecosystem- and ethnic community-specific. It exists in all rural communities, with different localities having different characteristics. A region's indigenous knowledge is inexorably tied to its biodiversity, since the biodiversity of an area represents an important component of the environment in which local knowledge is generated. Local practitioners dependent on indigenous knowledge and local biodiversity include:

- elderly ladies, grandmothers and housewives administering plant-based home remedies, special foods and nutritious diets;
- herbals and *kaviraj* (folk medicine men) offering plant-based remedies and spiritual recommendations, taking small amounts of money or items in exchange;
- bone-setters, the traditional orthopaedics specialising in treating broken bones;
- poison specialists, experts in treating snake bites, dog bites etc.;
- *dai* (traditional birth attendants) responsible for home child birth.

In addition to herbal medicine for treating human diseases, another important indigenous knowledge based medical system developed in the villages of Bangladesh, is the ethnoveterinary system for the treatment of domestic animals. It is also dependent upon local plants. A pilot survey in five villages of North-western Bangladesh (Zuberi 1997*a*) indicated that there are an average of 5.5 ethnoveterinary practitioners per village. They reported treating 17 diseases (mostly of cattle), using 47 local plant species, 18 of which were readily identifiable. All these herbals reported successful treatment of diseased cattle but complained about disappearing plants and lack of opportunities for training or support. The wealth of knowledge associated with ethnoveterinary practices has been confined to village families. This indigenous knowledge is not documented or codified, though in many countries especially in India and China intensive research is being carried out with a view to conserving it.

Social situation: Social factors are important in regulating the passage of indigenous knowledge. Exposure to this intricate and vast world of knowledge begins very early in life when children see parents and others determining livelihood strategies against the backdrop of the local environment. As children grow they acquire specialised knowledge and skills specific to their environment. The process is dynamic and individuals constantly adjust practices to suit the environment. They learn the local knowledge related to the identification, use and conservation of local plants used for food, fibre, medicine, fuel, etc. When a son follows his father to the field he learns about soil types, crop suitability, soil-water, land preparation, sowing of seed etc. If he fishes with his uncle he learns the most reliable techniques, what should not be caught, how to allow fish to reproduce, and so on. All these are incorporated into the individual's knowledge base. Through this learning many identify so closely with the environment that they refer to it as a 'living person' like themselves. Thus, for example the soil can be 'hungry', 'starving' or 'dead', the water of the *beel* (shallow waterbodies) can be 'sick' and they can 'read' and 'feel' the land, climate or crops. This 'holistic' perspective of indigenous knowledge makes it efficient and sustainable, while the 'reductionist' view of modern science separates the components of the environment thus destroying the 'system' and its interrelated nature.

Ongoing research into traditional medicine (Zuberi, unpublished) indicates that village elders have a far more detailed knowledge and appreciation of indigenous techniques and medicines and their use than do members of younger generations, who have only vague ideas and limited knowledge about traditional systems. Most of the young are sceptical about the efficacy and appropriateness of remedies based on traditional knowledge as shown in the data gathered by the study; only 7% of the 461 herbal practitioners located and interviewed, were below 30 years of age, 52% were between 31 to 50 years and 41% were above 50 years. The herbals often reported that they do not have candidates either within or outside their family willing to continue their profession.

It is useful to note the socioeconomic condition of traditional practitioners. Preliminary results of field surveys indicate that of 461 herbals interviewed, 33% are illiterate, 57% have primary education and 10% have completed school. Of all the herbals, 80% have another major profession and 57% are farmers. As many as 45% are landless and 26% own land less than 1.5 acres in area. More than 39% live below the poverty line, 29% are poor and only 32% consider themselves economically solvent. Of these 461 herbals, 30% have families with 2 to 4 members, 51% have 5 to 8 and 18% have more than 8 members. Thus in socioeconomic terms the practitioners of indigenous knowledge based traditional medicine are in a marginal position. Due to their poverty and neglect by the government and the Bangladeshi elite, the herbals are ignored in their own villages and their livelihood is under threat. The material and social poverty of the herbals is one factor that adds to the ascendancy of western allopathic medicines and medical practices.

Potential of the traditional system: The indigenous knowledge based traditional practices, especially the primary healthcare system, offer great potential for sustainable development. Poor, rural people would be the primary beneficiaries. Indigenous approaches are more appropriate, cheaper, readily available and easier to adopt than foreign alternatives. Moreover, according to local demand, indigenous knowledge based practices can be improved, modified or even blended with outside technologies if considered necessary. Unfortunately appreciation of indigenous knowledge and the role of traditional practices is yet to be generated among development planners, policy makers and NGO workers. Our state run (or private) medical training and delivery systems, NGO run development and community healthcare efforts, the formal animal care system and village-based poverty alleviation projects do not include any indigenous knowledge based traditional approaches. No research projects have been undertaken to evaluate the potential role of indigenous knowledge based traditional systems in sustainable development.

Documenting and revitalising indigenous knowledge and conserving biodiversity is of critical importance if we are to continue to benefit from the wealth of affordable, locally appropriate healthcare they provide to the rural poor (Zuberi 1997b). We know that present-day herbals are generally elderly, most of them are in remote villages with no apprentices. There is a grave danger that much indigenous knowledge will be lost with them. It should be noted that the existing knowledge based traditional healthcare system has an extensive network in all villages linking poor, rural communities. This can be easily used to develop an inexpensive but effective community based service delivery system of primary healthcare and education. Additional training of these herbals will affirm and conserve their own indigenous knowledge and skills, will add to and improve their ability to address the needs of the local community and will protect their livelihoods.

By the early 1970s the value of indigenous healthcare had been realised and some of the shortcomings of the modern system, such as dangerous side effects, were noted. This realisation generated a high demand for natural products for use as drugs, cosmetics, health food, dyes etc. A new worldwide wave of research and intervention activities is taking place with ethnobotanical, pharmaceutical and medical research. The World Health Organisation has recently published guidelines for the assessment of herbal medicine, taking into account its long presence. Intellectual property rights is an important related issue, which has direct implications on indigenous knowledge and biodiversity. India, for example, has very recently forced the US Patents and Trademarks Office to revoke a contentious patent it had granted to an American research group concerning the use of powdered turmeric (*halud*) for wound healing. Bangladesh should follow India in recognising the importance of protecting our indigenous knowledge. In its successful challenge of this patent claim, India backed up her arguments with documents from ancient *ayurvedic* literature on home remedies using turmeric. Documenting our indigenous knowledge can help to prevent biopiracy.

The conservation of our indigenous knowledge, biodiversity and natural heritage should assume paramount importance with the relentless pressures resulting in the vanishing of species, loss of genetic diversity, the disappearance of indigenous knowledge and destruction of livelihoods. There is a renewed interest in herbal systems all over the world. It is acknowledged that accessible and efficient healthcare systems are urgently needed, with the World Health Organisation launching the "Health for all by the year 2000" programme, and its adoption by national governments of less-developed countries. The age-old traditional healthcare system can partly fill this gap, if biodiversity and indigenous knowledge are preserved. This paper now goes on to report some of the results of efforts in North-western Bangladesh to introduce a participatory approach to the documentation, conservation and utilisation of medicinal plants. This programme concentrates on the under-utilised lands of villages, and aims to provide additional income to the poor with support from the International Development Research Centre and local NGOs. The programme recognises that a strong local knowledge base and rich biodiversity are valuable resources upon which a community can draw, and takes these features as a foundation for further developments.

Participatory approaches to medicinal plant conservation and use

Since over-population, agricultural expansion and over-exploitation have destroyed most of the habitats and natural populations of medicinal plants, the conservation of biodiversity should involve village, homesteads and farms. People should be reminded of the importance of biodiversity, especially the usefulness of the medicinal plants growing in and around their farmland, homesteads and roadsides. These plants should not be treated as 'weeds' and used as fuel. Indeed, the FAO Commission on Plant Genetic Resources has long recognised the role of farming communities in biodiversity and genetic resource conservation. Moreover, more than 50% of village farmers live below the poverty line and conservation should attempt to improve their subsistence and financial support through the sale of cultivated medicinal plants. This will give programmes sustainability. The team of conservationists and local NGO workers at Rajshahi have been involved in participatory documentation and conservation of local medicinal plant diversity as well as the indigenous knowledge associated with herbal medicine.

The Grameen Bank experience: We think we have something to learn in biodiversity conservation from the Grameen Bank success. Driven by a strong desire to help the poor, Dr Yunus, a lecturer in Economics at Chittagong University, in 1967 lent US$27 in total to 42 individuals. By May 1997 the resulting Grameen Bank had lent in micro-credit US$2 billion! About 94% of the loan recipients are poor women. It is reported that about 98% of the 4.5 million borrowers have paid their loans on time. Some salient features of the Grameen Bank system are:

- borrowers form a group;
- they have to pay a weekly instalment;
- they pay the loan as they earn;
- a defaulter is charged additional interest;
- a defaulter is persuaded by the rest of the group to be regular;
- a way out is provided if there is a valid reason for default.

The participatory biodiversity conservation programme has adopted some of these features. The advantages realised are:

- solidarity of group formations;
- conservation activities demand hard work and dedication, individuals who become fed-up can be positively influenced by others in the group;
- everyone monitors others' activities and achievements; all encourage one another;
- members share knowledge and resources, exchange seeds and seedlings;
- group activity is enjoyable and makes the work more attractive.

Sites selected: The indigenous knowledge relating to traditional medicine and medicinal plant diversity has a 'location specific' component: a particular agroecological region may have characteristic natural vegetation and a distinctive pattern of need or use of a species of medicinal plant. The customs of the inhabitants may have an impact on medicinal practice as well. Thus, it was intended that several distinct agroecological regions be included in the programme, including the Old Ganges Floodplains, the Recent Ganges Floodplains, the Tista Floodplains and the Barind Tract with its alluvial deposits.

Steps involved: As a first step, Rapid Rural Appraisal was adopted to collect first-hand information about traditional herbal practitioners and the state of the medicinal plant diversity in each village. The names and addresses of the 'herbals' were collected. Next, a Focus Group Discussion was arranged in villages with the herbals and the medicinal plant users. As the aim is not only the collection of information and creation of a database but also to involve the villagers in long-term conservation activities, several workshops were arranged. During the workshops informal discussions and group meetings were held to introduce the concept of participatory environment and biodiversity conservation. Those villagers who were interested in working without any direct financial benefit were recruited. Groups were formed with the herbal practitioners and poor farmers of the villages. The key persons identified were trained to motivate others and to collect, identify, document and propagate medicinal plants. The idea of marketing the cultivated medicinal plants was new and should hopefully promote conservation practices. The village group suggested land suitable for medicinal plant cultivation without affecting existing cropping; mostly fallow lands in and around homesteads, crop-field edges, graveyards, roadside verges and the banks leading to ponds were selected. Some much-needed seeds/seedlings of plants were arranged as gifts or exchanged to attract villagers and to help practitioners. In several villages some herbals were provided with support to establish "demonstration gardens". These familiarised the villagers with the medicinally important plant species and also supplied plant parts and propagules (seeds, cuttings) needed by users. The gardens acted as a source of enthusiasm for the activists and provided a forum for the discussion of indigenous techniques and knowledge. By collecting different species of medicinal plants they also played the role of a 'starter' for the conservationists. Also, large-scale cultivation of medicinal plants for sale or as a source of material for agro-based small industries began in these gardens. It is expected that the growers from the villages will pool their produce to satisfy the demand of the growing market for herbal products.

Difficulties encountered: During various stages of the project's implementation different types of difficulties had to be overcome. A few of these are discussed below:

- the approach had to be initiated on a small scale and gradually expanded to give it sustainability, the village situation made it difficult to realise this in practice;
- most of the villagers and field workers found the participatory, self-help approach hard to adopt. The usual idea of working for money prevails and many immediately lost interest upon seeing no promise of cash;
- other NGOs working in the villages usually provide the villagers with cash or other direct benefits. This has conditioned the poor villagers to expect cash or kind from projects. When they heard of the different approach of this programme the villagers wondered whether the biodiversity people were taking the money. However, though it was difficult in the beginning, many came to appreciate the idea, especially the sustainability aspect;
- the logic behind the idea of conserving the environment and biodiversity for present and future generations, and providing some cash as well, only won villagers over after a long period of interaction and rapport building. They adopted the approach when they realised that we meant to have a lasting association with them;
- early on progress was slow and many workers and participants lost patience. This proved to be an obstacle to keeping 'team spirit';
- the dry season climate and the low fertility of the fallow land made growing plants difficult. Many seedlings died and seeds failed to germinate. Extra expenditure for fertilising and watering was needed;

- in some areas women are very conservative and getting them involved in the initial stages was difficult. Homestead based production in particular needs women volunteers;
- the lack of a market for the small amounts of medicinal plants produced made conservation efforts difficult. The poor villagers did not believe that their produce would find a market, resulting in a low level of input;
- the traditional herbal practitioners are not recognised by the authorities (Government or Health Department), have no opportunity for training, or any support from the government or NGOs, and thus fail to meet the needs of contemporary society.

Conclusion

Social prejudice and ignorance often account for erroneous beliefs about the inefficacy of traditional healthcare systems. The dominance of the scientific medical system has undermined and eroded the once popular herbal system. But it has now been established that many indigenous medical practices are cheaper, more appropriate, readily available and lack any side effects. There is an urgent need to document and popularise herbal medicine and conserve plant diversity. In the face of rapid loss of indigenous knowledge and biodiversity in Bangladesh, the programme reported here adopted a grassroots level approach like the Grameen Bank, to document, conserve, cultivate and utilise medicinal plants. It thus provides primary healthcare to the poor villagers, whilst supplementing their income through better management of natural resources, and preserving biodiversity in homestead gardens.

Acknowledgements

Support from the Canadian International Development Research Centre, the Netherlands Embassy, the Centre for Environmental Research at Rajshahi University and the co-operation of the herbals and other villagers are gratefully acknowledged.

PART 4   INDIGENOUS KNOWLEDGE AND FISH RESOURCES

15 Indigenous Knowledge of Fish and Fisheries: A Pilot Study

Nurul Islam, Antonia Reihlen, Paul M. Thompson

FISH FEATURE PROMINENTLY in the lives of Bengalis. Large parts of their deltaic land disappear under the annual monsoon floods and large numbers of people turn to fishing to supplement their diets and incomes. At other times of year professional fishers, traditionally members of the *jele* Hindu fishing caste, exploit perennial waterbodies and rivers. This chapter summarises and assesses the findings of a pilot study into indigenous knowledge of fish, fisheries and aquatic ecology. Field research was carried out at two sites, both are flowing rivers located in Kishoreganj District and the fishers have free (open) access to these rivers. One is Moisharkandi-Boronpur section of the Ghora Uthra River in Mithamoin Thana. The area of this river section extends seasonally between 75 and 200 ha. The other is the Kali Nodi, which is a permanent side branch of the Meghna River. The water area extends seasonally between 800 and 1200 ha.

The study is part of the Community Based Fisheries Management (CBFM) project carried out jointly by a partnership of the International Centre for Living Aquatic Resources Management[1], the Department of Fisheries and several NGOs, and is funded by the Ford Foundation (CBFM 1998). The main objective of the CBFM project is to test community based fisheries management arrangements and determine if this ensures sustainable exploitation of openwater fish resources and a more equal distribution of benefits (Hossain *et al.* in press). Indigenous knowledge of fish and their ecology forms the basis for the existing pattern of exploitation and is thus the starting point for CBFM.

Methods

We employed two different methods for data collection in this pilot study: group interviews and participatory rural appraisal involving the drawing of maps. We worked with 11 groups of people, of these four comprised full-time fishers, six comprised part-time fishers (all were men as only men fish professionally in Bangladesh), the other group comprised women from a traditional Hindu fishing community who are involved in fish processing. Discussions lasted about one hour. First we asked the participants to name all the fish species they knew from their catches in the study area and to organise them into groups of fish that belonged together. The respondents usually described 5-10 different groups or categories of fish. After establishing these groups we asked the participants to tell us what the fish within each group had in common. Similarities of fish and reasons for groupings given by respondents were not restricted to biological features; economic, technical and other factors were also considered. The groups also gave information concerning spawning, fishing times, extinction of species, and sanctuaries.

In the participatory mapping we asked the fishers to map their area on large sheets of paper. They indicated the locations of the villages, fishing grounds, breeding places of fish, aquatic plants, *kata* (brushpile fish shelters — a traditional system used for attracting and catching fish), and any fish sanctuaries on the maps. The depth of water was also indicated in most of the maps. Different groups drew maps of the waterbodies representing either the monsoon or the dry season. Three groups also indicated on cross-sections of the river the depths at which fish were found. While the mapping exercises achieved their main objective of helping the fishers explain their knowledge of the linkages between fish habitats, fish, fishing and fishers, they were not a source of accurate maps (nor was this expected). Trying to make the waterbody outlines more accurate depends on the drawing skills of individuals, is time consuming, and is not critical to the fishers explanations of their fishing grounds.

Classification of fish

The participants were fully aware of the concept of classification. Nonetheless we needed to repeat several times at first what we were seeking in the grouping of the fish. The participants could see a list of fish they had reported to which they could refer when they forgot species. In Mithamoin, illustrations of common fish provided by the Thana fisheries officer proved helpful, either in remembering species or in pointing them out when local names were not known to the interviewer. Each group of fishers listed all of the species known to members in their river and then categorised them. The lists and answers were discussed constantly by the fishers. In most of the groups one participant tended to take the lead in answering after some time. We included the rest of the group by asking questions directly to persons who had not spoken recently. Progress by the groups could be confusing as fish were moved between categories when previously forgotten species were included. After some discussion the list of species seemed very clear to the fishers. However, the reasons for the classifications were more difficult to elicit and their validity is limited since possible reasons for categories were suggested (e.g. where do they live? what do they look like?) by the interviewer. In some cases the reasons appear unconvincing for the formation of a class.

Table 15.1 gives the number of species named by the different groups and the number of categories into which they were divided. The reasons for category assignment are listed broadly as ecological, economic or other. Identification to species of fish reported by local name was made using Ahmed (1953), Doha (1973) and Rahman (1989).

The different groups of fishers reported 23 to 67 different species compared with some 260 known from inland waters of Bangladesh (Rahman 1989), and categorised them into 4 to 10 groups. A comparison of the Mithamoin responses with the Kali Nodi ones shows that the Mithamoin groups gave more detailed information. The number of species and categories of fish exceed those obtained at Kali Nodi as do the reasons given for the classes. However, results of monitoring of catches in two years (1997 and 1998) indicate the reverse: 68 species recorded in Kali Nodi and only 55 species recorded in Mithamoin (CBFM project unpublished data). The traditional fishers of Kali Nodi based their categories more on technical (catch related) reasons. Muslim fishers tended to give ecological reasons for categorising fish, whereas traditional Hindu fishers also used economic and other reasons. The responses of the group of women suggest that their knowledge is comparable to men's in that they identified a similar number of species and categories.

Table 15.1:   Number of species and categories of fish named by fishers with reasons for groups

Village	Group participants	No. of species	No. of categories	Reasons for grouping fish[a]		
				ecological	economic	other
1. Mithamoin	Hindu, full time fishers	23	4	9	1	0
2. Mithamoin	Hindu, full time fishers	45	9	14	11	5
3. Mithamoin	Hindu, full time fishers	51	7	14	5	6
4. Mithamoin	Muslim, part time fishers	61	10	20	14	4
5. Mithamoin	Muslim, part time fishers	67	9	20	10	12
6. Mithamoin	Muslim, part time fishers	58	9	14	8	13
7. Kali Nodi	Muslim, part time fishers	60	5	20	0	4
8. Kali Nodi	Hindu, full time fishers	50	5	9	6	6
9. Kali Nodi	Hindu, part time fishers	50	5	9	2	4
10. Kali Nodi	Muslim, part time fishers	46	4	9	2	2
11. Kali Nodi	Hindu, wives of fishers, some dry fish	47	7	6	6	6

Note: [a]Numbers in the columns under 'reasons for grouping fish' are the number of times each group used that type of reason.

Table 15.2 summarises the groups of fish. Numbers indicate the frequency with which species was placed into the category. Fish named only once are not included in the table. The fishers' classes are in some cases similar to those of science, others are not. Where morphological aspects are a major factor in the categorisation, the classes are similar to the scientific order. Channiformes, for example, were always placed in the same group; similarly eels were grouped together. They usually put shrimps into one group, but some (*Gura icha, Katta icha*) appear in the "*Chela/Chapila*" group.

Table 15.2:   Categories of fish and their characteristics

Category	Species and number of times it was put into this category[a]	Reasons for grouping fish		
		ecological	economic	other
1.	*Chela, Chapila* (11) *Puti* (10) *Chanda, Dhala, Mola* (9) *Kachki* (8) *Kajoli, Kaikka* (7) *Shubol* (6) *Gura icha* (5) Kolisha, *Boicha, Aluni, Khorsula* (4) *Potka, Darkina, Poa, Baila, Katari* (3) *Rani, Laacho, Bojuri, Taka, Bacha, Ghaura, Hilsha* (2)	Small size and found in floodplains, *beels* and rivers. Available throughout the year.	Low market price. Can be sold mixed. Sold in local market. High demand by local consumers.	Can be dried. Caught by wide range of gears e.g. seine net, fencing, traps, current net, *mosari jal* (mosquito net).
2.	*Golsha* (7) *Batachi* (5) *Bojuri, Tengra, Poa, Ghaura, Bacha* (4) *Baila, Katari* (3) *Aluni, Kanla* (2)	Poisonous spines. Look similar. Found at surface, in shallow water, at riverbank and	High price and exported from area. Easy to sell. Can be sold mixed. Sold dried or alive.	Tasty. Always cooked on their own.

(Contd.)

(Continued)

Category	Species and number of times it was put into this category[a]	Reasons for grouping fish		
		ecological	economic	other
		floodplains. Plenty during monsoon. Some live in holes.		
3.	*Tara baim*, *Boro baim* (10) *Guti*, *Chikra baim* (8) *Rani*, *Bet*, *Ghora* (2)	Live in holes and clay. Eat clay and live at bottom level. Poisonous spines. Found in *haors*, ditches, bushes, *katas*, shallow water, riverbank and floodplains.	Fetch high price as dried fish.	No processing before drying. Damage other fish when stored together.
4.	*Shol*, *Koi*, *Shing*, *Magur* (10) *Taki*, *Gajar* (9) *Baila* (5) *Kolisha*, *Meni* (4)	Found in floodplains, *beels*, ditches. First fishes affected by fish disease (most likely Epizootic Ulcerative Syndrome). Some have poisonous spines. Live at bottom, hide in mud. Same breeding time, big, shelter in *kuas* (ditches).	High price and easy to sell – exported from area.	Can be kept alive in very little water. Easy to catch with spear, hook, cast net, trap, seine net, and fencing. Tasty.
5.	*Bacha*, *Ghaura* (8) *Laacho* (6) *Pabda* (5) *Golsha*, *Shilong* (4) *Batashi*, *Tengra*, *Kanla*, *Rani* (2)	Live at surface and at medium level. Some have poisonous spines. Look similar (two spines at head, white). Bottom feeder. Live together only in rivers.	High priced and exported from area. Medium market price.	Tasty and beautiful. Caught by seine net, cast net, current net.
6.	*Guchiair* (10) *Ayre*, *Boal* (8) *Rita*, *Ghagot*, *Chital*, *Pangas* (5) *Shilong*, *Pabda*, *Rui*, *Catla*, *Mrigel*, *Baghair* (4) *Kural* (3) *Mohashol*, *Behushi*, *Ghagla*, *Nandil*, Grass carp, *Karpoo*, *Baush*, *Ghainna* (2)	Big size. Live at bottom in rivers, canals and floodplains. Bottom feeder. Some have scales. Some have poisonous spines. Some are predators.	High priced and exported from area. Price in market depends on weight of individual fish.	Caught by seine net. Always cooked separately.
7.	*Rui*, *Mrigel* (10) *Catla* (9) *Baush* (8) *Karpoo* (7) *Ghainna*, *Chital* (6) Grass carp, *Kural*,	Big size. White scales. No spines. Live in rivers, canals and floodplains.	High priced and exported from area. Almost similar market price. High local demand.	Caught with spear, seine net, gill net. Do not have to be sorted from other fishes when stored.

(Contd.)

(Continued)

Category	Species and number of times it was put into this category[a]	Reasons for grouping fish		
		ecological	economic	other
	Kanla. *Boa* (5) **Mohashol. Nandil, Guchi baim** (4) *Rita, Pangas, Ayre, Sarputi* (3) **Khaila.** Mirror carp, *Baghair* (2)	Bottom feeder. Shelter in *kata*.	Price in market depends on weight of individual fish.	
8.	*Hilsha. Sarputi. Ghainna.* Silver carp (2)	Migratory, live in sea and river.	Exported.	Tasty.
9.	**Dima icha** (9) **Sharong icha** (7) **Tenga icha** (6) *Gura icha* (4) **Temba icha. Chata icha** (3) **Boiragi icha** (2)	Need shelter. Plenty in monsoon. Live in riverbanks, floodplains, and *beels*. Can walk and eat garbage. Some live in holes.	High price and export.	Caught with traps. Shelter in *kata* (brushpiles). Can be cooked with many different vegetables.

Note: [a]species names in bold indicate the most frequent placement of that species. Only species reported by more than one group are included in table.

Some fisher groups combined classes 2 and 5, and 6 and 7. Some fish (e.g. *Rani, Laacho*) appear in many different categories, as different fishers gave different reasons for their categorisation. Overall the fish categories could be summarised as: category 1-small fish; category 2-medium sized fish; category 3-eels; category 4-"live fish"; category 5-medium sized fish; category 6-larger fish (mainly catfish); category 7- larger fish (mainly carp); category 8-miscellaneous fish including *Hilsha* (which is rare in these rivers), and category 9-shrimps.

Fish breeding time and places

The fishers did not have detailed knowledge of the breeding times of fish. This may be because they rarely see the eggs of the fish. If they do see them, which is more probable with small fish that seem to spawn in more accessible shallow water, they do not know to which species they belong. Only group one gave detailed information about breeding times of different categories of fish, although all were asked (Table 15.3). The breeding places are derived from the maps drawn by the fishers.

Threatened species

All groups mentioned *Pangas, Nandil* and *Taka* as extinct or endangered (Table 15.4). Some named fish that have been extinct for a long time (e.g. *Kural* 20-30 years, *Mohashul* 25 years). This shows that knowledge of fish reaches back at least to when the fishers were young, and that knowledge passes on from parents to children. Extinction is mainly associated with environmental causes, largely the falling water level. No group mentioned over-fishing, and use of destructive gear was cited as a cause only once.

Table 15.3:   Fish breeding times and breeding places

Group	Breeding times	Breeding places
1. Mithamoin	Catfish (medium-large): Feb.-Apr. Catfish (small): Apr.-Jun. Snakehead: Apr.-Jun. Shrimp: May-Jun. Small fish: May-Jul.	—
2. Mithamoin	Spawning at full-moon.	Small fish breed mostly in floodplains close to the river and in areas with plants, also in shallow water of *beels* and riverbanks.
4. Mithamoin	—	Small fish breed close to the river in areas with plants.
1. Kali Nodi	All species: Mar.-May.	Large fish spawn in deep water.
2. Kali Nodi	—	Close to riverbanks, places with little current.
4. Kali Nodi	—	Small fish breed in shallow water in plant clusters.

Table 15.4:   Extinct and endangered fish species and reasons given

Group	Extinct species	Time extinct	Reasons
1. Mithamoin	*Pangas* *Taka* *Shilong* *Nandil* *Mrigel*	5 years 20 years	Lack of food (snails/*shamuk*) because the riverbed is shallower. New seasonality of *beels* and floodplains (water-loss because of irrigation, siltation etc.) Tides now weaker in the monsoon due to reduced depth and current in rivers (deep-water fish).
6. Mithamoin	*Nandil* *Taka* *Mohashul* *Kural* *Pangas, Koi, Meni* *Guchi-Ghagot*	15 years 12 years 25 years 30 years	Very few are caught. Very few are caught.
2. Kali Nodi	*Nandil, Mohashul* *Boro Potka* *Kural* *Ghora, Pangas*	20 years 25 years 10 years	Few are caught, declining for 8 years.
3. Kali Nodi	*Pangas, Nandil,* *Taka, Ghora*		They are deep water fish and the water level is decreasing.
4. Kali Nodi	*Pangas, Nandil,* *Taka, Ghora, Potka*		Due to the Farakka barrage at the Indian border and use of destructive gear (gill nets with small mesh).

Fish habitats

The information in Table 15.5 was derived using a standardised cross-section of a river and by asking the fishers to indicate where the fish live, not where they are caught or where they feed. Probably the fishers based their groupings of fish by preferred water depths from the gears they use and the depths reached with those gears. Different groups of fishers had conflicting ideas about which parts of the river they found fish in. Only a few species were placed into the same habitat by all the groups (e.g. *Kaikka, Puti, Chital*). More data is needed to verify the trends indicated here.

Table 15.5: Preferred water depths reported for different fishes

Top level[a]	Medium level	Bottom level
Kachki, Chela, Darkina, Chanda, Kaikka, Puti, Poa, Mola, Batashi, Pabda, Ghaura, Baush, Tenga icha, Dima icha, Sharong icha, Gura icha, Boal, Kajoli, Kolisha, Koi, Ghainna, Rani, Laacho, Kanla, Meni, Magur, Shing, Tara baim, Shilong, Baila, Taki, Chikra baim, Guti	*Bashpata, Laacho, Catla, Sarputi, Ghainna, Karpoo, Golsha, Icha, Poa, Baush, Catla, Boal, Mola,* Grass carp, *Ayre,* Silver carp, *Shol, Pabda, Ghaura,* Common carp	*Kajoli, Rani, Gila Kani, Baila, Shing, Koi, Magur, Chital, Ayre, Guchiair, Ghagot, Pangas, Shilong, Rita, Mrigel, Guti, Tara baim, Chikra baim, Icha, Kural, Dima icha, Kachki, Batashi, Tenga icha, Hilsha, Potka*
(Chapila, Bacha, Rui, Tengra, Gajar, Golsha, Chanda, Boro baim)	*(Chapila, Bacha, Rui, Tengra, Gajar, Golsha, Chanda, Boro baim)*	*(Chapila, Bacha, Rui, Tengra, Gajar, Golsha, Chanda, Boro baim)*

Note: [a]Species in parenthesis were placed in all three depth categories.

Fishing gear

Information about gear use was derived from maps. The groups pointed out places where they used each gear (e.g. *katas*). Only the most frequent gear was listed (Table 15.6), and categories (types) have been cross-checked with Ahmed (1970). A wide range of gear was used in the two areas. For fishing in the floodplains, fishers in both Mithamoin and Kali Nodi use different gear from those they employ in the rivers. The types of gear used differed between groups in the same river, but it is not clear if this is the result of traditions, lack of money to buy new gear, or a tactic for exploiting local fishing niches.

Table 15.6: Local names of fishing gears used in floodplains and rivers

Type of gear	Rivers		Flood plains	
	Mithamoin	Kali Nodi	Mithamoin	Kali Nodi
Seine/Drag net	*Goira jal, Pine jal, Pine ber, Khuna ber, Ghana ber, Gaitta jal, Dhani jal, Sandi jal, Jhapa jal, Gumaber, Katchitana jal.*	*Moshari jal, Konaber, Patan jal, Pine jal, Harhari jal, Ghana jal, Kachiber, Pine jal, Rana jal, Patni jal, Moi jal*	*Goira jal, Pine jal, Pineber, Khuna jal, Dhani jal, Gunaber, Katchkata jal, Sandi jal.*	*Atra jal, Ghana jal/Atta jal, Kachber, Pine jal, Rana jal.*
Gill net	*Pera jal, Current jal*	*Patni jal, Moi jal*	*Pera jal, Current jal*	*Fash jal, Current jal, Patni jal, Moi jal*
Cast net	*Uthar jal, Jhaki jal*	*Ram jal*	*Uthar jal, Talla jal*	
Hook and Line	*Borshi*	*Borshi*	*Borshi*	*Borshi*
Trap	*Chai*		*Chai*	
Set bag	*Harhari, Bhim, Baim jal*			*Harhari jal*
Lift net	*Jali*		*Jali*	
Spear			*Juita, koach*	
Fencing			*Patibund*	

Experience with sanctuaries

There was a fish sanctuary in the river in Mithamoin from 1994 to 1996. The fishers reported that it benefited them; they caught more large fish than before (e.g. *Ayre, Boal, Baush, Icha, Chital, Ghagot*) and more shrimp in areas outside the sanctuary. The sanctuary ceased when governmental support ended, but an aim of the CBFM project is for fishers themselves to take up such initiatives where they perceive a benefit. The fishers reported that *katas* are good shelters for big fish, but small fish are seldom found there. The fishers suggested that a sanctuary in future should be located at a place with little current and shallow water. In Kali Nodi there had also been a sanctuary, but the fishers did not obey the rules requiring them to only harvest it once a year. Few of the fishers had any idea about fish sanctuaries, but they agreed that sanctuaries result in an increase in large fish nearby. The fishers recommended areas with weak currents, deep water and little disturbance by river traffic for future installation of a sanctuary, and indicated that the main purpose of a sanctuary should be to protect fish breeding grounds.

Fishing times

Most of the survey participants said they fish at night because fish then come to the surface of the water (Table 15.7). Here they can be caught more easily using shorter nets. Full moon is believed to bring fish to the surface even more. However, one group of fishers did not agree with that and said that fish are afraid of too much light. During the day bigger fish are caught. Fishing between high and low tide in the dry season and at low tide during the monsoon indicates that better catches are achieved at low water levels.

Table 15.7:   Fishing times

Group	Fishing time	Reason
Mithamoin	Night Full moon, low tide, thunderstorms, moonshine	Fish gather at top level at night: no disturbance by boats, it's quiet, fish "enjoy leisure time", small fish eat at night, plenty of fish.
Kali Nodi	Night Full moon (between high and low tide in dry season, at low tide in monsoon) Little moonlight Jun.-Oct.	No boats, no disturbance by people: fish come to the top (nets of short length can be used). Fish surface when they see the light, and there are plenty at the top. Fish are at the bottom at full moon because they are afraid of the light. *Kachki, Chapila,* and *Puti* caught using *ram jal, felun, atra-jal.* Plenty of small fish at the top which do not come to the upper level in sunlight.

Conclusions

Participatory rural appraisal can help document and promote the use of existing traditional knowledge (e.g. local ideas on conservation, fishing, and sanctuaries). Regarding the methodology used, we make the following observations for future studies. It would be more efficient if researchers draw the outline of any waterbody on large sheets of paper before the group meeting. They can explain the map to the fishers and this would allow more time to add detailed information, and would help standardise for drawing skills. On the outline map the fishers could be asked to indicate villages, *beels*, fishing grounds, aquatic plants, fish breeding places (which species, when?), *katas* and sanctuaries, gears used (specific places), and other water uses (such as irrigation pumps, bathing places etc.).

A visual approach could be tested to simplify and hasten the classification of fish. Images of the most common species copied from books and posters could be cut out and pasted on card. This would help the fishers in categorising fish by moving around the cut-outs, would help ensure more equal participation of all fishers, and would make the process more efficient. Discussion of indigenous knowledge of fish could be structured around four main issues:

- Biological, relating to habitat, physiology, breeding etc.
- Economical, relating to prices, marketing etc.
- Technical, relating to fishing methods, processing, conservation etc.
- Other, relating to cooking methods, other uses of fish (medicine) etc.

There is a need for similar studies in a wide range of waterbodies and fisheries since there are large variations between regions, fisher communities, and other factors such as NGO activities. More importantly, indigenous knowledge also includes any unwritten rules and rights that traditionally govern access to and use of the fisheries. Involving local fishers in participatory planning for improving and formalising management systems should be based on an understanding of these traditional practices and local knowledge (Berkes 1998). Understanding traditional fishing practices and ecological knowledge will be useful in reaching local agreements to ensure sustainable fishing. It would be valuable to involve NGOs at the grass roots level in playing a role, from which they can go on to further community development and resource management. We should encourage communities to share their knowledge with participating organisations, so that improvements in planning and resource management of fisheries can advance from local ecological knowledge, practices and institutions. Development organisations also need to be flexible in incorporating local arrangements and indigenous knowledge in any projects and management improvements. Projects should have provision to exchange results of monitoring of catches, species diversity, disappearing species, indicator species and other biological aspects of the fisheries and their development with fishers, in addition to coming to grips with related indigenous knowledge, to give this a scientific reference.

Notes

1 ICLARM Contribution No. 1525.

16 Fresh Water Fisheries of Bangladesh: Issues of Sustainability

D. Mazumder, Z. Samina and T. Islam

IN THE AGRO-BASED ECONOMY of Bangladesh fish and fisheries play an important role in determining food security, nutrition and the income of marginal people. Due to intensive pressure on open water areas for food and income the total catch has declined and the habitat changed. Development initiatives to increase production are a potential cause of further ecological degradation. Aquaculture is considered to increasingly meet demand for food, though the technological constraints, as well as the growing presence (60%) of non-native species in ponds, need to be carefully considered to ensure the sustainable use of resources.

Fish are the world's fifth largest food resource and account for 7.5% of total global food production. About 100 million people in the developing world depend on fishing as their primary source of protein (Seshu *et al.* 1994; FAO 1995). Bangladesh has highly diversified fishery resources, with many species. The fisheries account for 80% of Bangladesh's total protein intake. The sector provides full-time employment for about 1.4 million people, and an additional 11 million people are involved in part-time fishing. The necessity for sustainable fisheries is now recognised with the decline in open water fish production due to resource depletion. The gap between supply and demand for fish has widened with a decline in production and an increasing human population. The per capita fish consumption has decreased and the fisher community has become impoverished.

Inland open water fisheries

Inland open water includes rivers, canals, floodplains, *beels,* lakes and reservoirs. In the past fish were abundant in open water. Rahman (1989) describes 260 species of fresh water fish in Bangladesh, the majority of small and medium size, widely distributed in the open water systems. The country has one of the largest floodplains in the world. Some 2.8 million ha. retain water for 4-7 months of the year. These floodplains provide good breeding and grazing grounds for many species and play an important role in repopulating the open water fish systems, including those of rivers and estuaries. The open water fisheries contribute substantially to fish production, and to the income of the rural poor of Bangladesh who are heavily reliant upon these for their subsistence (Ahmed 1997). The fishing communities have evolved highly effective technologies and knowledge systems over generations for the efficient exploitation of this resource. They were largely sustainable. Detrimental changes have occurred due to outside interference and ignoring indigenous knowledge and experience of fisheries.

Over the last decade the country's population has risen rapidly. Consequently the need to increase crop and fish production has become a priority. The pressure on open water resources has increased tremendously in the absence of diverse economic activity in the country. Resources have been exploited heavily and fish production from the open water systems has seriously declined due to overuse, and the range of species has changed (Tsai and Ali 1985; see Figure 16.1). Over the same time period fish habitats have decreased with people bringing floodplain areas into crop production. In addition, the use of pesticides and chemical fertilisers has increased, keeping pace with crop production, the cumulative effect adversely affecting open water fisheries. Annual fish production from the floodplains fell causing a decline in riverine fish populations as their breeding stock was disrupted with the intense pressure placed on open water systems (Mazid and Gupta 1995). The social impact of these ecological changes has been considerable. For example, Mazumder (1998) reported that a fisher community was displaced from the *beel* area of Churamonkathi in the Jessore region due to a decline in the availability of small, native species of fish.

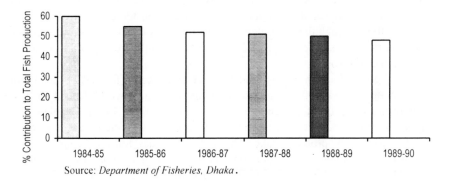

Source: *Department of Fisheries, Dhaka*.

Figure 16.1 *Decline in open water fish production*

In recent years, the Government has initiated programmes to boost fish production from open water systems through stocking fingerlings. The species selected for this were exotic and indigenous carp. The idea was to ensure the optimum utilisation of all the food niches in the open water system. Various reports have suggested that open water fish production increased slightly after the introduction of these fish species. Data from Hail Haor in Sylhet shows that the carp content in fish catches increased from 16.7% in 1990-91 to 30.8% in 1991 and 28% in 1992-93 (Jhingran 1997). This increase indicates that stocking can improve open water fish production, although the issues surrounding the long-term impacts of introducing exotic species into open water systems has yet to be assessed. It remains unknown whether these exotic fish species will harm native species over time. The impact of such introduction depends on the numbers of fish introduced, their size, and their ability to adapt to the new ecosystem and develop a breeding pattern in open water. In open water ecosystems the aquatic vegetation provides an ideal breeding ground for many of the native fish species. These habitats could be damaged by grass carp (*Ctenopharyngodon idella*), for example, due to its herbivorous feeding habits, or silver carp (*Hypophthalmichthys molitrix*) which feed on plankton, thereby competing with the native *catla* (*Catla catla*) for food and space. Both exotic fish have been introduced into open water systems to boost production. More attention should be paid to local knowledge of these issues and observations of changes in fisheries over time, and peoples' explanations of them.

Aquaculture

Aquaculture has been looked to, to help meet an increasing demand as open water catches are failing to meet fish requirements. In Bangladesh there are 146,890 ha. of ponds, 5,488 ha. of ox-bow lakes, 140,000 ha. of brackish water and 8 million ha. of paddy fields in which aquaculture could be undertaken. The potential of aquaculture in these water bodies is considerable (Mahabubullah 1983; Ahmed 1992; Shah and Townsley, this volume). Aquaculture is now considered an increasingly important source of protein and income for the people of Bangladesh. It is not a new technology however; people have maintained ponds for generations and have a rich heritage of knowledge pertaining to cultured fish production.

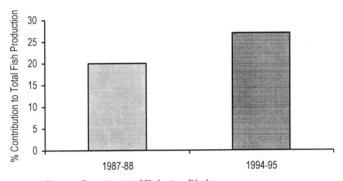

Source: *Department of Fisheries, Dhaka.*

Figure 16.2   *The contribution of aquaculture to national fish production between 1987 and 1995*

The issues of concern surrounding the further development of aquaculture include equity, technological constraints, the stunted growth of cultured carp and the use of exotic fish species. Aquaculture depends heavily on the supply of fish from hatcheries, but due to inbreeding, stocked fingerlings often fail to grow well in ponds. This reduces production and income generation from aquaculture. Small indigenous species are generally considered "weed fish" in culture ponds and are invariably eradicated because they are thought to compete with stocked species for food and space. The present introduced techniques of pond preparation have an adverse effect on these small species. Small indigenous species were found in 97% of ponds where only netting, the indigenous technique, was used to eliminate unwanted fish species, while they were found in only 22% of ponds where pesticides were used (Mazumder 1998). The introduction of exotic species of fish into ponds is another concern. About 60% of the stocked fish species are exotic and dominated by silver carp (Mazumder 1998). While aquaculture has the potential to increase food supply and help improve nutritional intake in Bangladesh, it is important to consider all related issues to ensure appropriate and sustainable use of resources. Where indigenous techniques are less harmful to the ecosystem and maintain a balanced and productive habitat, it seems reasonable that they should be used. We need to learn more about these indigenous practises and how they might be advanced upon to improve sustainable production.

Conclusion

An increase in fish production is not necessarily an indicator of sustainability. Fish production may increase through introduction of foreign species to an aquatic system, but the costs may be high due to the resulting loss of biodiversity. The careful screening of the ecology of fish is an important prerequisite for any development initiative relating to aquaculture. It is necessary to consider whether the increasing presence of exotic fish in the ecosystems disadvantages farmers by reducing the species available to them. In order to ensure the sustainable use of aquatic resources it is important to consider the knowledge of the local people whose livelihoods have depended on these resources for generations. The involvement of the local people in the planning and management processes is integral to the success of any intervention.

17 An Indigenously Developed Pond Aquaculture System

Wajed A. Shah and Philip Townsley

THE POTENTIAL FOR INCREASING fish production in Bangladesh through aquaculture development in the country's many under-utilised ponds, ditches and small waterbodies has often been noted. Estimates put the total area of "culturable" waterbody at about 150,000 ha. of which only about 50% is utilised for aquaculture (Nuruzzaman 1992). An attractive feature of many of these waterbodies is that they are located close to people's homesteads and may be owned by families that are otherwise landless (FAP 17, 1993). In spite of considerable efforts by development and extension agencies, the great potential of aquaculture for increasing the protein consumption and incomes of rural households has not been realised. The case study presented below describes an aquaculture system developed without intervention from extension agencies, by a community on the floodplain of the Jamuna River. The system is responsive to local conditions, indigenous knowledge and to the technical capabilities and requirements of its practitioners. In particular, it appears to overcome some of the technical, social and economic constraints commonly identified as impeding aquaculture development.

Study site

Saturia Thana, located about 50 kilometres North-west of the capital, Dhaka, is one of the most densely populated areas in Bangladesh. In a predominantly agricultural economy, levels of landlessness stand at over 50%. The twin villages of Bhatara and Char Bhatara, connected by road with the main Dhaka highway, support approximately 300 households made up of several distinct groups. About 200 households live primarily by farming, but a large group of about 100 households have worked for several generations as *nikari* 'fish traders'. It is within this latter group that aquaculture has, over the past decade, taken root. This development began in the 1950s when many of the traditional Hindu caste-fishermen in the area left the country for India. An employment niche was left vacant which Bhatara people, already involved in the fisheries sector, were quick to fill. The complex of wetlands which surround the village are still extensively fished by villagers, but are steadily disappearing due to siltation and changes in flooding pattern caused by roadways and settlement.

The fish culture system

In the 1980s a more or less chance combination of events initiated the development of aquaculture in the community. A villager with previous experience of fish culture whilst living in another district was repaid a loan in the form of fish fingerlings. Although early experiments met with limited success, a system was developed which functioned remarkably well, given the types of waterbody available in the area, and has since spread not only within the community but also to neighbouring villages.

Like most pond aquaculture systems in Bangladesh, the system in Bhatara is based on the polyculture of the Indian major Carps (*Labeo ruhita, Cirrhinus marigala, Catla catla*). It is notable for the degree to which it makes intensive use of existing water resources and integrates the production potential of some waterbody types with the input requirement of others. While some households have been able to carry out all stages of the fish culture cycle in a variety of ponds and ditches, others have specialised in particular stages of the cycle. Such activity, whether producing fingerlings or fish for consumption, integrates well with the fish trading activities that constitute the "traditional" livelihood of many of the households in the community.

The fish culture system in Bhatara can be divided into two stages: the nursery stage, which produces fish fry or fingerlings for stocking in other ponds; and the subsequent grow-out stage, aimed at the production of fish for the consumer market. The nursery stage is further divided into a primary stage (raising fish spawn to fish fry) and secondary stage (raising fish fry to fingerlings).

The primary nursery system generally utilises very small ponds located close to homesteads. The average size is 0.032 ha. Often these ponds are simply the borrow-pits from which soil for the raised homestead mounds was excavated to render them suitable for habitation. Most nurserers carry out multi-species fry production at the primary nursery stage although some concentrate on single species. The most commonly followed steps for primary nursery production are as follows:

- ponds are drained in early April at the end of dry season and left dry for about 15-20 days;
- where irrigation is available, water is pumped into the pond to a depth of 1.5-2 feet, (otherwise nurserers must wait for the first rain in late April or early May);
- ponds are poisoned for predatory insects and the following day limed at a rate of 16.46 kg/ha., fertilised with urea at 110 kg/ha. and manured with oil cake at 38.42 kg/ha.;
- one week after fertilisation, the pond is netted to remove frogs and insects;
- after netting fishermen collect wild spawn to stock ponds from the Jamuna River, about 25 kilometres west of Bhatara;
- fries are fed and reared for 16-20 days in the primary nursery, then sold to other culturists or used for stocking the owner's secondary ponds.

Villagers use numerous variations on these steps. Nurserers experiment to identify the best methods for their particular ponds, and establish relationships between rates of stocking and mortality, depth of water and survival, feeding patterns and the growth of fries. Some nurserers experienced serious losses in fry production. However, the number of nurserers is increasing steadily in response to demand as more local people take up aquaculture and because nursery systems can be established in smaller, more commonly available ponds. Fingerlings grown out from wild-collected spawn are generally regarded as superior to hatchery-produced fry.

Local methods of fingerling production in the secondary nursery system are not those generally recommended by extension agencies. Nurserers reported that the 'recommended' nursery technology is expensive and technically difficult to implement in rural conditions. The management methods used in secondary nursery production have developed through experience and observation. Secondary nursery production in Bhatara follows the same methods as the primary nursery system, but stocks fry, caught wild or bred in primary nursery ponds, and raises them to fingerling size to stock in grow-out ponds. Pond preparation is the same as in the primary nursery system. The size of secondary nursery ponds ranges from 0.08 to 0.16 ha. with a greater water depth than primary nursery ponds. Secondary nurseries produce stock both for the owner's grow-out ponds and for sale to other fish culturists. Villagers are aware of the risks associated with nursery production. The high mortality in fry/fingerling production has taught culturists the importance of adequate pond preparation. If successful, the returns are higher than crop production from the equivalent area of land, but if unsuccessful a considerable investment is lost. Despite the risks few culturists have abandoned this activity and two-stage nursery production has expanded so that the village has become an important local centre for fish, fry and fingerling supply.

The grow-out stage of the fish culture cycle is widely practiced in Bhatara and is conducted using a variety of input levels, stocking and management regimes. The methods employed are determined as much by the economic circumstances of a household as by their technical knowledge. Multi-species pond culture, stocking fingerlings from local nursery ponds and those caught by fishermen, is most common. Overstocking seems to be the rule but no set standards are followed. Results seem to satisfy those involved even if they do not represent the optimal yield from the available resources.

Table 17.1 shows the cost and returns for one pond operator carrying out all these stages of the culture system in different ponds (primary and secondary nursery and grow-out).

Table 17.1:   Cost and return analysis of integrated primary/secondary nursery and grow-out operation in Bhatara village, 1993

Fry production	Taka/acre	Fingerlings	Taka/acre	Grow-out	Taka/acre
Clean & de-watering	577	Pond preparation	1,250	Pond preparation	1,707
Poison & liming	375	Fries	8,756	Fingerlings	8,176
Fertiliser & netting	756	Feed & fertiliser	634	Feed & fertiliser	3,300
Spawn egg	4,000	–	–	Netting & caring	2,200
Feeding	346	–	–	Rent	10,000
Rent of pond	1,900	–	–	–	–
Total cost	**7,954**	**Total cost**	**10,640**	**Total cost**	**26,184**
Gross benefit	18,900	Gross benefit	24,000	Gross benefit	159,950
Gross Margin	**10,944**	**Gross Margin**	**13,360**	**Gross Margin**	**133,766**
BC Ratio	1.37	BC Ratio	1.25	BC Ratio	5.0
Rearing 1 month	–	Rearing 1 month	–	Rearing 9 months	–

Constraints and local solutions

Following years of research and extension work in aquaculture (Rahman 1986; Mazid 1993; Gill and Motahar 1982), it is widely accepted that the primary constraints on aquaculture development are social and economic rather than technical. A recent workshop on NGO involvement promoting pond fisheries and aquaculture identified the following constraints to widespread fish culture development: the supply of fish fry and fingerlings at the farm level; technology transfer; access to ponds and waterbody resources and multiple ownership of ponds. These constraints are discussed below:

Supply of fish fry and fingerlings: Villagers in Bhatara seem to have overcome this obstacle. Their experience in fisheries may have enabled them to acquire the necessary understanding of the biological cycle of cultivable species. Whilst a good local supply of wild spawn as a primary input is important, long-term dependence on natural sources of fish spawn seems unlikely. It is likely that similar development will occur in other areas as demand increases. In some areas of Bangladesh, small-scale hatcheries have developed in response to the growing demand from fish culturists.

Transfer of technology: Since its introduction eight years ago, aquaculture in Bhatara has steadily increased. The success of the technology and improved earnings for aquaculturalists has encouraged the transfer of technology.

Waterbody access: In Bhatara, as elsewhere in Bangladesh, the spread of aquaculture is limited by a lack of available waterbodies. This seems to contradict the widely believed idea of many unutilised waterbodies. Floods affect large areas of lowland Bangladesh and discourage investment in aquaculture. This is not to say that flooded ponds or ditches are not exploited, as when the flood recedes, leaving waterbodies stocked with wild fish, local people are quick to take advantage. In some cases, these stocks are improved by adding fish feed, providing artificial shelters for fish and by additional stocking of fingerlings. Flood prone ponds aside, the number of available waterbodies are few. In villages like Bhatara, there are scarcely any ponds available for further development. When the first household took up fish culture in the village, there was a choice of ponds. Today, owners of ponds realise the potential of these resources. Consequently terms of leasing are becoming less advantageous with lease-periods becoming shorter. Often owners will only lease ponds to local fish culturists for one year so that the pond is re-excavated and improved after which time the owners will take it over themselves. In the long term many small and medium landowners will probably acquire the necessary skills to manage their ponds themselves. But experience in Bhatara suggests that possibilities for experienced non-pond owners to become involved in aquaculture activities may exceed available resources. The tenure arrangements discussed below highlight this point.

Multiple ownership: Outsiders commonly perceive the multiple ownership of ponds as a potential constraint since disagreements over sharing of benefits and management responsibilities are common. While problems have undoubtedly occurred in Bhatara with regard to both these, it seems that local people are generally able to work out arrangements that overcome tenure problems. Although some 16 different tenure arrangements for culturable ponds and ditches were encountered in the village of Bhatara alone, in terms of their essential characteristics, they can be reduced to four principle systems:

1. *Share system*: The share system for pond fisheries essentially mirrors sharecropping in agriculture. All the production costs and labour is provided by the fish culturist/share-cropper. The harvest is then shared between him and the pond/landowner. There is no cost involved for the pond-owner. The exact rate at which the crop is shared between the two parties varies considerably depending primarily on the condition of the pond. If it requires much work in order to make it usable for culture the owner's share decreases. The maximum and minimum shares going to the pond owner are generally 50% and 25% respectively.

2. *Kot system*: The word *kot* is a local term for 'contract'. Contract periods range from one to six years and the pond owner or owners decide the terms. *Kot* holders reported that, under this arrangement, pond owners rent out only those ponds that require investment like re-digging, pond embankment raising and so on before stocking. The pond owners' interest is essentially to have the pond prepared for them so that at a later date they can take up aquaculture activities themselves. The length of these contracts is steadily reducing, as mentioned above.

3. *Lease system*: In this system, government-owned *khas* ponds are given on lease to private parties, generally through an open auction. Preferential bidding rights can be given to special groups, such as co-operatives, community groups or landless associations, but they usually go to the highest bidder. In bidding, contacts with local bureaucrats and political influence tend to dictate who may obtain the lease. While much has been made of the potential to redirect the benefits from aquaculture towards disadvantaged groups such as the landless (and some very successful programmes have been instigated) the scope for this is limited by the relatively small number of *khas* ponds available.

4. *Dow ani system*: This system appears to be a local innovation by the fishermen and fish traders of the study area. The word *dow* means two, and *ani* comes from *anna* meaning one-sixteenth of a taka. Thus *dow ani*, meaning one-eighth, refers to the share taken by the fish culturist under this arrangement. In this system, the fish culturist essentially sells his expertise and labour in return for a 12.5% share of the total harvest while the pond owner bears all the costs of production. The *dow ani* share holder guides and advises the pond owner as a consultant. This system seems to be gaining popularity in neighbouring villages.

Prospects and opportunities

The Bhatara case study illustrates several important points regarding the development of aquaculture in rural Bangladesh. Firstly, in spite of technical and social problems, where there is a market for fish, and an availability of inputs and suitable environmental conditions, aquaculture will probably develop. Concern about the "slow pace" of aquaculture development may reflect an unrealistic set of expectations among development workers rather than reluctance or tardiness among potential fish farmers. Secondly, while social problems such as pond tenure and multiple ownership have correctly been identified as important constraints, such problems can be overcome when the people involved can clearly see the benefits to be gained. Local fish culturists in Bhatara recognise the problems citing the political and social manoeuvres sometimes necessary to obtain access to waterbodies. In the long run the problem of access may create difficulties for landless people and non-pond owners who want to become involved in fish culture. As the potential benefits of aquaculture become apparent, pond owners are liable to become directly involved in culturing their own ponds. Thirdly, the development of the *dow ani* system in Bhatara shows that potential may exist for trained and experienced landless people to make a living through their technical expertise in aquaculture. The potential for using such experienced local people as extension agents should also be considered. While many of the factors influencing the development of aquaculture in Bhatara are probably specific to the region and its people, the case has implications for the development of aquaculture in the country as a whole and illustrates the resourcefulness of rural people and their capacity to build on indigenous knowledge when they perceive clear benefits from a new activity.

Acknowledgements

We should like to thank the members of the Flood Action Plan 17 Socioeconomic Field Team for drawing our attention to the case discussed in this report and for their assistance in collecting information and data. Particular thanks go to the villagers of Bhatara and Char Bhatara for their patience in describing and explaining their fish culture activities.

PART 5   INDIGENOUS KNOWLEDGE AND METHODOLOGICAL ISSUES

18 Indigenous Knowledge and Agricultural Research: Conflicts and Complementarities

S. B. Naseem

BANGLADESH IS OVERWHELMINGLY an agricultural country and society. But there is a gulf between those who purport to know about agriculture and those who practice it; that is between scientists and farmers. In Bangladesh the problem of understanding each other's views is acute. This chapter describes some of the conflicts and complementarities between indigenous knowledge and natural resource science for sustainable agricultural production. Natural resource researchers have comfortably placed themselves away from the reach of rural farmers. The scientists, with a college education, involve themselves in policy planning, dialogues with the scientific community and the introduction of advanced technology. They undertake all this in the name of agricultural development for rural people. Unfortunately, however, they tend to overlook the farmers' own aspirations, culture, traditions, knowledge and beliefs. The result has been a short-term increase in crop production that is proving to be unsustainable.

Natural resource scientists have tended to dismiss farmers' knowledge as non-scientific, being based on traditional faiths that have no importance in this age of technological advancement. They consider indigenous knowledge as native tales, proverbs and sayings of rural illiterates, devoid of any rational foundation or significance. Sometimes, following recent conventions and as required by some development programmes, natural resource scientists make a token gesture towards learning farmers' local knowledge. But they have failed in Bangladesh to recognise its relevance to development. They isolate themselves from the local environment and the people. Scientists with a modern education are influenced by western culture, they follow urban life styles that distance them, either consciously or subconsciously, from the heritage, culture and traditions of rural people. These outsider one-time researchers fail to acknowledge that local farmers, with their roots imbedded in their locality, could provide invaluable information for their scientific investigations. For example, agronomists recommend increased dosages of chemical fertilisers to increase crop yields, without regard for other sociocultural constraints affecting the adoption of high input technologies. Thus, in this country many scientifically conceived and well-planned development programmes devised in city-based offices by personnel who did not listen to those 'stupid' persons ended up as failures (see also Haque, this volume). We should recall the recommendations of the 1993 UN Earth Summit, 'Agenda 21', which explicitly spells out that sustainable agricultural interventions need to exploit the potential synergy between indigenous knowledge and modern science. We need to give an increased thrust to incorporate indigenous knowledge into sustainable development in Bangladesh.

The need for a socioculturally informed research dimension
Local knowledge underwrites the lives of rural people, informing natural resource management, health practices and other activities. Rural people in Bangladesh, on the floodplains and elsewhere, have evolved a range of farming systems and techniques through a process of innovation and adaptation, fine-tuned with the local environment, economy and sociocultural system. Agriculture has been practiced here for thousands of years. But unfortunately people's knowledge is not well documented and is disappearing fast (Chowdhury *et al.* 1996). While Bangladesh possesses a rich heritage of indigenous knowledge, much of it is threatened by the modernisation of agriculture. But rural people still nurture many myths, beliefs and traditions. The local technologies have evolved through long term experience of minimising farmers' risks. They have allowed the population to survive numerous natural calamities such as floods, droughts, cyclones and tornadoes, in addition to market input and pricing failures, all of which occur regularly in the country (Ahmed *et al.* 1996).

Agricultural research has recently been criticised for being too short-term oriented, incremental, production oriented and for ignoring wider issues (IRRI 1992). The plant and animal science research agenda is largely responsible, together with the demands of funding agencies. Contributions from social and environmental science are often credited with bringing back a broader, longer-term view to agricultural research in development (Gadgil *et al.* 1993). We are moving towards sustained production gains, in spite of the damage caused by natural disasters. Modern biological science combined with socioeconomic research can continue this trend. The choice of rural sociology and anthropology is deliberate. They are more appropriate than other applied social sciences, although in the Bangladeshi context they are poorly represented. Until very recently, sociology and anthropology were not active partners in agricultural research and development. This involvement of social scientists in the development process stems from a growing concern among biological scientists and administrators that they should be socially informed. They recognise that all too often agricultural research and development failed to fulfil their objectives because they were socially uninformed or ill conceived. This realisation, by default, has led to increasing attention to sociocultural variables in project design. Consequently there are increasing calls for multidisciplinary research with social scientists regularly included as team members prioritising the analysis of sociocultural context, contributing to the social acceptability of experimentally gained knowledge. They assess the implications of bio-technical knowledge in sociocultural terms, helping to advance sustainable agricultural technologies.

A key concept here is participation. Social research problems include the advancement of techniques for approaching and mobilising people to participate in projects. Under what conditions would they participate? What mechanisms would ensure maximum participation and fair distribution of benefits? There are many other questions that need to be addressed in the social analysis. For example what is the social organisation of the community and what are peoples' roles? What is the nature of kinship, political and hierarchical linkages and the social class composition? In particular, what is the structural composition of the target group population? What is its gender composition and so on? These data and their analysis, and other similar questions, are the basis of social enquiry. The motivation of people to participate in proposed project interventions relates closely to the function, needs and aspirations of their households and their perception of their productive activities. The participatory process is a complex one. Social scientists analyse the process and facilitate participatory methods to involve intended beneficiaries with project activities. Social scientists dealing with key concepts can draw people into the design and implementation of development projects.

Sociologists and anthropologists share with farming systems research specialists the assumption that farmers' productive activities amount to considerably more than producing a few important crops. They relate to the entire resource system of a locality and access to resources (Chowdhury 1996). The farming systems approach studies the biological-social system as a whole to advance improved agricultural practices, an approach particularly well suited to anthropology with its holistic frame of reference. Furthermore, farming systems research provides a challenging opportunity for sociologists and anthropologists to apply their knowledge in solving urgent contemporary agricultural problems at the farm level (BAA 1997).

Another role for indigenous knowledge researchers is to sensitise other team members to sociocultural considerations (see Alam, this volume). They can teach some social science considerations to the agronomists to familiarise them with the culture and life style of the people with whom they are working. This can be particularly valuable during the testing stage of farming systems research. The late arrival of both anthropology and sociology in Bangladesh makes the task of indigenous knowledge research all the more urgent. Social scientists inquiring into such key issues as household dynamics, participatory processes and class-gender issues must be equal partners with their biological science colleagues in agricultural and natural resource management research and development. Social and environmental appraisals have to be integrated with the agro-scientific in designing and implementing projects.

Cropping practices and indigenous knowledge at Charan

I now provide an example of the issues discussed from a Department for International Development project (DFID, UK) in which I have been involved as a rice agronomist with help from an ethnographer. The project site is situated at Charan *beel* in Tangail District. People living around Charan *beel* have experienced large changes in their agricultural practices in recent decades, with the arrival of modern scientific interventions. In the last thirty years in particular, significant changes have occurred around the *beel*, with the introduction of high yielding varieties of crops, which have had a dramatic impact on people's practices, and on their social and natural environments. Previously, they relied on their indigenously evolved cropping regimes. There was no use of inorganic fertilisers. Farmers maintained the fertility of the land by following a range of indigenous methods. The *B. Aman* variety called *chamara* produces long stems that farmers used to leave in the fields during harvesting. They used to allow this '*narra*' straw to decompose on the ground or they burnt it, thereby returning organic matter to the soil. Similarly, people did not remove the crop residues from pulses but left them to rot and promote soil fertility. Furthermore, the deepwater, tall *chamara* rice plant, which grows according to floodwater depth, provides good shelter for spawning fish. Fish from the *beel* obtained their food from the *chamara* field. These are natural age-old practices. Although the crops did not give high yields, they had a very acceptable taste. Today the area around Charan *beel* is under intensive paddy cultivation. Farmers transplant different high yielding *boro* varieties in the month of *Poush* (December-January) and harvest in the month of *Baishakh* (April-May) or *Jaistaya* (May-June). They depend on local cultivars of *T. Aman* called *patjak* and the faster growing *B. Aman* called *chamara* for the second rice crop. Those farmers growing *patjak* cannot squeeze in a third cash crop, which would usually be mustard. Those growing *chamara* sow a mustard cash crop in the month of *Kartic* (October-November), after the *chamara* harvest, and harvest it in the months of *Poush* or *Magh* (January-February). This demands a large amount of fertiliser, which often makes it inaccessible to very poor farmers. After the introduction of high yielding rice varieties farmers started using fertiliser, for which demand greatly increased. During *boro* transplantation farmers may decide not to apply any fertiliser, relying on the residual effect of fertilisers used during mustard cultivation. Water too is expensive during the dry season. There are several shallow tube wells providing irrigation for high yielding varieties. Now crop production has become dependent on fertilisers and yield significantly decreases without fertiliser application. *Aus* cultivation is now totally absent from the area, and some people are growing *chamara* with greatly reduced yields.

Also, changes in flood character and inundation pattern caused by various flood management infrastructures have harmed agricultural production. Floodwater no longer comes gradually, but rises rapidly, hindering the growth of *chamara* paddy. The sudden rise in water drowns the crop, and this local cultivar is becoming less common. The farmers' cropping calendar has changed in response to these changes in inundation patterns and the amount of water coming into the *beel*. Presently the lean period is in the month of *Chaitra* (March-April) known as "*uinnaya mash*" when families survive on savings from the high yielding varieties of *boro*. This practice is captured in the folk rhyme "*Sara bachare khaio, Ashin-Kartice thuio*" (eat all year but save for the months of *Ashin* and *Kartic*, September-November). These were previously the lean months when people used to cultivate *chamara, Aus,* etc. Nowadays, with the introduction of high yielding varieties of *boro*, people say "*Sara bachare khaio, Chaitra, Baishakhe thuio*" (eat all year but save for the months of *Chaitra* and *Baishakh*, March-May), because this is the new *boro* cultivation period when they need to spend a lot of money on inputs.

High yielding paddies helped people to avoid potential food shortages like those experienced in the recent past. But they have created other problems. People say that the high yielding varieties of rice are tasteless. The excessive use of fertiliser is damaging soil fertility. Farmers maintain that while fertilisers keep the topsoil fertile they are damaging the subsoil, which is becoming harder like burnt bricks. The use of inorganic fertiliser and pesticides in paddy fields is also depleting fish resources in the *beel*. People believe that water contaminated by fertilisers and pesticides is flowing from higher land into the *beel*, destroying eggs and fry of various fish, particularly the *kai* fish, which lay eggs in paddy fields. People also blame recent fish diseases on the contaminated water. Some say that today there is an increase in digestive problems because of the heavy use of fertilisers and pesticide used to grow high yielding paddies. The increased extraction of water for irrigation of the *boro* crop has also proved detrimental for fish resources. Some farmers are taking water directly from the *beel* for irrigation, threatening to dry up the *beel* completely. The result is loss of fish habitat, reducing numbers of fish in the *beel*. Those remaining are easily caught, further reducing numbers. The continuous pumping of water is also depleting underground reserves.

Conclusion

All of these unfriendly environmental impacts have resulted as a consequence of farmers moving away from indigenous agricultural knowledge and practices in order to meet purported increased demands for food. Previously, traditional practices worked in harmony with the natural environment; they were self sufficient without any foreign high production technologies. Rural people are paying a high price with the arrival of high input-output technologies in the form of natural degradation, social disturbances, increasing inequalities and unstable production systems. People face massive new environmental problems in their environment as they change from their tried and tested agricultural practices. The imposed new technologies and practices have, some argue, helped overcome food shortages to an extent but the poor farmers are paying dearly. If current trends continue we may all pay dearly, with a chronically destabilised agricultural system. It is time for us to get back to basics, to review our cultural heritage and how indigenous knowledge might help us. We have declining fish populations, falling soil fertility, increasing social conflicts, loss of biodiversity and so on. The people at Charan believe that this is happening because they have been separated from their age-old indigenous knowledge. Anthropology and sociology may be relatively recent to Bangladesh but their insights are urgently needed. Indigenous knowledge researchers working with households and facilitating participatory processes must be equal partners with natural resource scientist colleagues in agricultural and environmental management and development. Indigenous knowledge informed social and environmental appraisal has to be integrated into agro-technology in agricultural research and development programmes in an attempt to reverse the disturbing trends witnessed in the Bangladeshi countryside.

19 Cultivating Indigenous Knowledge on Bangladeshi Soil: An Essay in Definition

Paul Sillitoe

WHEN IS KNOWLEDGE INDIGENOUS? There appears to be some confusion in development contexts, where indigenous knowledge has been increasingly sought after of late, as I have intimated in the introduction to this book and as some of the foregoing chapters have shown. While lexicography is widely perceived as a dry pursuit, it is nonetheless necessary to agree about the meaning of the words that we use in our arguments, or else we are in danger of talking past one another and engaging in pointless debates, taking the words we use to mean different things. There is some tendency towards this in current development discourse over the employment of the term indigenous knowledge and the usefulness of attempts to incorporate this knowledge into development research and interventions. This is seen in the range of other terms to be found in the literature for indigenous knowledge, vying for prominence and claiming to be more representative of whatever it is this field is taken to encompass. They include local knowledge, popular knowledge, rural people's knowledge, indigenous technical knowledge, traditional environmental knowledge, folk agricultural knowledge. It would take another paper to unravel the various meanings with which writers invest these terms, sometimes using different ones to cover the same ideas, others the same one to label different ideas. It is difficult to draw lines between them, even the word indigenous itself is fraught with obscurity. I shall argue for the continued use of the term indigenous knowledge on pragmatic grounds, as the term of widest currency in contemporary development discourse (De Walt 1994). Some writers contrast it with scientific knowledge, even implying that it applies only to non-Western knowledge, prompting others to query the status of 'non-scientific' Western beliefs and the implications of contemporary accelerating globalising trends, particularly with the explosion in communications. These differences have a contentious political edge, with connotations of superiority and inferiority. The absence of any consensus over terms intimates the flux that characterises this fast moving and exciting field in development practice.

The term indigenous knowledge has emerged, within the broad context of recent participatory approaches to development (Farrington and Martin 1988; Sillitoe 1998c), to label a new field of specialism in development circles. It is an emerging area of expertise, in the process of establishing a place for itself within development practice where it has recently become popular to point out that indigenous peoples have their own effective 'science' and resource use practices, and that to assist them outsiders need to understand something about their knowledge and management systems (Brokensha, Warren and Werner 1980; Warren 1991). There is a growing acknowledgement that effective development assistance benefits from some understanding of this knowledge and related practices (Sillitoe 1998*a*; Warren and Cashman 1988). Indigenous knowledge may refer to any understanding held collectively by a population, informing interpretation of the world, currently in development particularly that pertaining to natural resource management. It is conditioned by sociocultural tradition, being culturally relative understanding inculcated into individuals from birth, informing how they interface with their environments. The difference with anthropology is one of emphasis. Indigenous knowledge research relates to development issues and problems, its objective is to introduce a locally informed perspective into development, to promote an appreciation of indigenous know-how and power structures.

The definition of indigenous knowledge is no straightforward endeavour in rapidly changing contemporary societies subject to the forces of globalisation. If we put the knowledge of Bangladeshi small farmers into historical and developmental context, what is indigenous and what is foreign? In the context of a Department for International Development (DFID) research programme in Bangladesh[1], in which I have been involved, we conceived of the relation between scientists and farmers as comprising a continuum. This takes us to the heart of the debate over the definition of indigenous knowledge, and its correctness. At one end we have poor farmers who have no formal education, whom we may take to be as close as we might hypothetically come to 'unalloyed' indigenous knowledge, derived from their own cultural tradition. At the other end of the continuum we come to Western scientists, who are trying to incorporate some empathy with local perceptions and practices into their work, wrestling with the problems of interdisciplinary research (Dixon *et al.* 1998). In between we have various intergradations of local insider and global outsider knowledge depending on community of origin and formal education. Each has some varying impact on the other, in which process indigenous knowledge research tries to mediate. But what is indigenous knowledge and what is not?

A review of Bangladeshi farmers' knowledge of their land and soil fertility in historical perspective is used here as an ethnographic vehicle to illustrate what we might understand to comprise indigenous knowledge, and the implications of the continuum concept (see Hussain 1992 for technical details on soils). At a project workshop in Dhaka (Barr *et al.* 1996*b*), our collaborators identified declining soil fertility and shortage of biomass (with falling organic matter content) as a serious constraint to which farmers attribute declining productivity. Some of the chapters in this book likewise express concerns about sustainability. Bengali farmers talk about the *jore* (or *shokti* or *bol*) 'strength' of soil when discussing its fertility. They refer to strong soils giving good crop yields (*jore beshi*, enough strength, as opposed to *jore kam*, less strength). This strength can be felt in the soil, *balu* or *bele* sandy soil crumbling when dry whereas *etel* or *metel* clayey soil forms hard clods. Some soils that are *jore* 'strong' may also be relatively infertile for other reasons than 'weakness'. These are complex relative concepts influenced by other pedological factors. Farmers also refer, for example, to the *ras* (or *pum*) of the soil as contributing to fertility. It is what is left behind in the soil after flood water has receded. It also comes with the rain, and comes up in the groundwater. It is associated with moisture. For some farmers *ras* appears to refer to soil moisture content alone. According to others it is something more, imparted by the soil to water, that is taken up by plants. The soil water has *ras*, it is something with the water (*pani*), which is necessary for plant growth. There are no *ras* particles. If soil dries out the *ras* goes too, it becomes 'lifeless' and will yield poorly. Soils vary in their capacity to hold the *ras*. A *jore* 'strong' soil will hold more *ras* for longer and so be more fertile than a *jore nai* 'weak' soil which will retain *ras* for less time. If there is *ras* then the soil will express its *jore*.

A common misapprehension is that the term indigenous knowledge refers to some notion of traditional untrammelled 'other' knowledge, the property of homogenous, culturally independent communities that maintain intact some local tradition pertaining to soil fertility or whatever, unaffected by foreign ideas. This is what the Romantics called the *Volk* view, that of the original autochthonous people. And in Bangladesh currently there is the notion that indigenous knowledge research will rescue and document this knowledge as it is perceived to be rapidly lost under the onslaught of modernisation. There is the danger of paternalism, of promoting cultural 'preservation'. Anthropologists have recently criticised heavily the idea of a timeless 'other', which the synchronic ethnographic writing of this century has sometimes seemed to imply, notably when dominated by structural-functional equilibrium thinking with its roots in nineteenth century social theory. It is incorrect. The idea of an 'original' and 'unalloyed' indigenous perspective that we need to catch is untenable, even among the world's recently contacted tribes, for example of 'stone age' New Guinea (Sillitoe 1996). It is untenable on several grounds, environmental, cultural and historical.

Environmental change

On environmental grounds it is unacceptable because indigenous knowledge shifts with the changes that occur in any region's natural conditions over time. And no ecological system is static. Any indigenous knowledge has of necessity to accommodate to changes as they occur. On the floodplains of Bangladesh these changes can be dramatic, occurring in short periods of time, as rivers for example change course across the delta, leaving new land exposed in one place while inundating somewhere else (Huq and Rahman 1994). All floodplain dwellers are acutely aware of them. They are cognisant of environmental history recorded in the landscape. Farmers for example, know that there are variations (*parthakkaya*) in soil across any area of land, and that the soil environment is dynamic and subject to constant change.

While looking at a survey pit dug by soil surveyors adjacent to Charan *Beel* in Tangail District those present made some interesting comments which indicate that they not only have a good idea of the geographical history of their area but also how this has informed their knowledge of its resources, notably how differing sedimentation regimes have resulted in different soils with varying cultivation potentials. The profile pit, 120 cm deep, comprised four locally named horizons: *balu, ret, kumairamaati* and *etel* which can be read, as people explained, as a record of the region's environmental history. Some two to three hundred years ago there were only large braided river channels in the area, and no people farmed there — some people say that it was on the course of the old Brahmaputra river — oral history says that there were two ports at nearby Kalihati and Moricha (on the edge of the Madhupur tract) with boats plying between them. At this time *balu* sands were deposited on *char* lands (alluvial islands of coarse material deposited in braided channels — Brammer 1996). People refer to the *balu* sand as *matir janma* (lit. soil birth), that is the first soil deposited in the area, brought by the river long ago. The river gradually changed its course, people being acutely aware that their riverine landscape is particularly dynamic, watercourses changing over time. People gradually started to settle in the region, as the river changed course, and to use the emergent land — the name Charan means 'grazing land', indicating the early use of the area for agisting animals, together with fishing which is assumed to have been practised continuously, largely by Hindus, many Muslims not arriving until later. The rule is that as *char* land appears in a river course it belongs to those who have lost land in erosion nearby — but there is much disputation about this, over who has rights to occupy such land (e.g. contemporarily on the Jamuna).

Since that time other horizons, called *vaz* locally, have been deposited, as annual flood waters have brought sediment in. At first the annually flooding river remained nearby and the land continued to receive heavy depositions of silt, called *ret* locally. As the river course moved further away to the west, so the *ret* deposition declined, and the deposition of clay increased with the annual inundation. Farmers readily explain how flood waters carry the fine particles in suspension, leaving the coarser *balu* sand particles behind. The heavy *kumairamaati* clay gradually washed into lower areas adjacent to the *beel* waterbody, such as that where the profile pit was situated, from the marginally higher surrounding land. This clay was said to have extended up to the surface before cultivation of the area. Today the surface horizon has changed with farming into a lighter *etel* clay topsoil (through the incorporation of rotting plant material, breaking up in cultivation, use of fertilisers etc.). The changes in soil resources were continuous, and go on contemporarily with annual monsoon flooding moving and depositing soil. The floods constantly change the edaphic conditions on farmers' plots, importantly in their eyes contributing to continued fertility by replenishing the soil. They are alive to these changes and can relate how the topsoil they cultivate has been deposited over the soil below during floods.

The highly dynamic nature of land resources is not only due to natural processes but also human behaviour. The activities of people change the pattern and occurrence of soils, giving rise to Anthrosols. The *kumairamaati* clay for example, is taken by potters, who sometimes excavate considerable areas to collect it. If in suitable locations, landowners may continue with the excavations to produce *kua* refuges for fish as flood waters recede or ponds for aquaculture, stocking the holes with fish. They excavate these waterbodies regularly elsewhere too about the floodplain. Farmers also regularly engage in the levelling of paddies, sometimes moving considerable volumes of soil about the landscape. Likewise the building up of ridges over the generations, called locally *vita,* for the location of *bari* homesteads above the level of floods, has resulted in the movement of very large amounts of soil. These changes in soil distribution necessitate appropriate management responses based on sound knowledge of natural processes. They may change the cultivation potential of land, even when subsequent floods ameliorate the damage with the deposition of new silt.

This local interference with land resources might be expected to be guided by indigenous understanding of its implications, but not so with outside interference, which has been extensive during the latter half of the twentieth century. The widespread flood protection defences constructed under the Flood Action Plan have so upset the seasonal hydrological cycle of the Bangladesh floodplain, notably changing flooding patterns and fish migrations, that a considerable amount of indigenous knowledge demands revision or has become redundant. People are struggling to come to terms with the changed environment. The interference to the monsoon flooding regime has soil fertility implications where farmers traditionally rely on the annual deposition of *ret* or *pulimaati* silt by floodwater as part of their farmland fertility management. While it is invariably only a thin layer (rarely more than four fingers deep), it is important, farmers say, to the continued fertility of cultivated soil. It varies in colour from ash (*chai*) to reddish, and a thicker layer may be a gleyed blue colour underneath the surface (potters use the reddish silt as slip to colour pots red). It is *vasavasa* non-adhesive (not sticky), and displays *fupa* swelling (expands when wet). Farmers comment that it is deposited in far less quantities today with the Flood Action Plan embankments and sluice defences and that this will prove detrimental to the maintenance of soil fertility. Their previous indigenous practices are being subverted and they are having to turn to other means to ensure good crop yields, notably the use of inorganic fertilisers, but these not only have other environmental costs but also economic ones as many small farmers have to enter into uncertain financial arrangements to afford them. It is not merely a technical issue of coming up with revised farming and fishing practices, it has a sociopolitical dimension to it too. These changes affect all those who secure their livelihood from the floodplain. When agencies alter the nature of the communal fishing resource for example, making it more controllable with flood protection devices, management of it becomes a viable commercial proposition, and powerful local interest groups move in to assume control and manage the resource at the expense of poor local fishermen whom they try to marginalise and exclude.

Cultural change

The objections on cultural grounds to the idea that indigenous knowledge relates to some sort of timeless tradition go considerably beyond human practices changing and interfering with the natural environment, necessitating constant revision of related knowledge. There is the problem initially of defining the sociocultural group which is assumed collectively to possess the knowledge. Distinguishing one society or culture from another is contentious. By what criteria should we differentiate between them: according to different languages or histories, different nations or governments, different religions or other cultural traits? In South Asia, should we treat Bangladesh as separate from West Bengal, where people speak the same language, and if not, in what regards is Bengal separate from India, and India from Bangladesh? In turn does Pakistan differ from these two countries, Urdu speaking West Pakistan recently dominating Bengali speaking East Pakistan. When we come down to a local level the problems remain the same. Our Department for International Development funded project on the Bangladesh floodplains has revealed considerable differences between two communities, one in Tangail and the other Rajshahi District, in their knowledge and management of natural resources, so should we distinguish between their indigenous knowledge traditions and those elsewhere in Sylhet, Khulna and so on? The problem is drawing the lines. There is even evidence that knowledge varies between communities on opposite sides of the same *beel* lake.

When we venture to attempt a definition of the knowledge bearing group on geographical, linguistic or cultural grounds, it is dubious to suggest such societies ever existed in isolation from others. All human societies everywhere have on occasion embraced outside knowledge. There is nothing new in this: diffusion of traits between cultures has been occurring since our ancient African ancestors reared up on their back legs. It has occurred and continues extensively in Bangladesh. It underlines the speciousness of attempts to find and document untrammelled indigenous knowledge. When did it exist: before the British colonial invasion, before the Moghul invasion? Diffusion and change have occurred throughout the historical period. We are unsure what pertained before, but the archaeological record suggests much the same picture.

This change is evident today when we pass along the indigenous-to-scientific-knowledge-continuum. From farmer-fishers whose entire experience is of the nearby floodplain, to local people who have received some formal schooling, and have some passing acquaintance with science, which they will blend with their locally derived knowledge and cultural heritage. Their education conditions the status of their community's indigenous knowledge, and it concerns not only their own knowledge but also that of their uneducated relatives, to whom they will in some measure impart their foreign derived understanding. Furthermore they will all be subject to extension advice, either first or second hand, received from government agencies, non-governmental organisations and so on.

It is not always easy, nor necessarily fruitful to try and distinguish the source of knowledge; either in cultural and historical terms, as inherited from previous genera-tions; or in terms of evolution and invention, as generated internally from perceived changes in social and natural environments; or in terms of diffusion and education, including extension activities, as imported from elsewhere outside the culture. A review of farmers' knowledge and practices regarding the manipulation of organic matter in the management of soil fertility illustrates both the continually changing complexion of indigenous knowledge and how contemporary understanding is a blend of elements and not discrete parcels of knowledge which we can label as indigenous, extension, scientific or whatever. It is evident that farmers have long been aware of the importance of organic matter to soil fertility. A soil that is expressing the benefit of organic matter content has *quyat*, which is not visible but contributes significantly farmers say to the *jore* 'strength' or fertility of the soil. It increases in soil that is left under fallow. They attribute it to completely rotted and incorporated plant material. It makes *bele* sandy soil 'stronger' and more coherent, sticky and slippery (noticeable when farmers 'ladder' the soil in rice cultivation), but reduces the stickiness and cloddiness of *etel* clayey soil.

While they have a number of long-standing practices to increase the organic matter content of soils, these have been coming under pressure recently with population growth and the increased demand for fuel. One such practice is the *gorto* pit in the *bari* houseyard for the collection of *paush* manure, the family throwing into it vegetable waste (banana and mango skins etc.), *gobor* cow-dung, the *leda* droppings of chickens and ducks, and other houseyard sweepings of leaves and so on. At intervals they carry the contents to their fields and tip it on and plough it in. But it has declined considerably today, poor people collecting and drying dung for fuel and farmers increasingly depending on inorganic fertilisers. Another practice on the decline is the *nara purano* burning of rice stems following harvest, which people say promoted soil fertility. It was also said to be good for pest management, particularly of fungal pests. It returned considerable amounts of burnt organic matter to the soil, particularly when farmers fired the long stems of *chamara* deepwater rice cultivars, the cultivation of which is now declining too. Changes in agricultural practices after harvest with the introduction of new cultivars and associated cultivation technologies, notably high yielding rice varieties, are reducing the return of organic matter. And what stems there are people may gather for fuel. The fuel crisis is depleting soil of organic matter.

There is also the use of green manure called *jaibosar*, a term which refers more broadly to rotting plant material. The evidence is that farmers have recently increased their use of this as they have become increasingly aware of the implications for soil fertility of declining organic matter contents, which they are witnessing with the relentless growth in population and growing fuel crisis removing plant material that would otherwise be left to rot into the soil. Farmers comment on the importance for soil fertility of *jalaja udvid* or water plants, especially water hyacinths, that are deposited on the land after monsoon flooding, which they subsequently plough in. This practice stops the soil becoming *matano* hard they say, keeping it friable and cultivable. Some practices are fortuitous developments, farmers adapting to changed circumstances, as in their use of the *kachuripana* water hyacinth. This exotic plant, imported into Bengal sometime during colonial times, is commonly cited as an ecological hazard, spreading rapidly and choking waterways. But farmers have incorporated it beneficially into their farming system, some collecting it and spreading it on their land and working it into the soil as green manure. It is another example of environmental change reorienting knowledge. Areas of standing water in which water plants like the hyacinth may grow are seen to assist the supply of rotting plant material beneficial to soil fertility. In some places people are growing *dhaincha* shrubs (*Sesbania* sp.) on plots for one to two months until two to three feet high, when they cut the plants down and incorporate them into the soil, transplanting paddy after ten days or so (this practice features mainly in the cultivation of *aman* paddy). It is probable that some of these practices have spread as the result of extension advice. It is common for extension workers to convey messages based on scientific advice reinforcing the importance of organic matter to soil fertility. The farmers' understanding of these issues is a blend of knowledge from various sources, which it is difficult to disentangle. It is syncretic knowledge.

Population and change

The environmental and cultural aspects of change meet under the issue of demography. Population growth has been formidable in Bangladesh, as several of the contributions to this volume point out, putting ever increased pressure on land resources and promoting changes in people's perceptions of resource management. At the beginning of the 1990s the population was 115 million (756 persons km^2), and with an annual growth rate of 2.4% it is expected to exceed 161 million by 2010 (Bangladesh Bureau of Statistics 1995; Sobhan 1991). This growth in numbers of mouths to feed has been matched in food production by the breeding of high yielding varieties (HYVs) of crops, notably rice, and associated technologies of shallow and deep tube well irrigation and increased use of fertilisers and pesticides. Many commentators attribute the prevention of famine and starvation to these technical innovations. They are another example of how outside technical interventions, like the flood defences, can impact heavily on indigenous knowledge and practice. The small farmers have had to adapt their know-how to manage in the new technical environment. It remains their farming system informed by their local knowledge.

The changes, in a short period of time, have been considerable. In some places farmers have gone from taking one crop a year, to which previous indigenous knowledge related, to three a year, to which today's indigenous knowledge relates. This has had a considerable impact on agricultural practices, even influencing the way in which people may distinguish between different land resources, according to the number of crops that they may take from them. On the lowest land they may only have enough time between inundations to cultivate one crop of either a local *boro* variety of rice or an introduced *irri* rice crop (after IRRI the International Rice Research Institute in the Philippines which has played a central role in the development of HYVs) both called a *faram* crop (from English 'farm'). This land is *ek fashali* (lit. one crop), and equates with the land adjacent to *beel* lake margins. On higher land which is under water for less time they may be able to take two crops: an *aus* and *rabi* (including *irri* or *boro* rice and vegetables like onions), called *dui fashala*. And on the highest land they may be able to cultivate three crops called *tin fashala* (lit. three crops): *aus* and two *rabi* crops *(chaitaly* and *boro*), or *aus* and *aman* mix (staggered harvest) and *boro*, or *irri* and *rabi*. The crop seasons overlap and demand careful calculations regarding cultivation timing, which has required a commensurate change in indigenous knowledge and farming practices. This varies between regions, illustrating the non-standard nature of indigenous knowledge within a single cultural tradition, as noted previously.[2]

The changes wrought in peasant agricultural practice have been dramatic, not only in technical terms but also in sociopolitical ones, widening inequalities, on which grounds some commentators have criticised the so-called HYV 'green revolution' (e.g. Griffin 1979). Although some governments in Bangladesh have attempted to legislate land reforms since independence, wide differences remain in land holdings between families, which the HYVs, although nominally scale-neutral, have tended to exacerbate by allowing some concentration of holdings in the hands of those who can afford the necessary inputs, largely irrigation water and fertilisers. The gap between rich and poor has if anything widened, and the families of many larger and wealthy landowners have effectively absented themselves from land management, frequently moving into cities and towns where they work in government service and business, leaving sharecroppers to cultivate their land. The link with the land is broken. The implications for any indigenous knowledge tradition are profound. The wealthy large landowners who no longer actively farm land may, as in the Charan district, lease it out to in-migrating sharecroppers from other poorer surrounding districts. The landowner indigenous knowledge is 'lost'. This is the knowledge of persons assumed to have inherited the longest standing connections to the land resources, heirs to appropriate management practices evolved over the generations with a vested interest in the sustainable use of resources, if not their improvement. The sharecroppers may come from communities elsewhere and have to tune their knowledge and practices to the new local environment. The newcomers have to learn and adapt the knowledge they bring with them from their regions. The tenuousness of their tenure further militates against them developing a deep association with place which is a significant aspect of indigenous knowledge, contributing to its depth and richness.

The more advantaged may progress through school to college and university, some to study agricultural subjects, environmental science, geography and so on. This takes us further along our continuum. We come to national collaborators on research and development projects such as our Department for International Development funded one, whom we might take to be mid-way in some senses along the continuum. They have an extensive formal scientific background, with higher degrees and some occupy senior university posts, but they also have a familiarity with the indigenous culture, as native speaking members of its metropolitan society. This gives a unique perspective, with its own potential insights and blind spots. Some of them come from farming families and are themselves landowners, a further conduit of scientific understanding into local communities. They inevitably pass on some of their learning to relatives and friends when they return home to rural areas, even if they do not themselves engage in cultivation. Their rural kith and kin are also subject, as pointed out, to the varying attentions of the government's extension services, grounded in the same science. The imported knowledge passes into the local pool, is blended with what is known to inform today's understanding and practice. There is no repository of traditional indigenous knowledge: it is always changing and continually influenced by outside ideas. While this kind of diffusion may have occurred for all time, the rate has accelerated dramatically in recent times, as the knowledge continuum and newly emergent global epistemology make clear.

History and contemporary change

The pace of change appears to have been increasing during this century with, as it draws to a close, the emergence of the notion of globalisation. This further undermines dramatically any attempts to find a static indigenous knowledge tradition anywhere. It is change of a different order to the previous diffusionary processes — the theory of diffusion, which dates from the beginning of the century, and which has long been out of favour, having re-emerged in globalisation discourse. The rate of diffusion has accelerated markedly with the burgeoning growth of global communications, such that few, if any places on the globe are now unaware of diesel tractors and inorganic fertilisers. Development itself is an agent of this diffusion, a contributor to the process of globalisation.

While it is questionable in history to fix upon some date as a benchmark, time passing in a continuous stream, the period from the Second World War until the present day has been characterised by this acceleration of change. During this time Bangladesh has emerged from colonial rule, and endured a bitter independence struggle to become a nation. Its citizens are now self-governing, one consequence being an increase in educational opportunities and self-determination, with all of the aforementioned implications for notions of indigenous knowledge. If we restrict ourselves to the last fifty years, we see that the peasant farmer has had to cope with considerable change which has reinformed his understanding of the world. During the disorienting and violent events of 1947 with partition from India and its aftermath, large numbers of Hindu farmers fled Bangladesh and Muslims replaced them on the land. This represented a profound dislocation of traditional ways, the newcomers having in some sense to adapt their knowledge and practices to the new local environment, even reinvent them to manage the new conditions. The fleeing of Hindu landowners meant that much accumulated indigenous knowledge left regions like Charan, and new Muslim 'landowners'/occupiers had to some extent to 'concoct' their own indigenous repertoire through experience.

The political implications of these events are still working themselves out in Bangladesh, governments having declared that the land of Hindus with interests and assets in West Bengal to be enemy property which may be annexed, and powerful Muslim interests bribing government officials to forge ownership details in their favour. Others have no legal title, however obtained, having taken over Hindu land without ever paying anyone for it. There is also the illegal occupation of *khas* government owned land. Some of this land, previously uncultivable, has become exposed around the edges of *beels* with the lowering of water levels due to a combination of natural and human processes, including sedimentation and excessive groundwater pumping for irrigation. Again some persons bribe Government settlement officers to alter the official records to show them owning such land. There are many disputes over access to agricultural land and tenure, and sometimes fights. Land is scarce with the high population densities, particularly good farm land. Disputes over land ownership also occur between relatives. Some men calculate where they may take possession of land and manipulate their relations accordingly, sometimes to the anger of other relatives, for example manoeuvre to inherit land from maternal grandparents or in-laws if they have no male kin to take it over. The politics of dowry payments may also feature an element of compensation to daughters forgoing land rights. The evidence suggests that connivance and disputes over land ownership have gone on for generations. The unfair acquisition of land by the wealthy and powerful is even celebrated in the poetry of Tagore (1985:55-56).

> *I had forfeited all my land except for one half-acre.*
> *The landlord said, 'Upon, I'll buy it, you must hand it over.'*
> *I said, 'You're rich, you've endless land, can't you see*
> *That all I've got is a patch on which to die?'*
> *'Old man,' he sneered, 'you know I've made a garden;*
> *If I have your half-acre its length and breadth will be even.*
> *You'll have to sell.' Then I said with my hands on my heart*
> *And tears in my eyes, 'Don't take my only plot!*
> *It's more than gold — for seven generations my family*
> *Has owned it: must I sell my own mother through poverty?'*
> *He was silent for a while as his eyes grew red with fury.*
> *'All right, we'll see,' he said, smiling cruelly.*
>
> *Six weeks later I had left and was out on the road;*
> *Everything was sold, debt claimed through a fraudulent deed.*
> *For those want most, alas, who already have plenty:*
> *The rich zamindar steals the beggar-man's property.*
> *I decided God did not now intend me for worldliness:*
> *In exchange for my land he had given me the universe.*
> *I became disciple to a sadhu — I roamed the world.*

Looking back further in history we see that these recent events are not new. Invasions and population movements have long characterised the history of Bengal. They are recalled in place names. It is assumed, for example, that Hindus have always fished in the Charan *beel* region of Tangail District, and that they long ago established the village of Agcharan, which means 'ahead (i.e. first) Charan', whereas neighbouring Pachcharan, which means 'behind Charan', was settled later by Muslims who subsequently arrived. Sometimes the extent of the accompanying changes are so large and rapid that they represent the virtual overthrow of aspects of extant indigenous knowledge, demanding its dramatic modification. This presents a particular development challenge. It is evident in Bangladesh, where our collaborating project partners consistently cite 'lack of knowledge' as a problem. They point to conflicts over proper resource use and besieged local understanding assailed by many unfamiliar technological interventions (input heavy HYV crops, cultured fish species, centrally imposed FCD/I schemes etc.).

Many farmers, dislocated several times from the land and seeing their floodplain management heritage heavily buffeted by forces beyond their control, are struggling to cope. This is evident in their use of, and growing dependence on inorganic fertilisers, and also pesticides. Their generic name for inorganic fertilisers is *shar* meaning literally 'main-part' (e.g. summary of important points in a book is *sharangsha*), reflecting their importance in maintaining crop yields. They increasingly depend on these under pressure not only to sustain yields but also to grow more food to keep pace with their growing population. The arrival of HYV rice cultivars and associated technology, and related market impacts are further factors. These changes in agricultural practice have been rapid and the long term implications unclear. Charan farmers, for example, are currently using urea (called *shada guti* [lit. white grains]) which is 46% N, potash (called *lal shar* [lit. red fertiliser]) which is muriate of potash K_2O, and a little triple super phosphate (called *maita guti* [lit. soil-coloured grains]) which is 46% P. They are tending to apply uniform amounts to all land. There is little or no field extension advice, farmers are learning from one anothers' experiences.[3] They copy one another. They have become increasingly dependent on fertilisers to keep up yields, particularly the high yields of IRRI varieties.

Farmers say that the use of fertilisers is undermining the natural fertility of the soil, and that crops will not now yield well without fertiliser applications. Over use of fertilisers is making the soil dependent on them they say, the soil is 'habituated', even 'addicted' to fertilisers. The soil is also becoming *jao* very hard, farmers comparing it to ovenburnt *jhama* bricks. On the surface the soil condition looks all right, but the fertilisers are changing it below in the subsoil, making it hard. The experience of farmers is that they are having to increase the amounts of fertilisers that they are applying to the land as time goes by, worsening the problem and their dependency, although over use of fertiliser can 'burn' crops. The change in the flooding regime with the Flood Action Plan defences also prevents farmers from reverting back to their previous cultivation regime (when they cultivated more *chamara* [broadcast *aman*] deepwater rice and pulses). They are locked into a vicious circle, reinforced by changed market conditions and prices with HYV rice, and an expanding population dependent on rice as a staple food. They are rapidly revising their indigenous knowledge in the light of these experiences, as they search for more sustainable solutions to their production problems. It is here that local knowledge informed agricultural research may have an important contribution to make, to help rectify the downside of previous interventions.

Sociocultural context

Another point regarding the definition of indigenous knowledge is that it does not refer to technical issues alone, although in natural resources projects like ours in Bangladesh there is considerable interest in technical matters. Local knowledge research comprises more than technical enquiries into other's pest control measures or fertility management strategies, to improve or maybe learn from these (perhaps finding some unheard of biological agent or whatever). It is not a quest for technical fixes alone, although these maybe important. It is necessary that resource management strategies are set in sociocultural context, otherwise there is the danger of misunderstanding and distortion. The decisions that people make and the practices that they follow are not driven by available natural resources alone but have a social and political component. Even where aspects of people's technical knowledge appear to be overwhelmed by rapid change, we still need to set their problems within sociocultural context. An appreciation of local, socially embedded strategies remains central to any meaningful understanding of peoples' practices. They are subject to continual negotiation.

People do not reach decisions about land use on technical grounds alone, that is pertaining only to the physical condition of the natural resources available to them. They manoeuvre within a sociopolitical environment too. This is evident in sharecropping arrangements. While landowners and sharecroppers recognise customary responsibilities to one another for inputs, crop sharing, labour, deciding what crops to cultivate and so on, there is an element of negotiation too. If they are related this is likely to affect the outcome, as is any previous interaction between them and attendant obligations. The local politics can become complex. When deciding what crops to grow for example, farmers are frequently obliged to comply with each other and fit in with surrounding plots to manage irrigation demands, crop protection needs (e.g. from browsing goats or sheep), and power brokerage is evident. Some farmers may be obliged to go along with cultivation strategies that are not in their best interests, like putting a sandy droughty soil under rice, knowing that the large water demands will be difficult to meet. If someone has a tubewell near to a plot, the landowner may agree to him sharecropping it because this will reduce water costs. The waterlord is likely to use any influence that his control of this capital equipment gives him to maximum effect. There are physical issues too; small plots are less economic to cultivate and so may be more readily given to sharecroppers, and so on.

The supply of inputs, and how farmers afford these, has a significant sociopolitical aspect too, revealed by an historical review of how pest and disease management has changed over time. Farmers say that one of the reasons they cultivate less *chamara* and *aus* varieties of rice today is because of chronic pest and disease attack. Traditional practices to control and eradicate these include sprinkling wood ash on fields. People also talk of *chokh laga* the 'evil eye' causing disease to some crops (e.g. lodging due to stem rot). They paint earthern pots black and decorate them with white spots, called *thula paila* (literally, black pot), and hang them up in fields to protect the crop. They hang old brooms from poles to the same effect. But they are increasingly coming to rely on biocides, *bish* (literally, poison) or *gash*, such as the trade organo-phosphates Basodin and Faradin and malathion insecticides, which they spray onto crops when they can afford them. They recognise that these chemicals are more effective than traditional measures at controlling diseases and pests but their expanding use takes farming decisions increasingly out of their hands. They regularly experience problems with the supply of these and other inputs. For example in 1995 there was a shortage of fertilisers. Wealthy farmers could afford them but they were unobtainable to poorer ones who lost their crops. There was violence at this time and the shortage contributed to the defeat of the government in subsequent elections. The poorer farmers also regularly have trouble in raising the cash they need to purchase the inputs that they need and frequently have to resort to *kot* leasing of their land, using it as an asset to secure a loan from *mahajan* moneylenders. If anything happens to their crop and they fail to repay the loan they lose their land. The gambling that small farmers have been obliged to do to remain solvent and afford needed inputs to produce economically viable yields has been blamed for the rise in the numbers of landless families and the consolidation of wealth in rich families which have taken over their land. The HYV technological fix has had unforeseen social consequences (Griffin 1979; Lipton and Longhurst 1989), underlining the sociocultural implications of any technical intervention and the embeddedness of indigenous knowledge.

Indigenous and scientific knowledge

The political dimension extends to all stakeholders in the development field, including researchers, relations of power and domination extending from top to bottom. Development, a contested domain, has many actors trying to promote different interests and agendas (Grillo and Stirrat 1997). Some argue against distinguishing indigenous knowledge because it promotes unequal relations, privileges the scientific perspective, diminishing the views of the poor (Nader 1996). The implication is that this paper's continuum of knowledge should be compressed to a single point. But the existence of differences, however defined, creates the potential for inequality. The upshot of differentiating between different knowledge traditions, whether different folk ones or indigenous and scientific, is not that one is necessarily privileged above another. Any privileging that occurs is not inevitable. It is arguably dubious to privilege scientific discourse as its costs become increasingly evident, both environmental (with pollution, non-sustainability etc.), and social (with redundancy, alienation etc.). The parallels some see with earlier colonial indirect rule, in today's attempts to relate local knowledge to development initiatives, are misplaced, as are accusations of encouraging cultural chauvinism, which flow from the equation of indigenous with 'native', the colonised and subordinated. If anything, the use of the term indigenous in contemporary development discourse is anticolonial in intent, relating as it does to participation and empowerment.

It has been argued that the conflation of others' knowledge traditions into an indigenous category distinct from a universal scientific one is insupportable because it overlooks differences within each tradition and similarities between various indigenous and scientific perspectives. It fails on three grounds: substantive because of similarities in the essentials and content of these different knowledge systems; epistemological because of certain similarities in the methods used to investigate reality; and contextual because science is no less culturally located than other knowledge traditions (Agrawal 1995; *Indigenous Knowledge and Development Monitor* 1995, 1996). Firstly, to talk about indigenous knowledge implies no belittling of the intellectual achievements of humans from different cultures, and many would agree that there are substantial similarities and overlaps in the substantive contents of various knowledge traditions (Lévi-Strauss 1966; Atran 1990). Secondly, it is undeniably questionable to attempt to distinguish scientific from any other knowledge on formal grounds, that it is more objective for example, or exclusively tests deductive models using experimentation (local farmers are probably some of the world's most avid experimenters — Richards 1989; Haverkort *et al.* 1991; Rhoades 1987). Thirdly, scientific knowledge is indisputably anchored culturally in western society where it largely originated (Pickering 1992), although with contemporary communications and associated globalisation, hybridisation is occurring and blurring distinctions between scientific and other knowledge on sociocultural grounds.

Regardless of globalising trends, different cultures have differingly formulated and expressed understandings of the world. We have no single point but many continua. Currently, in different regions we find people with unique cultural traditions and histories, which continue to condition in significant regards their views of their environment, life and so on. They concern different issues and priorities, reflect different experiences and interests, and will be codified in different idioms and styles, which we come to understand to varying, currently postmodern debated extents. They are informed by cultural repertoires that have evolved over generations, albeit not in isolation, being influenced by others, having some points of similarity and overlap, yet maintaining a distinctiveness; the contrast between different traditions correlating closely until recently with geographical distance. This leaves the definition of society and culture begging, but is sufficient to locate the meaning of indigenous knowledge. While not replicating one another, individuals share a sufficient indetermined amount in common to comprise a distinct cultural order with common historical tradition, values, dialect and so on. We expect some variation between persons, sometimes in a patterned manner, along gender, age, class and other lines. Indigenous knowledge is not uniform. Individual farmers for example, have to contend with different locations and soils, and are likely to have parcels of land in several different locations on differing soils and so have a range of different experiences informing their decisions.

It is undeniable that scientific knowledge has underpinned massive technological change, allowing human beings to interfere with, and extend considerable control over nature, and that it is the dissemination of this technology for the betterment of humankind that underpins the notion of development (even where it is a cynical front to further political control). It is the wish of the majority of the populations of lesser developed countries to share in this technological advance, not just to increase their standard of living, but sometimes, as in Bangladesh, to stave off starvation, sickness and death, particularly with the relentless expansion of population. The bottom-line with development is that it assumes that the technologically (not morally or culturally) superior West has something to offer the poverty-stricken Rest as defined from "our" materialistic perspective, and that most human-beings wish at least to have enough to eat and be healthy, if not the latest in high-tech gizmos. But these "others" understandably want any developments on their own terms. One of the objectives of Indigenous Knowledge research is to try and facilitate this.

It follows from this that the "we" and "them" dichotomy is inescapable in some measure and to argue in effect that we should not distinguish between different cultural traditions is unrealistic. The distinction between indigenous and scientific, local and global knowledge is defensible, differences within, and similarities between knowledge traditions notwithstanding. Knowledge systems are not the same whatever the culture, although the current trend towards globally interconnected cultures and histories is eroding distinctions, but the struggle for ideological prominence, values and beliefs, looks set to be never-ending. But the corollary of difference is not that one, invariably scientific "us", is superior to local "them". The idea of a continuum extending from poor local resource managers to research scientists should help us to overcome the "we" and "them" divide by uniting us all. We are not talking about two unconnected poles, rather a spectrum of relations. Advocates of indigenous knowledge in development argue that we should aim to play off the different perspectives, the strengths and weaknesses, advantages and disadvantages of different knowledge traditions to improve our overall understanding of issues and problems by generating synergy (Blaikie *et al.* 1997). But conflict is inherent in the process too because we are not just talking about furthering understanding, of advancing more rounded views, but of facilitating interaction between actors with different agendas and employing knowledge to effect some action, and the values that underpin these are sometimes not readily reconcilable. Perhaps the aim should be equitable negotiation, which is a central tenet of local knowledge in participatory development. The negotiations become far more complex but the development initiatives are more likely to be appropriate for more people and hence more sustainable.

Conclusion

It may be distorting, as several commentators rightly point out, to counterpoise global scientific knowledge with local indigenous knowledge when in many communities today persons hold both simultaneously. This chapter underlines the speciousness of attempts to find 'real' indigenous knowledge, asking when and where it came from, as if it existed in some untrammelled form somewhere. But the term "indigenous knowledge" is now widely in vogue and firmly established in current development discourse (De Walt 1994). The recommendation is that we should learn to live with it and agree in what senses we understand it to refer to local understanding and practices, and rejoice that at last ordinary grass-roots folk are getting a voice, indigenous knowledge being part of the participation movement, with its associated empowerment objectives. Those concerned to see local people's knowledge incorporated into the development process should be busy building on this bridgehead, and not spend time debating the term used for it. We have indigenous knowledge. It is common for new English terms to be ambiguous, take 'information technology' or 'mass media'. To suggest changing it could be counterproductive. I have arrived at this conclusion after toying with various alternatives. Two of the more interesting candidates were, firstly the neologism glocal (Robertson 1996), an inventive combination of global and local, giving glocal knowledge (GLK) or glocal knowledge in development (GLOKID); and secondly insider knowledge which recommends itself for having the same acronym IK as indigenous knowledge but presents us with the problem of defining insiders.

Indigenous knowledge is the property of ambiguously defined cultural entities with their own historical heritage and language traditions, unique contemporary worldview and behaviours, a singular pastiche of old and new, ever in process of change and reformulation from within and without. It is the local view. The increasingly rapid change to which the content and context of indigenous knowledge is subject with global communications, underlines what has always been the case, that it is both a pluralistic and moving target, making it particularly challenging intellectually. Never static, it is ambiguous by nature. It recalls Heisenberg's uncertainty principle: a static electron-like focus on the current social order unavoidably restricts our understanding of its momentum, the changing social order. We attempt to understand both, putting our interpretation of contemporary society into historical perspective and trying to see change into the future. The indigenous knowledge we try to understand and accommodate today is not yesterday's local knowledge nor is it tomorrow's. Knowledge is always in flux.

It is erroneous to think in terms of locating an 'original' indigenous knowledge for any culture, which has been subject to various, largely externally generated changes. We should focus instead on the ever ongoing indigenisation of knowledge. At what point does knowledge go from outsider knowledge to insider knowledge? The curry, tandoori and balti are now for many, part of Western culture and not thought of as Bengali indigenous cuisine; likewise tobacco, potatoes and some drugs are not thought of as Amerindian cultural property, they are now indigenised European knowledge. What makes some foreign knowledge attractive and susceptible to incorporation as insider knowledge? What part does utility play, sociocultural salience and political domination? People make culturally informed decisions when they select and reject, and we need to research these indigenously rooted mechanisms to understand these aspects of change and development. The fact that indigenous knowledge is eclectic and hybrid, dynamic and continually evolving, presents us with methodological challenges, of how to document it without petrifying and so distorting it. What is the status of such research and how can we ensure that it is not just the appropriation of others' knowledge into foreign contexts where they lose control of it? If we all have a partial understanding of the world how can we promote a partnership, not a dominance relationship, that generates the synergy that may flow from a combination of perspectives, the scientific and folk, global and local? No one stakeholder can guide the process having only some relevant knowledge, and one set of priorities. It is to these challenges that we have to address ourselves.

Notes

1 In its investigation of the meaning of the term indigenous knowledge, this paper draws on the experiences of this group of natural and social scientists working collaboratively on the floodplains of Bangladesh, attempting to incorporate local understanding and practices into research projects intended to further understanding of production systems and identify constraints to productivity. I thank all my colleagues on these projects for stimulating discussions that have helped to clarify my ideas, and particularly Julian Barr and Peter Dixon. There are two closely related projects funded by the Department for International Development of the UK Government in its Natural Resources Systems Programme of research, one under the Socio-Economic Methodologies component (Project R6744) and the other under the Land-Water Interface component (Project R6756). The views expressed here are those of the author and not necessarily those of DFID.

2 In Tangail: *aus* (early rice variety) = April-August, *aman* (late rice variety) = April-October, *rabi* = October-January, *boro* = December-April, and *irri* = January to May. In Rajshahi: *aus* (early rice variety) = Feb-August, *aman* (late rice variety) = May-December, *rabi* comprises two sub-seasons, one is *chaitaly* = October-January, and the other is *boro* = December-May (this includes time that farmers cultivate *irri* varieties, and also some local *boro* varieties).

3 The rate for mustard crop currently is urea: 0.5 kg per dcml (100 dcml = 1 acre; it is an introduced European measure, the Bengali area measure is the *bakhi* or *bigha*, which varies in extent from region to region), for potash: 0.25 kg per dcml, and for phosphate: 1.0 kg per dcml. For *irri* rice cultivation some farmers put on half these amounts, while others only put on 1kg per dcml of urea (this latter application gives a lower yield).

20 Actors and Rural Livelihoods: Integrating Interdisciplinary Research and Local Knowledge

P.J. Dixon, J. J. F. Barr and P. Sillitoe

IN THE BIBLICAL STORY OF BABEL, humankind tried to restore its lapsed relationship with God by building a tower reaching to the heavens. God smashed the tower in anger at this challenge to his authority, and scattered the people of Babel to the four corners of the earth. They lost their common language and were thereafter condemned to 'babble' uncomprehendingly at each other, with ensuing misunderstanding and conflict.[1] There are parallels here with contemporary development discourse and practice, logical positivism and its consequences. As Chambers (1979, 1993) and others (e.g. Hobart 1993) argue, the insistence of western development scientists that only they have valid knowledge of the world and can build the technologies of the future, is not only hubris akin to Babel's citizens but also stymies meaningful communication and dialogue. They too have fallen from grace, for foisting inappropriate technologies under the transfer-of-technology model on farmers who do not understand them or cannot use them, and sometimes causing environmental degradation. By contrast it is part of the indigenous knowledge agenda to foster meaningful and equitable dialogue between all parties.

We have to go beyond 'politically correct' assertions and portrayals of other knowledges as 'faulty', to challenge the dominance of scientific 'truth' and assess the implication that *all* knowledge, whether about God or the phenomenological world, is interpretation, is partial and provisional. This relates to the context-dependent nature of all knowledge. For example prior knowledge inflects understanding; new knowledge changes the meaning of older knowledge previously held 'valid'; while absence of knowledge (which may become known in the future) inevitably means that any 'truth' must be incomplete. The point is that it is 'good to talk' and, after Babel's disastrous insistence on one 'grand design', that it is 'better to listen' to the points of view and reasoning of others if we are to develop together technologies for achieving sustainable development. We need to beware of delusions of certainty if the edifice of 'development' is not to come crashing down. We live in an increasingly complex and interconnected, so-called 'post-positivist' and 'post-modern' world, which demands a spirit of ecumenecalism and tolerance towards others' beliefs, knowledge and practices and a willingness to learn from others — such as has long been part of many eastern cultures and religions (see Eyre 1979).

After Babel: dialogue and process learning

This shift to uncertainty and provisionality has come about with the decline of logical positivism and the emergence of constructivist, relativist approaches in the social and more recently natural sciences, which direct us to take account of other ways of knowing and others' knowledge (see Denzin and Lincoln 1994). As a result an increasing number of development practitioners have called for greater attention to be paid to the indigenous knowledge of natural resource users (see Chambers 1979; Chambers *et al.* 1989; Warren *et al.* 1995). The indigenous perspectives of others can be instructive and useful. Reasons given include utilitarian functionality and greater equity in technology delivery (see Biggs 1989; Brundtland Commission 1987 in Chambers *et al.* 1989:xvi). These arguments have broadly been accepted by policy and donor organisations, who now seek to promote synergy between local people's knowledge and western scientific knowledge and to replace 'supply-side' technology development with 'client-focused' approaches targeted more directly on the needs of the poor. Implicit is that science has something to offer poor natural resource users. Explicit is that the relevance of science and its products can be improved by learning from indigenous knowledge (see Sillitoe 1998*a*, 1998*b*), while the comparative advantage of each can assist in achieving sustainable rural livelihoods.

There have primarily been two mechanisms for progressing the match between appropriate technology-supply and client-demand in the natural resource sector. Firstly, through a participatory approach to the assessment of client need — as in Participatory Rural Appraisal. These recently popularised methodologies facilitate learning about natural resource users' knowledge and different 'stakeholder' perspectives and the mutual exploration of how these might assist in resolving identified development constraints. Secondly, through a systems approach which, because of the complex social and bio-physical problems encountered, involves interdisciplinary research teams of both natural and social scientists, and increasingly natural resource users themselves. Technology development and its transfer to end-users remain important, but under a 'people-first' policy which pays closer attention to end-users' expressed needs, and considers technical assistance as subservient to the higher goal of human and social development (see Cernea 1985; Chambers *et al.* 1989). Social scientists — particularly social anthropologists — are increasingly joining natural resource research and development teams both in order to facilitate the process of consultation with local resource-users, and to access the latters' indigenous knowledge — that is both their technical and natural resource management knowledge.

The British government's Department for International Development (DFID) is seeking to integrate participatory practice and systems thinking into its Natural Resources Systems Programme by adopting an interdisciplinary research framework. This paper draws on data and experiences from two inter-linked DFID projects in Bangladesh, one with a natural resource focus the other an indigenous knowledge one, which take an interdisciplinary research systems approach. By investigating the livelihood strategies and natural resource management knowledge of key socio-economic groups on the floodplain, the aim is to develop an understanding of the interrelationships between different production strategies, particularly agriculture and fisheries, and advance a planning and evaluation framework highlighting the systems implications of development interventions. The natural resource project is farming systems focused and is gathering quantitative bio-physical and socio-economic data to investigate different natural resource use patterns. The indigenous knowledge project, primarily collecting qualitative data which is also spatially, temporally and socio-economically referenced, seeks to provide insight into the decision-making process that leads to the observed outcomes and offers alternative, 'stakeholder', perspectives on natural resource management strategies. Both are using database technology (see Barr and Sillitoe, this volume).

Interdisciplinary systems research: the social construction of scientific 'truth'

Some development specialists divide knowledge into two distinct categories (see chapter 19): scientific knowledge and the rest (i.e. indigenous knowledge), implicitly suggesting they are incommensurate, and prioritise the former over the latter (Table 20.1 — see Barnes 1974; Chambers 1986; Wolfe *et al.* 1992; Whickam 1993).

Table 20.1:   Indigenous knowledge and scientific knowledge (after Wolfe *et al.* 1992)

Knowledge	Indigenous Knowledge	Western Scientific Knowledge
Relationship	Subordinate	Dominant
Communication	Oral Teaching through doing	Literate Didactic
Dominant Mode of Thinking	Intuitive	Analytical
Characteristics	Holistic Subjective Experiential	Reductionist Objective Positivist

While differences between science and indigenous knowledge may sometimes be apparent, the distinction derives in part from the development model held (see Blaikie *et al.* 1997). The transfer-of-technology approach belongs to a discourse which constructs difference and defines the terms according to which evidence and validity are assessed. The process learning approach (see below) dissolves difference and contextualises evidence and validity. The former approach resists dialogue, privileging scientific analysis over indigenous knowledge, whereas the latter fosters dialogue (in interdisciplinary research) between natural and social scientists and natural resource users.

Sociologists of science, drawing on Kuhn (1962), locate science in culture and time as cultural practice and historical social construct. It is 'situated knowledge', and as such is a provisional social construction, not absolute 'truth'. Knowledge, dependent on time and place, is inevitably limited and partial. Science recognised that this was so for indigenous knowledge, which it saw as a constraint to development, to be replaced not built upon. It did not judge itself similarly circumscribed until the advent of post-positivism. Some bemoan the passing of old certainties and 'truths'; but others point out that they were an illusion, dogmatism linked to the exercise of power rather than truth (see Foucault 1980; Scoones *et al.* 1994). Post-positivist science has created space for indigenous knowledge and the rehabilitation of different actors' perspectives as potentially both constraints and aids to development. The demise of certainty has a liberating rather than constraining effect. There is a renewed quest for provisional understanding and meaning, with scientific knowledge in its proper place as one player among others. Rather than one dominant world-view, other formerly muted voices may be heard. For all it remains a socio-cultural enterprise in which knowledge about the world and acting effectively in it is sought through experimentation, validated to the satisfaction of users, and reproduced as reliable cultural knowledge to be acted and built on.

Drawing on Kuhn, Chambers (1986, 1993) argues that historically natural resource research and development has been typified by 'normal professionalism' which reproduces itself in development institutions, and 'defends itself against threat by specialisation, simplification, rejection and assimilation'. Knowledge that does not 'fit', such as indigenous knowledge and the qualitative information of anthropologists, is rejected as 'unscientific' or accorded functional utility only. By contrast the advocated 'new professionalism' reverses the power relations implicit in 'normal professionalism', promotes interdisciplinary research and the participation of natural resource users in the identification and resolution of livelihood constraints, seeks indigenous knowledge and institutes a process-learning approach to development.

In this 'brave new uncertain world' interdisciplinary research is to be encouraged, is perhaps even a necessity, ensuring a variety of perspectives on any problem, and providing individuals and groups with new information. While there may be arguments for distinguishing between scientific and indigenous knowledge, there is a growing consensus that the synergy of 'knowledge negotiated' at the development interface may advance more sustainable interventions (see Figure 20.1).

Indigenous knowledge held by farmers and fishers **Scientific knowledge held by disciplinary specialists**

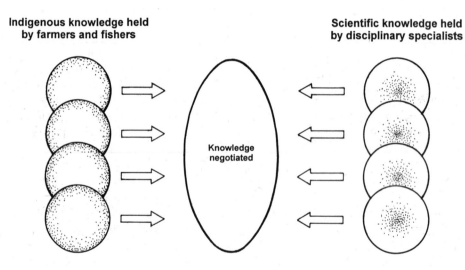

Figure 20.1 *Integrating indigenous knowledge and natural resources research*

The drive for interdisciplinary research within development has come from demands for systems thinking — for example in agroecology (see Altieri 1987) and farming systems research (see Gilbert *et al.* 1980; Shaner *et al.* 1982; Wilson and Morren 1990). In some social sciences (and particularly anthropology) systems-thinking (or holism) is more or less *de rigour* (see Chambers 1997; Senge 1990).[2] We accept that holistic and reductive approaches may complement each other, reductive approaches proceeding within a holistic framework. In many disciplines, however, the privileging of structure over agency has limited systems thinking by focusing on homeostatic rather than complex emergent systems.

We can see the implications of the shift from structure to process in farming systems research. 'Early' farming systems research was notable for going on-farm, and using interdisciplinary research teams with a systems perspective (see Gilbert *et al.* 1980;

Shaner *et al.* 1982; Collinson 1981). However, the approach over-privileged scientific analysis (rarely collecting indigenous knowledge data), employed a formal economistic model in analysis, and unconsciously promoted a western conception of farming (see Chambers and Jiggins 1986). In short, it tended towards formal structuralism and reductionism, conceiving of farms as 'hard' closed systems and studying them componentially. As a result, 'early' farming systems research recommendations, while potentially useful to resource-rich farmers, were largely irrelevant to resource-poor natural resource users in complex, risk-prone environments. 'Later' farming systems research is more participatory, shifting from a crop-only perspective ignoring farmers' knowledge, towards an appreciation of complexity and farmer decision-making. It combines a holistic approach, integrating social and natural sciences, with one which attempts to 'minimise outsider ethnocentric assumptions' (Gardner and Lewis 1996:119-120). The methodology still privileges outsiders' over insiders' development goals (as in its preoccupation with optimisation through the intervention of 'experts' — Bawden 1992); has further to go in seeing diverse livelihood practices as interacting 'soft systems' (the lived experience and perspectives of different user groups — see Bawden 1992; Cornwall, Guijt and Welbourn 1993:16-17; Scoones *et al.* 1994:30); and needs to go beyond the farm boundary (the farm-unit preoccupation indicating a limited conception of holism and stakeholder interest — see Altieri 1987; Conway and Barbier 1990; Uphoff 1996*b*; Gibbon 1994).

The idea of 'hard' systems objectively defined by privileged outside experts gives way to a relativistic conception of 'soft' systems (or 'human activity systems') knowable as social constructs; where individuals and groups define reality and reproduce it through their activities. They will likely have different understandings and points of view. It encompasses what Bourdieu (1977) refers to as *habitus,* the 'taken-for-granted' world underpinning human decision-making and action. A simple example would be the acceptance of a social status such as 'husband' or 'wife', or allocation to others of the identity of 'untouchable', and activities (i.e. role-playing) which make these and the relations between them 'concrete'. The individuals and groups may share the same activity system (as husband and wife agree on the allocation of their respective roles), may negotiate a new shared system (for example Bangladeshi wives working in the fields rather than remaining in *purdah*) or may have different perspectives and activity systems (for example as natural resource scientists and Bengali farmer-fishers have about natural resource inter-relationships.)

Systems learning and livelihood archetypes

It is necessary to learn about systems from a variety of perspectives. Under the transfer-of-technology approach, learning and research was largely by scientists alone. They generated knowledge off-farm according to their own assumptions and goals, for example research to improve cultivar yield. The knowledge was transferred to the farmers as discrete technology packages. Scientists assumed that they were right in their analysis of natural resource systems, of client need, and in their proposals for the removal of system constraints. No wonder there was patchy uptake by farmers, there was a gap between their and scientists' understanding of the world, about how it worked and could be improved, and about what the priorities were. They should learn by rote how to use the technologies produced, but if their goals and the contexts did not match that of scientists, they were of limited use to them. Farmers either had to adapt the technologies to their situation, change the contexts in which they could be used, or change their livelihood goals. For resource-poor farmers in complex risk-prone environments, rejection of these technologies was often the only option open to them. This sent an implicit, but misunderstood, message to agricultural development specialists; they interpreted adaptation and poor uptake as evidence of farmers' 'ignorance' and 'backwardness' — they 'blamed the farmer.' The solution to this was for development agencies to provide more support to farmers via extension services — the Training and Visit system being perhaps the apogee of this — and it failed because it generally consisted of a reiteration of the 'instructions for use' which scientists had developed together with the technologies back on the research station. Extension services, with their own institutional agendas and paid to support scientific technology distribution rather than farmers' real needs, became an integral part of the edifice. The extension services and farmers were expected to fit the needs of the technology, not the technology to fit the needs of farmers.

In this 'human activity system' the legacy of Babel is evident, everyone talked past each other, while 'feedback' reinforced stereotypical assumptions about the 'problem' and how to tackle it. No deeper learning occurred, by one 'culture' from another and particularly by scientists from and about farmers and their livelihood needs. The transfer-of-technology paradigm, and 'early' farming systems research, co-opted farmers as the lowest rung of the food production system, with optimisation of production by farmers as the superordinate goal of the development enterprise. Some resource-rich farmers could be co-opted to this goal through policy instruments and for them the Green Revolution was a success. However, there remained many farmers with different goals and different needs; farmers who are as much 'consumers' as 'producers'.

The poor rate of uptake of many technologies by natural resource users for whom they were designed suggested to some that the transfer-of-technology approach was inappropriate, in that the analysis and identification of constraints were not the same for natural resource users as they were for scientists. They had different perspectives on the system. The first steps in the shift from supply-side to demand-side technology development led to consultations with members of target populations, but these persons tended to be drawn from the more articulate and well resourced sections of the community and their views, needs and capacities were taken as 'representative' of all. Improvements in technology uptake and the improving ability of countries to meet food security requirements were initially taken as evidence that a consultative approach to client need was sufficient. However, the approach was increasingly criticised for 'studying down', for failing to take account of the needs of the less articulate or well-resourced members of communities, and for working with a homogenous picture of rural communities. But worse, it led to a covert bias in favour of better-resourced farmers who were consulted on technology design and had the resources with which to make use of it. This represents a hidden transfer of resources to those natural resource users who least require them and away from those who do, and contributes to a growing gap between rich and poor.[3] The policy may or may not contribute to overall national food-security, but Dreze and Sen (1989) have shown that famine and hunger relate as much to lack of access to food (for example due to poverty) as they do overall scarcity.

We can see the need firstly, to consider system characteristics — to understand the linkages between parts of the system, the role of feedback, and so on. Interdisciplinary research using participatory methodologies institutes feedback within process-learning. Secondly, we can appreciate that it is necessary to identify groups with different livelihood strategies (that is different 'livelihood archetypes', see Long and Van der Ploeg 1994), both to capture their perspectives and indigenous knowledge, and because these 'ego-focused' human activity systems ('soft systems') are interdependent. The above criticisms have been taken on board by the development community. There is now greater effort to disaggregate a population according to socio-economic, gender, age and other criteria in order to target aid, and in particular to identify the most needy and marginalised members of society and their needs — which includes identifying the structural constraints which marginalise them (whether due for example to occupation, gender, religion, or ethnicity). Technology and policy assistance can then be targeted on lessening these constraints and building these groups' 'capital' requirements to secure their social inclusion into the mainstream economy.

In the two research projects on the floodplains we have used participatory wealth ranking exercises to identify poverty, while relying on quantitative and qualitative data to identify livelihood archetypes and their key 'capital' endowments (see Pretty 1998). We take a livelihoods approach (see Ellis 1998; Carney 1998*a*, 1998*b*), recognising that rural families diversify to offset risk to their food security and have 'portfolios of livelihood strategies' which sector-specific approaches (such as a focus on rice or fish) cannot adequately capture because these strategies 'cut across a number of self-bounded policy arenas' (Ellis 1998:2). In addition, we advocate a wider systems approach in seeking to identify the complex interdependencies that may exist between livelihood archetypes. We aim to develop an understanding of the (competitive and complementary) relationships which exist between production systems, and particularly agriculture and fisheries, and to model the systems implications of development interventions.

Local perspectives and natural resource management: science and the political economy of outcomes

There are three practical reasons for instituting a process-learning approach. Firstly, as farming systems research realised, the on-farm context is far more complex than the experimental station.[4] Secondly, scientific models are social constructs, observer bias is inescapable, and facts — dependent on the position of the observer — can support more than one interpretation. Different interpretations (including farmers' and fishers') have validity and should be sought. Thirdly, evidence suggests natural resource users view the world holistically and take a process learning approach to it — that is they are prepared to change their minds and management practices in the light of experience.

An example from our field data. To the external observer, Bangladeshi farm households appear to shift between 'plan' and 'performance' (Richards 1993) in planning annual cropping series for their farm plots but changing these when necessary in response to current environmental and social opportunities and constraints. Farmers who plan to grow a cash crop of onions as their *rabi* (or dry) season crop on *beel* land may switch to *boro* paddy in response to their up-slope neighbours' intentions to plant irrigated paddy, or they may negotiate with farmers up-slope of their neighbours to plant onion and deny irrigation water to down-slope paddy farmers who may then have to grow onions too — unless they are able to negotiate a different outcome.

The outcome of this negotiation process is a human activity system made visible on the *beel* landscape as a distinctive wedge of cropland extending from higher to lower land near the *beel* during the *boro* season. It stands out from land planted to different rice varieties on plots elsewhere around the *beel*. Whether the cropping pattern will be repeated in future years or appear elsewhere on the *beel* landscape will be dependent on the individual, yet interdependent, decision-making of farmers in response to the various opportunities and constraints that arise in the future. Such 'self-organising behaviour', as systems theorists have named it, indicates the need to take context into account and its potential impact even when there are established ideas of individual ownership.

The floodplain cropping mozaic, as represented by scientific modelling (in Geographical Information Systems) is a 'negotiated outcome' of the totality of livelihood 'performances'. Each performance is predicated on individual households' perspectives of livelihood opportunities and constraints and their capacity to respond. Individual households may have a conception of 'their farm', but the fragmentation of landholdings, the interdigitation of the plots of different households, and the flexible definition of rights to natural resources on plots at different seasons of the year suggest households routinely take into account the performance of households beyond their own. The total farming/fishing system is dynamic in time and space not only in response to the marked seasons, but also because there is a dynamic tension between plan and performance by individual households, which in turn are interlinked through human activity systems involving both private and common property resources. Stakeholders' indigenous knowledge which informs their natural resource management reasoning, takes account of a host of social and cultural factors, while the floodplain mozaic which farming systems research models is an 'emergent' property of these causal factors.

The floodplains represent one of the world's most intensively farmed and fished landscapes. The extreme population density results in a mosaic of intimately associated rural production units. These units are commonly called farms, but are better viewed from a human rather than physical perspective, as family based units which depend variously on fishing and farming and on off-farm income sources. However the production system on the floodplain is not merely the sum of these units. The conceptual model of 'farms' as discrete units (albeit very fragmented ones) managed as such by farm families taking independent decisions within their farm boundary, based upon reliable physical and economic information, does not hold well for the floodplain. The 'floodplain production systems' are complex adaptive systems which emerge from the organisation of many individual but coupled production strategies on the floodplain. This pattern of floodplain production is an emergent property of natural resource use. Although dynamic and never exactly repeatable, such patterns exhibit consistent themes (Waldrop 1992). It is these themes or relationships which we need to understand to promote more sustainable, positive-sum (win-win) development on the floodplains. We need to be particularly conscious of the impact of interventions on the livelihoods of the poor and other marginalised groups.

Formal science can model the changing mozaic over time and space as a series of 'snapshots' and can make hypotheses about the rationale driving the system changes. These 'etic' explanations while valid are limited, particularly when it comes to predicting future changes in the system, because they do not consider the political-economy of resource management. They are not good at modelling the 'culture' in 'agriculture', for example the micro-politics which underlie the allocation of resources. From a 'social constructivist' position the system perspectives of different parties are as valid in their context and in relation to their livelihood goals as those of natural scientists. We are not arguing that scientific knowledge should be set aside. Science gives a different perspective, one which can add value to local livelihood strategies by filling information gaps, and suggesting potential ways natural resource users might move forward in their quest for more sustainable livelihoods.

The above points suggest that scientists should seek to appreciate user-groups' goals, their perceptions of risk and reward, of opportunity and constraint (in both socio-economic and biophysical terms) in relation to their livelihood strategies, and their implications for other households. It is also necessary to retain a certain critical detachment, not the 'objectivity' of science, but a critical and reflexive stance towards context-dependent values which may sometimes be an asset in some situations but a constraint to progress in others. It is an attempt to 'see both the wood and the trees', the elements and the wider system, the 'facts' and the paradigm which organises them. It provides a different, not necessarily better, perspective to the local one. At the same time, scientists' detachment from the 'human-activity systems' of rural Bangladeshis puts them in a position potentially to assist natural resource users to explore their relationships and reconsider and revise their indigenous knowledge where appropriate.

Complexity and social equity

We may assume that each farm household has a good idea of the rice it needs to grow or purchase to feed itself. They can make provisional plans to allocate land on that basis, including owned or sharecropped plots, to subsistence or cash crops. New knowledge, hearing what neighbours are planning to grow on adjacent plots, leads them to adapt their cropping plan and/or to seek to influence their neighbours' cropping plans where these impact on their own. After negotiations, in which a range of non-agricultural considerations (including power relations between different parties) are undoubtedly involved, a collective cropping plan for the season is agreed. The totality of individual provisional 'blueprints' gives way to a processually-derived mutually-agreed outcome. This 'emergent' outcome may or may not lead to adjustments in individual households' allocation of resources to other livelihood strategies, and/or to changes in the cropping pattern in the *beel*. It is not clear what outcome may result — that is what the area devoted to any crop is going to be, if any. This only 'emerges' as a result of the negotiating process. This 'self-organising' outcome is the result of a host of micro decisions made by interested parties in relation to each other and on the basis of their individual needs. Other self-organised interest groups may emerge around other issues, but need be no more permanent.

There are analogies with the co-evolution of organisms in ecosystems (i.e. adapting in relation to each others' ongoing evolution; Capra 1996). Such self-organising human activity might be thought to produce a stable system. This is generally the way structuralist anthropology presents it with its focus on 'the rules of the game'. And there may be a kind of homeostasis at this level — though complexity theory suggests this is better conceptualised as an 'approximation to homeostasis' or oscillations around 'attractors'. There has been a shift in systems thinking from closed- to open-systems (from homeostatic to evolutionary systems), and the consideration of externalities (such as policy decisions which skew options). Homeostatic conditions are more points (or 'snap-shots') in an evolving system. More usually the political economy of capital and associated feedback leads to accumulation for some individuals and groups at the expense — impoverishment, marginalisation, vulnerability — of others. Analysis of the decision-making involved is required to understand the terms on which the system operates.

From farming systems to livelihood archetypes

There is a well-established tradition of farming systems research in Bangladesh (Hossain 1990; Chowdhury *et al.* 1993; Siddique *et al.* 1994; Roy 1996), from government to NGO research and extension. There is a broad spectrum of production activity on the floodplains, depending differentially on farming and fishing as the main components. Farming systems research has traditionally approached this diversity by aggregating like production units into homogenous 'recommendation domains' which can be targeted by researchers to adapt technologies specific to that group of farms (Norman *et al.* 1995). The inference is that 'the farm' as the unit of study, many consisting of only an homestead and less than 0.2 ha of cultivable paddy, and sometimes a pond, is a discrete management unit. The approach has been 'research into farming systems' rather than 'systems research about farming' (Bawden 1995).

But farming systems researchers have increasingly realised poorer families, particularly in the developing world, develop a 'portfolio of livelihood strategies' (Ellis 1998) only one of which is farming, and that there is cross-subsidisation between various enterprises and between household members (see FAO 1998). Diversification into non-farm activities reduces risk to food security and smooths out income and expenditure flows over the year where farming activities are seasonal. While farming systems research is adept at disaggregating farming households into archetypes and constructing 'recommendation domains' for extension services and policy makers, it has generally failed to recognise the implications of interdependencies between livelihoods. The Bangladesh evidence suggests that different farm archetypes have different mixes of strategies, with greater or lesser diversification into non-farm activities, with different needs relating to different 'recommendation domains'.

Many farmers in the developing world not only exploit farm and non-farm opportunities, but are also directly interrelated, for example through the interdigitation of farm plots in Bangladesh. On the floodplains farmers' actions impact on the livelihoods of neighbours immediately and directly. Also, there is a politico-economic dimension to natural resource use, different floodplain livelihood archetypes have differential access to natural, social and human 'capital', and individual households use these to further their own goals vis-à-vis neighbouring households. Development needs to consider the interdependencies between livelihood archetypes and the implications that supporting one type can have for others. A systems framework which can evaluate the relationships between groups of producers (farming systems 'in the large' {Norman *et al.* 1995}) is necessary if the aim is to achieve a net improvement in floodplain output, not just certain parts of it, possibly at the expense of others. It would for example determine the benefits or otherwise to farmers within a recommendation domain of a change in their *rabi* cropping technology, but not how that change might affect another groups' *beel* fisheries, say, through the crops' use of surface and ground water for irrigation. Such a framework must encompass competing, complementary and neutral activities to determine positive-sum ('win-win') and zero-sum ('win-lose') or negative-sum ('lose-lose') impacts (Uphoff 1996*b*).

From a wider systems perspective it is appropriate to look closely at what the various livelihood archetypes' needs are and what the potential impact of any intervention may be both for a specified target group and for other groups on the floodplain. Using this approach we can focus on rural livelihoods, identify appropriate livelihood archetypes (for example through participatory wealth ranking), construct farming systems research models for each, employ appropriate business-studies methods to identify constraints to their sustainability, and construct recommendation domains. Problem census and village workshop exercises with representatives of identified livelihood archetypes are two useful methods in this work.

Problem censuses and village workshops[5]

In our linked DFID projects we firstly identified livelihood archetypes through reconnaissance social surveys at the two project sites. These generated socio-economic strata based on land-holding according to common Bangladesh governmental practice. The robustness of these strata as representing livelihood archetypes was supported through participatory wealth-ranking exercises. Throughout the project cycle the household was treated as the smallest unit of study and intra-household disparities in resource allocation were not considered, though we recognise that when households gain overall through a development intervention, individuals (for example women and children) may still lose out as individuals.[6] Representatives for the problem census and village workshops were drawn from the various identified socio-economic strata, with some collapsing of strata to make the exercise more manageable. Discussion groups were formed on the basis of commonality of livelihood, plus a gender dimension.

During the problem census exercises the different groups identified a range of different constraints to their livelihoods. The hypothesis was that different groups would identify different constraints according to their primary livelihood strategy and that this would particularly hold for wealthier farmers versus full-time fishers, but that there might be some commonality in the problems identified by groups. There were some problems that were common to all groups (e.g. problems with seed supply, lack of access to credit), suggesting the potential for community-wide interventions to address these. These are potentially collectively empowering rather than divisive, although demanding careful thought and planning prior to implementation. For example, improving community-wide seed-supply may merely provide a hidden subsidy to those who can afford to rely on the market rather than supporting access to seed by the poorest. If the primary target group is defined by policy-makers as the poorest, an intervention or a policy instrument has to be carefully designed to proportionally benefit them most (while not being seen as a threat to the livelihoods of wealthier members of the community). For example, improving access by women to seed for seedbed preparation, which they usually undertake on a sharecropping basis, with them keeping the income earned. This would be particularly beneficial to poorer households who have limited resources for buying seed and may have consumed reserves of seed from the last harvest during the lean period.

It is not easy to identify such an intervention (and even more difficult to implement one) as shown by the exploration in village workshops of a hypothetical intervention — the management of water ingress and egress from a *beel* during the monsoon season. There is a continuum from those whose livelihood portfolios are primarily land-based, through those who have an decreasing interest in land-based/increasing interest in water-based activities, to those whose livelihood is primarily water-based:

1. Large and medium landowners (farmers);
2. Smaller owning and sharecropping farmers/fishers with a mix of seasonal livelihood strategies including farming and fishing, (and van-pullers/boat owners);
3. Those who are primarily full-time fishers with some dry season livelihood strategies.

Large and medium land-owners: In the problem census exercises, groups of large and medium landowners readily identified a range of natural resource problems which they saw as constraints to their agriculturally-based livelihood strategies. In village workshops these groups (and also their wives in separate discussion groups) supported land-based interventions, and in particular improving *beel* drainage to release land for agriculture for longer periods (e.g. to enable the earlier planting of *boro* crops, and to reduce the fallow period for land). The possibility of draining the *beel* altogether during the dry season, which would release more land for cultivation by those who had title to it, was also raised at one project site. However, the potential impact of such an intervention on *beel* fish stocks through drainage of permanent water (acting as a fish refuge) was not raised by them. Their main interest was optimising returns from their privately owned land.

The deepening of a channel to a *beel* to improve drainage may also make fishing more efficient during flood. Self-interest is again evident. The need for political contacts, the cost of a license to fish here and the fishing gear needed (large lift-nets) suggest its likely monopoly by wealthier people (larger landowners) with access denied to the poor. The longer-term impact on fish stocks of a practice which seeks to capture a large proportion of all fish that pass through a channel is uncertain, but may cumulatively reduce the number and varieties of fish in the *beel*, both young fish (since very fine-mesh lift-nets are used) and larger, breeding, fish. There would probably be a more immediate impact on the livelihoods of those who rely on opportunistic fishing in the open waters of a *beel* — including landless and near-landless poor. In brief, 'community' investment in improving *beel* drainage may reduce access to a common property resource (capture fisheries), transferring this food and income source to private hands, from poorer to wealthier people, while potentially threatening its sustainability.

Seasonal mix of livelihood strategies: The problem census identified the following livelihood strategies spanning the land-water interface: (a) landless labourers/ sharecroppers and part-time fishers; (b) sharecroppers/medium farmers and part-time fishers; and (c) women from landless labourer/sharecropper households. The main problems concerned access to land, other natural and economic resources and employment, the scarcity of common property resources (such as fish, grazing for livestock, and fuel), and the cost and poor quality of inputs (such as fertiliser) required for agriculture. Access issues were a major concern of the poorest (those in groups a. and c.), while more practical difficulties (such as scarcity of good quality fertiliser and seed, and poor drainage from the *beel*) predominated for those (group b.) who had some limited access to land. Access issues were particularly pressing for women from the poorest strata. Their identified problems suggest they not only lack access to land (even homestead land) and other resources (such as credit), but also have to compete with everyone else for common property resources (such as grazing and fuel). Additionally, they identified pay and employment discrimination when they work outside the home, which many have to do to support their household. They also identified negligence and physical abuse by their husbands as a problem. Finally, an age dimension to poverty also emerged, women from the poorest strata stressing that as couples aged illness and incapacity — particularly of the husband — made it increasingly difficult to make ends meet.

Significantly, group (c.) women from the poorest strata were unable (or unwilling) to propose solutions to their problems other than micro-enterprise training, interest-free loans and/or grants of land. The same was true of group (a.) landless labourers/ sharecroppers. By contrast group (b.) sharecroppers/medium farmers put forward a variety of practical solutions to their input and output constraints. It appears that where groups have little or no access to land they are unlikely to be interested in the removal of constraints to land based livelihood strategies. It is noteworthy that none of these groups put much emphasis on problems associated with the common property natural resource which is probably a significant part of their livelihood portfolio for part of the year — *beel* water and capture fisheries during the monsoon season, although they noted scarcity of fish.

The indications are that these groups have similar land focused concerns to wealthier farmers. They depend on wealthier farmers for access to land and employment. This may account for them identifying *beel* drainage as an issue. In sum, these poorer groups are more likely to be co-opted to support the goals of farmers rather than fishers. Reducing these groups' dependence on access to land and agricultural labouring — for example through non-farm work — could potentially shift their support more towards capture fisheries and their sustainability.

Full-time fishers: These groups mentioned problems relating to water resources. There were several. Fish-stock decline through sluice-gates impeding migration, disease, removal of small breeding fish through the use of fine-mesh nets, over-fishing by 'non-fishermen', and siltation of the *beel* and depletion of *beel* water through irrigation use. Also access issues with control of *beel* fishing by non-fishers, land-owners excluding fishing near *kua* (refuge pits) they have dug, rich farmers leasing *khas* (government-owned water-bodies), and fishing by non-fishers in *khas* leased by fishers. Proposed solutions to these constraints focused on improving the fish-stock and optimising yield. Only one (keeping the sluice gates open during the beginning of the flood) appeared to conflict with the interests of farmers who might wish to prevent flood ingress for as long as possible. The proposal that government should only lease *khas* to 'true fishers' probably reflects the common regional tendency towards group identity and occupational monopoly (while in many areas of Bangladesh full-time fishers are predominantly Hindu), while the lack of enthusiasm for policing flood-season fishing by non-fishers probably reflects the practical difficulties of doing so on behalf of politically marginal groups (for example a minority Hindu group living in a predominantly Muslim community).

Same resources, different views

All rural Bangladeshis depend on farming and fishing for their food security. Farmers' and fishers' livelihood strategies are complementary, and indeed many invest in both natural resource domains; e.g. wealthy farmers lease *khas* waterbodies, own large lift-nets, etc. while fishers may buy or lease land. However, the predominant activity in their livelihood strategy brings them into competition over natural resource use and control at certain periods of the year. The balance of power is skewed in favour of farmers and land-based production. The power differential between the two groups is partly a function of numbers, of religious affiliation and of access to public bodies controlling access to resources. But it is also linked to the general perception (with associated negative connotations) among the Bangladeshi urban élite, the government, international donor- and research-bodies that the floodplain is *land* which is annually flooded, the flood doing considerable damage to land, infrastructure and crops. Instead of a perception that it is neither just a 'plain which floods' nor a true 'wet-land' but a seasonal land-water interface the natural resources of which support the harvesting of a large volume and variety of fish, and the production of between one and three crops a year, which supports a variety of interdependent livelihood archetypes.

Concerted development of minor irrigation has shifted cropping towards intensive production of high yielding varieties of irrigated *boro* and wheat, at the expense of dry season oilseeds and pulses and to some extent *aman*. Additionally, flood control and drainage works have reduced the depth and duration of flooding, and have shifted *aman* production from traditional varieties to HYV *aman* grown in shallower water. This picture of environmental modification (less water in the monsoon, additional water in the dry season) to increase food grain production has not benefited all floodplain producers. The focus on food grain production has led to a more intensive and risk-prone agriculture. It has also negatively impacted the floodplain fishery, principally due to flood control, but also due to the premium for water in the dry season. Seasonal wetlands have been converted to drier cultivable land, resulting in loss of fish habitat. Perennial wetlands are becoming increasingly ephemeral with reduced effectiveness as fish refuges (CNRS 1996). Flood control has reduced migration and recruitment of floodplain fish and reduced species diversity. The overall impact is reported to be a 70% reduction in production from floodplain fisheries (NEMAP 1995).

The precedence given to land over water may also be a function of the difference between land as a private-property resource and water as common property. Individuals can exercise monopoly control over land and will invest in it, but not water. Private sector initiatives aimed at water resources, for example to address the 'the tragedy of the commons', have not been successful. They restrict access of those who rely on aquatic resources — in Bangladesh those who have a diversified mix of livelihood strategies exploiting both land and water resources, as well as non-farm opportunities.

Evidence from village workshops shows that different livelihood groups see the *beel* differently and suggests there has been a skewing of the system in favour of land-versus water-based livelihoods. The definition of the floodplain itself by non-Bengali outsiders and by government may be based on one which sees it as 'land which is periodically flooded', a definition that may underlie the historical focus on flood-control measures, crop improvement and the like. When fish feature they are generally seen as 'fish in agricultural systems' (e.g. pond aquaculture, rice-fish, and so on). For fishermen, and for many of the poor who depend on seasonal capture fisheries, the difference may be that they perceive of the floodplain and *beels* not as '*land* which is periodically flooded' but as '*water* which periodically recedes to reveal farm land'.

The development of the present 'human activity system' is biased towards land and its individual ownership and away from water and common property resources. When land appears from the flood, it is claimed by individuals. Title is claimed to land under perennial *beels*, which individuals expect — and encourage — to become 'dry' over the years. Squatters struggle to settle government *khas* land (along roadsides etc.). The 'tragedy of the commons' is not necessarily the destruction of common property resources by all through over-exploitation (though this is happening as pressure on them increases), but their depletion through transfer to individual ownership. We have accumulation of land resources by the wealthy, and marginalisation of the poor who, denied access to land, have increasingly to rely on diminishing common property resources (floodplain fisheries). On the other hand, community-based management is not a guarantee of sustainable and systemic improvements. Implementation of the New Fisheries Management Policy, which aimed to place the control of waterbodies in the hands of *bona fide* fishers, has been largely subverted by powerful local interests (Toufique 1997). Attempts to establish water user forums with representatives of different interest groups have been similarly captured by locally influential people (Soussan *et al.* 1998).

Development on the floodplains has poorly addressed the needs of small and marginal Bangladeshi farmers and fishers (Haggart 1994; FPCO 1995; Ministry of Agriculture 1997). It has failed to take account of interrelationships between different users, and has instigated interventions with negative impacts on the poor who continue to face declining income and unsustainable livelihoods. Nonetheless, Bangladesh's Fourth Five Year Plan had a major objective to "ensure sustained agricultural growth through more efficient and balanced utilisation of the country's land, water and other natural resources." A balance which can only be achieved by recognising the importance of these resources to all those who use them. In order to progress towards more balanced and systemic increases in productivity, we need to advance a conceptual model of the floodplain that centres on relationships between diverse livelihood strategies, and one that is derived from peoples' own perceptions. It should emerge from interdisciplinary understanding of the system and group consensus from interactions between floodplain stakeholders.

Conclusions

There is need for structures (policies, local institutions and supporting methodologies) that can draw on the conceptual model and implement more systemic improvement in floodplain production. It will require the integration of indigenous knowledge with more formal scientific knowledge, and an understanding of the perspectives of all stakeholders. We need an understanding of the heterogeneity of the livelihood strategies of primary stakeholders and of how they interact. It is the interdependencies between their 'human activity systems' which constitute the social and biophysical dimensions of the floodplain system. The system is 'soft', and open, complex and emergent. Whether it is sustainable or not is in question.

We are moving from scientific monologue to stakeholder dialogue in which indigenous knowledge has a role to play. In doing so we go from a blueprint to a process approach involving co-learning (see Mosse, Farrington and Rew 1998; Cornwall, Guijt and Welbourn 1993). Additionally, as the social and biophysical dimensions of systems are considered together, so we become critically aware of the political dimensions of knowledge and action (see Blaikie *et al.* 1997; Scoones *et al.* 1994). In their decision-making farmers respond to social and physical opportunities and constraints at the micro-level, as well as to opportunities and constraints at the macro-level such as the policy environment. Previously, policy-makers in Bangladesh have taken a reductive and additive approach to the social and biophysical system of the floodplains. This approach has outlived its usefulness. Many interventions designed to improve production have considered only parts of the 'system', be it food grain cultivation or carp capture fisheries, while other ignored parts of the system have been negatively affected. The negative impacts may off-set the improvements, resulting in no net gain in production or nutrition (a zero-sum game). Furthermore it is often the most disadvantaged — the landless or women and children — who are the losers, with wealthier medium and large land-owning farmers as the winners (Ministry of Agriculture 1997).

When there is no mutual understanding, people talk past each other or 'babble' uncomprehendingly at each other. The outcome, as evidenced by transfer-of-technology development, is an illusion of unity and of working towards a common end. Technology development and policy design cannot be appropriate and effective unless the needs and skills of all clients and practitioners are taken into consideration. Either there will be poor design and a failure of uptake, or interventions may be ingeniously adapted locally, or they may be appropriated by particular social groups to further their own interests. Interdisciplinary research and co-learning is an inclusive, 'deliberative', development practice which draws on the different knowledge of many in seeking better and more sustainable livelihoods for the heterogeneous population of the floodplains. In doing so, we hope to avoid the fate of Babel.

Notes

1 There is a passage in the Koran which possibly refers to the tower of Babel and its destruction by God, but it does not carry the same connotations as it does in the Bible.

2 Calls for a systems approach are not new. They can be traced back to the 1940s in work by cyberneticists and linguists. Indeed, systems-thinking characterised the perspectives of many scientists in earlier centuries before the separation of science into more distinct sub-disciplines with the rise of reductive approaches.

3 A similar argument has been made by feminists with regard to intra-familial transfers and the need to incorporate a gender perspective into development.

4 While causal factors can be simplified and held steady on-station (and a mechanistic linear notion of causality may be sufficient), the on-farm context is typified by multiplex non-linear causality and dynamic co-evolution.

5 Problem census is a farmer-centred approach used in Bangladesh by Government agencies and NGOs to identify and prioritise production constraints (Crouch 1991). The world views of different stakeholders were expressed in the problem census. The village workshops drew on soft systems and stakeholders methods to provide a framework for the expression of multiple perspectives and system learning to progress towards an accommodation — though not necessarily a consensus about natural resource management. It is useful in complex situations with groups of different people dealing with value-laden problems and situations where there are different goals. Bangladesh's floodplains where there is a dynamic interaction between social groups as floods spread and contract across the land is just one such complex situation.

6 There is a considerable literature on differential access to resources within households (for example see Moorehead and Bhargava 1999), but for practical

reasons the issues are not considered here. Our definition of 'the household' follows that which is usual in Bangladesh, that is the group which shares a common cooking hearth.

Acknowledgements

We could not have written this paper without the teamwork and intellectual contribution of all those involved in the two research projects referred to — both project staff and many local people at the field sites. It is invidious to name individuals, but we would wish to acknowledge here those most closely involved with the problem census and village workshop exercises mentioned in the second half of the paper. They are Mahbub 'Pial' Alam and Gour Pada Ghosh, Dr. S. B. Naseem and Professor M. I. Zuberi; Drs Graham Haylor and Colin Bean (University of Stirling); Alice A. McGlynn and Dr. Robert Payton (University of Newcastle); M. Moklesur Rahman and Anisur Rahman (Center for Natural Resource Studies, Dhaka). The research on which the paper is based is funded by the Natural Resources Systems Programme of DFID, under contracts R6744 and R 6756. However the views expressed are those of the authors and not necessarily DFID.

21 Databases, Indigenous Knowledge and Interdisciplinary Research

J. J. F. Barr and P. Sillitoe

INTERDISCIPLINARY RESEARCH is central to enquiries into indigenous knowledge. Effective communication is essential in this research. At a time when many of us feel that we are suffering from chronic information overload and are finding it increasingly difficult to handle the flood of words in the narrow specialisms where we build our careers — be it identity in the New Guinea Highlands or gender in the Caribbean islands, Islamic fundamentalism in the Arab world or ethnic relations in Europe — how feasible is this demand for greater interdisciplinarity? Who has the cerebral capacity and necessary time? To what extent might we use the new information technology — electronic databases and so forth — to control the tide instead of magnifying it, to make the task more manageable? How might information technology further communication and understanding? To what extent might database software, and associated tools such as graphical 'cognitive mapping', facilitate the exchange of qualitative data pertaining to indigenous knowledge across the interface with natural scientists, help us to negotiate paradigmatic differences between knowledge traditions?

The computer database, as a modelling tool, is potentially a powerful instrument for furthering interdisciplinary work. The potential benefits of databases in indigenous knowledge contributions to interdisciplinary natural resources research in development are several. They are a useful aid in the complex management of interdisciplinary research teams. They organise data efficiently, and make it readily available simultaneously to several researchers. All collaborating disciplines should interact at each step of a research project, though it is in the conceptual modelling stage that interdisciplinary interaction is likely to be particularly fruitful (Swanson 1979). Databases facilitate such complex joint analyses of information. They are amenable to burgeoning electronic communication between team members in different places and facilitate dissemination of results (email, WWW, internet, etc.).

The sharing of computer software when modelling natural resource use may advance the contribution of each discipline by revealing complementarities and highlighting contrasts. Computers may oblige a group working together to scrutinise its thinking and analysis closely, and blur the boundaries between individual contributions, so facilitating a joint narrative. The use of computers in indigenous knowledge research may reduce some of the mutual scepticism between disciplines about the validity of their understanding of problems where founded on differing epistemologies. They should also better place indigenous knowledge to contribute to natural resources research by making it more accessible to scientists. They are familiar to scientists, as an integral part of their research culture today, for example in modelling natural systems. The biophysical sciences now regularly use computer databases in the building of elegant systems models, for example modelling watersheds, landscapes and hydrology (e.g. the North-East Land Use Project (U.K.); O'Callaghan 1996). They too collect masses of data to formulate their models. The geologists' plate tectonic model is one of the most impressive, unifying a wide range of data (e.g. seismology readings, flux of minerals etc.), and explaining a range of previously disparate phenomena.

The use of databases may, as a consequence, help further the legitimacy of indigenous knowledge in the eyes of scientists and others, presenting others' knowledge through state of the art technology. But we should not anticipate any ready epistemological breakthroughs. The research paradigms and strategies that inform natural and social sciences differ significantly. Research on natural resources management commonly proceeds by first identifying a problem and then devising a scientific model to advance its understanding and hopefully its solution (Wilson and Morren 1990). The use of qualitative databases for the recording and analysis of social data does not proceed in the same way. We have no elegant social models to which deductively to work, the data being too complex and chaotic. In addition, research in the social sciences continually runs into intractable political issues, of the sort that can subvert development interventions, whether based on elegant natural resource management models or not. The natural scientists' quantitative data contrasts with the social scientists' qualitative data, particularly anthropologists wrestling with local knowledge. Nonetheless databases may help bridge the gap.

Databases in indigenous knowledge research

The storage and manipulation of indigenous knowledge in databases is taking off. The use of qualitative computer software is increasing in ethnographic research and is set to become an important methodological tool (Coffey *et al.* 1996). The term 'indigenous knowledge database' is increasingly coming into use, although something of a misnomer. A database is a programme that facilitates storage, selective retrieval and manipulation of numerical, textual and graphical data, 'an organised collection of information held for some common purpose' (Bagg 1992). It is not strictly speaking an analytical tool. 'Indigenous knowledge database' covers both data manipulation software and more sophisticated software for coding and tools to assist analysis. Local knowledge data being largely qualitative, demands interpretation to draw out evident trends and patterns. Indigenous knowledge research usually generates textual data, including interview transcripts, field observations and secondary reports — qualitative data that are interpreted within one or more of several possible theoretical frameworks. The computer is useful for storing, rapidly retrieving, comparing and contrasting data fragments, and can aid in the analysis of complicated patterns (Padilla 1991).

A database, as a tool to organise and assist in the interrogation of ethnographic material, is a sophisticated technological aid to long established methodology. In his discussion of ethnographic methodology, Malinowski (1922:17), for example, recommended that "results ought to be tabulated into some sort of synoptic chart, both to be used as an instrument of study, and to be presented as an ethnological document. With the help of such documents and such study of actualities the clear outline of the framework of the natives' culture in the widest sense of the word, and the constitution of their society, can be presented. This method could be called *the method of statistic documentation by concrete evidence.*" He expanded further on this method in his later development-related work on culture change, to which he was led by a concern for injecting some anthropological education into the training of colonial officers, describing himself as an advocate of 'practical anthropology' (Malinowski 1939:38). He recommended as part of his applied anthropology methodology the use of three-column tables, listing under separate headings the traits of the two cultures in contact (metropolitan power and colonial subjects) and in the middle column the 'new cultural reality' resulting from the interaction (Malinowski 1945). But lacking today's electronic technology he was unable to operationalise this method to any significant extent in his research. Nonetheless the database concept was there.

The field of text-based software is well established, mainly in the field of sociology, to analyse qualitative data such as direct transcripts of interviews and focus groups, known collectively as computer-assisted qualitative data analysis software (CAQDAS) (Tesch 1990; Miles and Huberman 1994; Weitzmann and Miles 1995; Fielding and Lee 1998). It should be useful in the exchange of indigenous knowledge with natural resources scientists. These qualitative data analysis software packages, either on their own or combined with cognitive mapping software, attempt to combine computer-based modelling and qualitative data analysis, commonly using textual data collected in interviews as their raw material. They should facilitate two related processes: (1) the storage of indigenous knowledge data/transcripts in a way available and accessible to natural resources scientists, without the interpretative intervention of social scientists, and (2) the analysis and exchange of processed information on indigenous knowledge with natural resources scientists. Other researchers are starting to use spatial databases, largely geographic information systems (GIS), to analyse cultural relations with the environment, mapping ecosystems and human interference. Although there is potential for spatial analysis of knowledge, they concentrate largely on the outcome of people's actions rather than what they know (Aldenderfer and Maschner 1996). However a general caveat, that applies to much computer software, but especially CAQDAS, is necessary. Many users expect that the software will 'do the analysis' at the 'push of a button'. In this regard the 'Analysis' in the CAQDAS acronym is an illusion. CAQDAS facilitates the human analyst to do analysis by more readily structuring data to examine patterns and test theories. Although the myth of analysis continues, it is now commonly recognised that CAQDAS is a data management tool more than a truly analytical one (Kelle 1999).

Other researchers are taking a different approach, developing software to capture and formally represent indigenous knowledge, to facilitate analysis and reasoning with it. They are using computers as modelling devices to generate rule-based knowledge systems and diagrammatic outputs to represent indigenous knowledge (e.g. the Agroforestry Knowledge Toolkit — see Walker *et al.* 1994. Also Walker *et al.* 1995; Walker and Sinclair 1998; Sinclair and Walker 1998*b*; Joshi 1998; and Fisher *et al.* 1997). These packages disaggregate indigenous knowledge into basic natural language extracts or unitary statements and use artificial intelligence tools to create a knowledge system based on these template extracts that others can interrogate (Dent *et al.* 1996: 120). The developers argue that the approach provides a formal method to "develop knowledge bases that are an explicit and representative abstraction" of what farmers know, and are thus a "testable, comprehensive and coherent model of current knowl-edge on a domain", essentially an expert system based on local knowledge (Walker and Sinclair 1998). The indigenous knowledge, translated into a computer storable syntax, is accessible to the user who may interrogate the electronic representation to learn about peoples' practices. It cuts farmers out, divorcing them from their knowledge, which the machine reifies. There are fierce arguments ahead about the feasibility or otherwise of devising artificial intelligence databases to accommodate the sociocultural dimensions of decision making, for postmodern critiques make us unsure about the extent to which we can even aspire in cross-cultural contexts to understand these issues. And these are magnified greatly when we go on to consider the problems that surround the documentation of the tacit and experiential dimensions of knowledge, that which it is difficult to articulate, which in some profound senses may be unutterable.

These automated reasoning procedures and diagrammatic representations have been developed for a range of cultural and biophysical contexts. They claim to indicate, among other things, that key ecological processes are widely and generally understood by respondents, that knowledge distribution is only weakly related to socioeconomic, gender and cultural distinctions. Although studies report both uniformity and diversity (individuality) in the knowledge held by farmers in different communities, this is attributed to differences in the level of detail asked for and in the life experiences of the respondents (Walker and Sinclair 1998). It is assumed that a community shares basic terminologies and theories of fundamental processes as common knowledge. This equates with general, 'long-term' environmental knowledge, one of the classes of knowledge distinguished by van Beek (1993) in his work with the Dogon in Mali. The rule-based approach does not cope well with van Beek's second class of knowledge, which is specific, largely individual and is "less dependent on 'tradition' than personal experience" (1993:56). An abstractive approach which conflates the two types of knowledge into a single category of 'local ecological knowledge' focuses on uniformity, and is thus likely to represent knowledge as fixed, inflexible and 'traditional', over-looking its dynamic, personal and innovative aspects (Murdoch and Clark 1994). The result could be to miss the occurrence of knowledge about a given phenomenon which might be highly significant, particularly in development contexts (Hesse-Biber 1995).

While proponents of knowledge-based systems suggest that indigenous knowledge is more sophisticated than extension services generally allow, they assume a significant role for science. While local respondents may have a better awareness of causal relationships in some fields than scientists, they have more superficial knowledge of the important processes that are difficult to observe (e.g. action of pathogenic micro-organisms and competition for water and nutrients among trees and crops — Bentley 1989). This general observation, it is argued, suggests that there is an opportunity for scientists to focus their research on constraints in those areas where indigenous knowledge is weak. It is here that databases afford an opportunity to interface between local and scientific knowledge. These are contentious assertions, which have important implications for any emerging indigenous knowledge methodology.

The holistic approach of anthropological research, which should inform culturally contextualised indigenous knowledge research, parallels interdisciplinary systems research. Systems theorists normally make a distinction between 'soft systems', which are qualitative systems and involve humans ('human activity systems'; Checkland and Scholes 1990), which may draw on ethnographic techniques for data acquisition, and 'hard systems', which are quantitative systems amenable to numerical and rule-based modelling (Ison *et al.* 1997). Agricultural and natural resources research focuses to a large extent on the collection and statistical analysis of continuous or categorical numerical data. It has more recently expanded with the arrival of GIS, to include spatial and spatio-statistical analyses. The rule based approach to indigenous knowledge tries to imitate them. In an interesting attempt to compare indigenous knowledge and

Western spatially-oriented knowledge about the environment, rule based systems have also been combined with GIS (Gonzalez 1995).

The increasing acceptance of participatory approaches in development (Chambers 1995) has introduced a new dimension into this 'hard' natural resources research — the collection of qualitative data requiring interpretative analysis. This 'soft-hard systems' combination is evident in interdisciplinary research combining natural resources sciences and local knowledge, and is now promoted as an approach in the study of sustainable rural livelihoods (Scoones 1998). The combination of qualitative and quantitative methods, as advocated here, should give a more comprehensive view of any problem viewed from different perspectives or 'levels of reality', and may further corroboration of results (Prein and Kuchartz 1995). The differences in the data collected and analysed by different disciplines, notably natural and social scientists suggests that interdisciplinary projects could benefit from using a range of different databases, seeking to establish working linkages between them. In our work in Bangladesh we are using three software packages: Microsoft Access for quantitative data, Arcview GIS for spatial data and QSR NUD*IST for qualitative data.

Data collection issues

On the Bangladesh project two Bengali field researchers, resident at separate sites in Tangail and Rajshahi Districts, are collecting the ethnographic data, primarily through unstructured interviews, supervised by an English academic. They are Masters graduates, with backgrounds in botany and anthropology respectively, and both have received anthropological training in the UK. They interview and take notes with farmers, fishers and their families in Bengali, and transcribe the results into English directly into laptop computers, though key vernacular terms are not translated. The resulting rich text covers general discussion, context and common terms (e.g. rice grains, oilseeds, etc.) in English, while significant local terms are left in Bengali. We import these interview transcripts subsequently into the QSR NUD*IST computer-assisted qualitative data analysis package for coding and structuring to facilitate analysis. We have resorted to unstructured interviewing of people about selected natural resource topics in an attempt to stop the scientific paradigm dominating the research, and to reduce postmodern identified outsider distortion of others' knowledge. But the result is an ethnographic mess. We have a large number of unstructured transcripts. In some senses the database archive of interview transcripts might be taken as a postmodern ethnography, being an unordered multivocal record of many views or 'voices'. It approximates to Lindholm's (1997:759) caricature 'of vagrant snippets of texts, jokes and ruminations collected at random, as fragmented and compelling as a Menippean satire'. We could even arrange for the computer to nullify the author's distorting and privileged position by randomly selecting material from the archive. But the resulting text would be difficult to comprehend, lacking any intellectual structure.

In an effort to structure this ethnographic morass we are turning to CAQDAS technology. We can use this to search the database and assist us in arranging the material it contains. In the process we assume analytical authority and make choices in undertaking our investigation of the data. Nonetheless the data remain untainted in the database, partly meeting the complaints of postmodern purists who will criticise us as outside agents for ordering them. These are not pure 'native' accounts because our ethnographic researchers have made selections in writing their field notes, and further ones when subsequently translating from Bengali into English and entering their notes into database files. Initially there was also a tendency by the scientifically trained researcher to approximate respondents' words to what he considered would be more suitable technical language. This experience to some extent agrees with Niemeijer's (1995) opinion that all interview based approaches to eliciting indigenous classificatory systems (e.g. of soil) result in an etic taxonomy, as consciously or unconsciously the scientific paradigm influences the interviewer. Niemeijer proposes an ethnographic approach using sorting procedures and cross-checking with many informants as a preferred alternative. However our anthropologically trained field researcher had no preconceived scientific model of the farming and fishing world, and we think that his interviewing, as a native Bengali himself, probably did probe the emic perspective. It is the collection of indigenous knowledge by natural scientists that is more problematic.

In computer-assisted qualitative data analysis, the ethnographic information is not translated into a computer syntax, but imported into the machine as field notes, possibly tape-recorded text, often as transcripts of interviews with informants. Stored in the database, researchers can subsequently code and analyse it for patterns. It allows at the very least, the common storage of diverse textual and other data, previously kept in field notes, survey returns, case histories, reports of events, research diaries and the like, making them accessible to a team of researchers and others (natural scientists, policy makers etc.). It also allows for diagrammatic representations of knowledge. Those who have not collected the ethnographic data can access them verbatim, break them into 'text units', code and index them, and search them for topics relevant to their interests. The software reduces the drudgery of manual data coding and processing (Richards 1995). It is possible to code by a range of criteria such as different categories of respondent (by gender, class, age etc.), which helps to combat the tendency for non-anthropologists to think indigenous knowledge is homogenous in any rural community. It is also possible to use the local vernacular to explore the content of terms and concepts, and attempt to explore the data according to indigenous structures and categories (e.g. Birmingham 1998). This may then be used to discover the extent to which these may match Western scientific understanding of the phenomena. The use of vernacular search terms ideally requires the presence of a technical translator or a working knowledge of the language.

There are some important ethical issues here that we need to address. How should we 'sterilise' data, particularly that in the headers of transcripts, so that informants and sensitive information are protected? If we protect the data, by using pseudonyms, fictitious locales etc., in what senses might we violate the integrity of the data, that is distort and misrepresent it by not giving all the information? If we do not know the source of certain information or the relation of the person giving it to others featuring in the data set we may misconstrue it. For example, the 'axe that someone may have to grind' as a result of their personal history with others may imbue the comments they make with a particular significance. This relates to issues of relationships and identity that situate the information culturally, socially and historically, without which it may not make full sense. Furthermore, should people be given a warning before talking to indigenous knowledge researchers, and if so what kind, that what they have to say will find its way on to a database, and could be used against their interests? In an attempt to prevent the latter eventuality we need to consider who will have access to the database, which relates to power issues. If we have open access to all, which is what the goal of databases accessible to and accessed by farmers implies, how are we going to protect individual rights to privacy?

We run into another series of paradoxes here (see Introduction to this volume). We need to ask if a democratic open access database is feasible or whether the data stored on it will be too banal as a result. The reverse, the idea of restricted access databases, raises difficult problems of power relations with gatekeepers controlling access, potentially manipulating what others have to say, and acting or assuming to speak on their behalf. This relates to the currently criticised role of the expert. But can we meaningfully escape from them? Do ethical issues of the sort cited need to be formulated within the context of a professional code, as has been common practice up until the present? Currently anthropology has little professional presence in the development domain. Should it strive to have one? A professional presence implies a recognised place in the development business, of which anthropology is in some profound senses critical, even questioning the legitimacy of development as, according to some, an instrument of continued neo-colonial domination. We have another potential conflict and paradox here, in relation to current critiques of 'expert' culture in development (Chambers 1997), of warnings about the dangers of experts, persons who may furthermore militate against interdisciplinary research. Anthropology is broadly sympathetic to these criticisms. We wish in some senses to do away with the notion of narrow specialists to foster interdisciplinary research and create a more equitable development environment, or at least to reduce the power of their professional presence. On the other hand anthropology needs to advance a professional identity to address collectively some of the moral problems attending indigenous knowledge research and to contribute effectively to its integration into development.

The coding process, pattern searches and analysis

The procedure that we have followed in our Bangladesh project, as outlined, is to work initially along disciplinary lines during the data collection phase and seek subsequently to promote interdisciplinary interaction during the analysis phase. Both the natural scientists and social scientists/anthropologists are collecting data by discipline, using orthodox methods. This is followed by preliminary mono-disciplinary analysis and summarising of data, discipline experts seeking patterns using the standard procedures of their subjects. Next comes the creation of interdisciplinary databases and their exploration from an interdisciplinary perspective (featuring complex coding etc.), with on-going discussions during this analysis phase, as we explore implications of findings further. In regard to indigenous knowledge, we started coding after the ethnographers had spent one year in the field and had returned a sizeable sample of interview transcripts, and we were confident that they had the farmers' and fishers' confidence, and had sufficient day-to-day contact with them to have some understanding of their thoughts about their natural environment. We used the main emerging indigenous concepts for an anthropologically sensitive version of a coding structure, thus generally adhering to the precepts of grounded theory (Glaser and Strauss 1967).

We begin by coding all interviews with a header of factual information about the respondent (name, age, gender, socioeconomic status, home location, religion), which gives us a sociocultural framework by which to sort the data (Figure 21.1). The programme allows us to recall all the data on a specified topic according to specified sociocultural parameters, retrieving like respondents and searching for trends in what

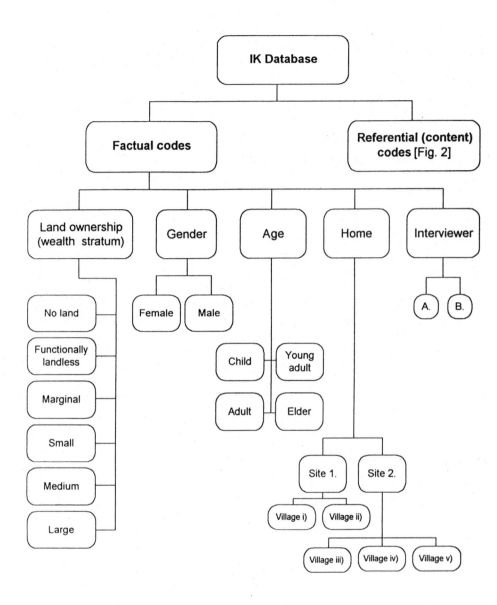

Figure 21.1   *Coding structure for factual data about transcripts*

they say and think about some topic — for example all the interviews from landless men aged 20 to 29 in which they refer to fishing and the annual monsoon floods. After 'factual' coding, we 'referentially' code the interview transcripts. Referential coding refers to 'what the text is about' (Richards and Richards 1995), and involves assigning a selected code to lines of text. The particular software allows one to organise codes into either hierarchical structures or free unstructured associations, though this device is absent in the very latest version of the software, which depends on non-exclusive 'sets'of codes rather than hierarchical trees. We find that the tree structure helps natural resources scientists to interrogate and build models from the data. Various data combinations can be analysed and compared. The software facilitates data exploration and theory building, by allowing a researcher to bring together all the text units from different sources with the same code. It encourages iterative analysis with coding, data searching, hypothesis building, further coding, searching and theory testing and so on. The enquiry benefits from effective data organisation, several heads thinking about issues and iteratively exploring themes. The software even allows different team members to build their own coding structures, which can then be compared, revealing something about contrasting epistemologies, or joined together. The approach encourages the development of hypotheses from, and the testing of theories against, the data (Richards 1995).

The coding proceeds as a two-stage process. Firstly, automated referential coding on batches of interviews, searching and coding for particular key vernacular terms or phrases relating to natural resources management issues, using the Bengali categories, such as *beel* lake, *dighi* large pond, *doba* small pond, *nodi* river and so on, which have emerged during field work (Blyth 1998). These refer to various floodplain waterbodies and text units where respondents refer to them. Others include terms such as *pukur* pond, *beeler kanda* lake margin, *khal* canals, *boro ghona* bays in lakes, all of which are assigned to a higher level coded category called '*jaladhar*: submerged land' (Figure 21.2). Similarly, text that includes names of fish, such as *rui, cutla, chapila, mola, bicharangi* are assigned to the coded category '*mach*: fish species'. Secondly, we do manual interpretative coding on the same interviews. We read the text and refine and add further coding according to respondents' comments on topics. This obliges us to think about the import of the interview, when we start theorising about the subject matter. A danger at this stage, in allowing researchers untrained in cross-cultural approaches to structure the data, is that they will impose their theoretical views on them, rather than allowing hypotheses to emerge from a review of interviewees' responses. The risk is that natural scientists will impose their own disciplinary categories; for example that a soil scientist will code for soil colour, texture, water content, horizon depth, parent material and so on or a botanist code local flora according to Linnean genera, which may not parallel local perceptions. But they cannot violate the integrity of the raw ethnographic data.

When we have completed the interactive coding, the software allows us to advance our theory building and search for patterns in the data. It has several functions for this such as Boolean and proximity searches. We have found the matrix analysis function useful in encouraging scientists to explore the heterogeneity of a community's knowledge. A two-way matrix of factually and referentially coded information — for example 'socioeconomic status' with 'fishing gears' — allows us to see how persons with different resources view fishing practices. It also assists in the compilation of local classificatory schemes — for example criteria used in the identification of fish — which facilitates natural and social scientists working jointly. The codes 'waterbodies' and 'fish names' can be compared in a matrix as part of an investigation of local notions of fish ecology (Figure 21.3). The results of searches can reveal data gaps and suggest further enquiries, comprising part of the iterative process of coding and hypothesis development — for example that people appear to think that certain fish favour specified aquatic environments, what environmental signals do they look for?

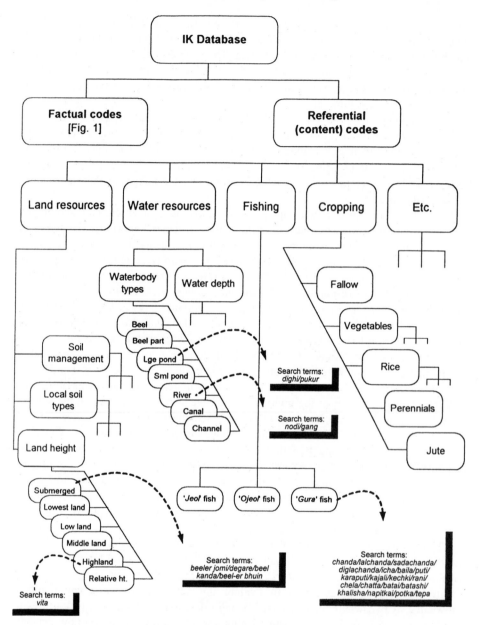

Figure 21.2   *Coding structure for referential content of transcripts, with examples of search terms I*

Computer knowledge versus indigenous knowledge

When we code indigenous knowledge data we are starting to impose our own structure on them. We have to guard against the danger of scientific models coming to dominate any analysis, in the same manner that it may during the interviewing stage. There is the problem of ethnocentric coding, mentioned above, thus the decision about who does the coding does not have neutral consequences. Indeed we may have the compound

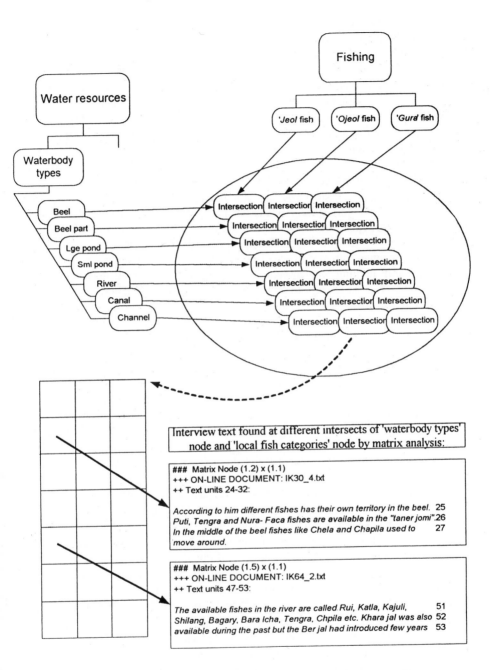

Figure 21.3 *Coding structure for referential content of transcripts, with examples of search terms II*

problem of researchers possibly unfamiliar with database programmes which themselves contain culturally unfamiliar and unstructured data. How should we decide what to code for? We might try to obviate this problem by using indigenous words and categories in coding, as described, but this assumes a high level of familiarity with the data. If we structure the data to make it more accessible to scientists and others we have the danger of ethnocentric distortion and misrepresentation, but if we do not organise the data in some way scientists will have difficulty accessing it because it remains an amorphous mass of notes on conversations, field observations etc. A danger in putting structured ethnographic information into a database is that it may promote the idea among scientists that they can abstract pieces of technically related information of interest to them out of sociocultural context. They can, for example, just search for information on soils or livestock or whatever. This relates to the idea of indigenous technical knowledge, that one can focus on technical issues alone, and ignore their social embeddedness (Sillitoe 1998*d*).

An overly scientific approach to indigenous knowledge research is contradictory, aiming to record and store systematically what is essentially fragmented, dynamic and discontinuous for other researchers and development workers to consult (Warren, Slikkerveer and Brokensha 1995; Grenier 1998). It defines what is useful in an ethnocentric manner, threatening to disenfranchise the original owners from their knowledge and fuelling contemporary heated debate on indigenous intellectual property rights. It is an attempt to archive the essentials for manipulation and transfer what is vital and dispersed. It is to immobilise and emasculate others' knowledge, cutting it off from their society where it has life, in some senses killing the knowledge. It may, without suitable safeguards, reify indigenous knowledge, placing a synchronic record of it into a computer so that it is fossilised in the machine. This approach repeats the error of earlier ethnographic work which presented other cultures as bounded, static and timeless, overlooking how knowledge changes and expands as people manipulate and use it, particularly when they come into contact with others, which is the condition that defines development, which seeks to promote change. Further, it is arguable that since local knowledge is partly the outcome of processes and improvisational capacities, its commoditisation or reification may obscure instances of adaptation of knowledge and the acquisition of skills. But information technology may offer some scope for tackling these issues, it may represent an opportunity for a more continuous, contextualised diachronic record.

We also have the tricky issue of what happens to indigenous knowledge when entered into a database. A database is a construction, used for manipulating information, and as such it produces a particular version of the world, of knowledge. It is not just a technology but a process for managing information. It imposes a particular way of knowing and representing the world. How faithful are these representations to the indigenous view, are databases 'toxic to human diversity' (Rundstrom 1995)? They are not culturally neutral. They are vulnerable to both structural distortion and our socially informed construction of knowledge. We need to beware that they are not more culturally insensitive than necessary. They will privilege certain information above other information. Again, over-emphasis on positivistic views and empirical science. There is a danger that database presentation will ignore multiple realities. We know that communities are not homogenous, and we need to devise databases that can accommodate diverse views, inconsistencies, contradictions and ultimately disputes over what is known (Scoones and Thompson 1994). In short we need to move towards, as is now possible in CAQDAS, overlapping sets of knowledge domains or even fuzzy logic.

We should not allow electronic magic to blind us to the fact that many of the old epistemological conundrums remain. The use of databases does not overcome some of the perennial problems of ethnographic enquiry. The inevitable distortions that creep in with translation from one culture and language to another are not addressed. Nor are the transformations that occur given the biases of all researchers, not only scientists with their dominant theories of the world, and the manner in which their assumptions and agendas inform the record and analysis, particularly important in development contexts with their politically informed goals. Not even a database can record it all! We also have the issue of representing experiential knowledge. The documentation of knowledge which in large measure is experience and skill based — "a performance" — threatens "misplaced abstraction", for it is intrinsically interactive environmentally and culturally, drawing on multiple domains (Richards 1993; Sillitoe 1996). We need to explore the extent to which the incorporation and integration of oral histories, disputes, narratives, photographs, film sequences, quantitative data, observations, interview transcripts and so on into databases might capture this complex cultural reality on one level, while allowing us on another to present a more organised and structured view along the lines of customary ethnography.

Representation and databases

It is not only a question of database representation, or misrepresentation of knowledge, but also political representation of the knowledge bearers and use of their knowledge. The storage and manipulation of indigenous knowledge in databases is potentially a two-edged sword. It has the potential to be either a marginalising or an empowering technology depending on how it is employed.

On the one hand we have the danger of increasing differential access to data. The tendency to reduce others' knowledge to packages of practices or culturally decontextualised inventories (Sillitoe, this volume) which might be passed on 'up', to be manipulated and drawn upon for development ends not only threatens to deprive it of creative agency and potential, it also thwarts their participation in the process. While the use of database technology may make indigenous knowledge more accessible to researchers in other disciplines, the one-way extraction of data and their subsequent computer input and analysis, may paradoxically disenfranchise the owners. The storage and management of indigenous knowledge in databases may be criticised like Western science for divorcing it from peoples' everyday lives, where it gains meaning, and making it non-responsive to their needs (Agrawal 1995). It increases the likelihood of 'expert' analysis out of the field, militating against action research, distancing knowledge and decisions from farmers and fishers, though this is not always the case (Sowerine *et al.* 1994). In separating owners and end-users from 'their' knowledge, it discourages their participation in the research and development process (Coffey *et al.* 1996:8). Researchers must therefore be clear that the manner in which local knowledge is handled will differ according to their purpose. Approaches will necessarily vary if aiming to "legitimise local knowledge solely in the eyes of the scientific community" rather than using it as a means of empowering local people in their own development (Thrupp 1989).

The technological transference, effectively separating owners from their heritage, blocks their active participation, the promotion of which is one of the objectives of indigenous knowledge work in development. It separates people from their knowledge, depositing it beyond their reach in inaccessible databases. The data become totally inaccessible to local people from whom it derives. The technology is beyond the capacity of those untrained to use it, it privileges the expert further, who controls access to the knowledge in the database. It may place someone, possibly an anthropologist and almost certainly not an owner or end-user, in the position of indigenous knowledge 'gatekeeper' with all the power implications (Sillitoe 1998*a*). The indigenous knowledge becomes a commodity, accessible at a price. It comes to comprise part of the information complex of the bureaucracy; at the worst we can imagine it having a subversive effect for the poor, even increasing state surveillance capacity. Confidentiality is a particular problem, as already mentioned (Hesse-Biber 1995). Open systems accessible to users other than the ethnographer increase the risk that interviewees' statements may be interpreted or used in ways of which they would not approve. We have development workers again legitimising themselves and their theories, promoting the appropriation of others' resource management techniques and practices for manipulation, further disguising the imposition of top-down plans and control. It perpetuates the current day development 'crisis', undermining radical empowerment alternatives.

Regarding problems with databases distorting, misrepresenting and disenfranchising indigenous knowledge, we should beware of repeating long-worn arguments and conundrums. In several regards the problems encountered are no different to those we face in committing peoples' testimonies, practices, oral traditions and so on to paper. If we are dealing with a non-literate cultural tradition, any representation is distorting other than an oral and practical one (see Goody 1968; Goody and Watt 1963; Street 1993; Bloch 1998 on literacy and its implications). And where literacy rates are low, as they are in many societies such as rural Bangladesh, the recording and interpretation of information on paper and storing it in libraries and archives, just as effectively puts it out of peoples' reach as any database.

The issues of knowledge distortion and computer literacy are more or less academic when we address economic and political barriers to participation. The technology is expensive and currently way beyond the reach of the poor, though the proliferation of ISD telephone booths and growth of internet cafés in Asia, and the Grameen Phone rural cellphone initiative in Bangladesh, do point the way towards more popular participation in the communication and information revolution in the future. If however, for the present, databases are only going to be accessible to those who can afford the technology, these persons alone are in a position to legitimate their knowledge or view of the world. We have power relations twisted further. Indeed those with access can distort the interpretation of the ethnographic data to suit their own ends, those in power may use it to legitimate claims to represent the true culture bearers. We have the reconstruction of local knowledge for outside agency consumption amounting to the potential wilful distortion of ethnographic reality, on top of the aforementioned epistemological distortions. This raises the contentious issue of the relation of database technology to power structures, its impact on these, from within the local community up through various regional structures to the national and international levels. The contrast between outsider and local knowledge reveals another contradiction inherent in indigenous knowledge database development, namely that many political and policy decisions are made at a national and international level, whereas many problems are often specifically local. Is it possible to relate the different levels? These different levels within development contexts — the national, regional and local — demand different information and knowledge, so we might expect conflict of expectations, with indigenous knowledge relating to local solutions whereas many development problems are essentially regional, national and international in scale.

On the other hand the use of databases in indigenous knowledge research could potentially help us advance methodologies to address these perennial anthropological problems more effectively and further the empowerment of the poor. We need to consider the feasibility of community participation in constructing and running indigenous knowledge databases, devising applications which can incorporate indigenous people, local communities and development projects. How can we democratise indigenous knowledge database use? We need to ensure that these further popular participation, and are not used as a 'smokescreen' by agencies to legitimate their own interference, in which event they become stores of extracted information and party to the manipulation of people. In other words, peoples' participation in the creation of databases should empower them and their communities rather than serve the functional objectives of external agencies (Farrington 1998). The use of databases may help to legitimate indigenous knowledge by presenting it in 'modern' high-tech format, increasing its credibility in the eyes not only of scientists, as mentioned, but also policy makers, politicians, development agencies and so on. They offer local communities a new way in which to represent their interests, potentially empowering them to make their argument using modern technology. It is arguable that with the development of the new generation of voice activated computers, together with the increasing use of film images, featuring hot-links to video sequences of activities, interviewees talking and so on we shall see database stores of information made more available to non-literate farmers. It seems likely, given a free choice and ignoring technical and financial constraints, that farmers and fishers would choose to represent their experiential and orally held body of knowledge using video rather than typed text.

Databases afford us a way methodologically to accommodate to the postmodern observation that each individual has his/her own idiosyncratic understanding of the world. Some of those working in the indigenous knowledge field are increasingly acknowledging that knowledge in any community is not uniformly held nor homogenous but structured and influenced by a range of factors. Communication is partially structured 'politically' according to social differences and relations. We can try to ascertain the extent of variation using a survey device, as we are in Bangladesh, using the findings of a community survey to structure data according to respondents' social position, correlating social status with indigenous knowledge variation. A database allows us not only to assess the extent of indigenous knowledge variation between individuals (by age, gender, class etc.), but also to start to understand the political power dimension which it is critical to assess from the point of view of the participation agenda. We can see if certain persons put a different 'spin' on knowledge, or seem to know different things, and use it to push a certain agenda in their favour. A database of raw ethnographic transcripts should also allow us better to define the content and source of indigenous knowledge; we can attempt to assess the extent to which ideas from elsewhere (e.g. formal scientific notions) have permeated into local ideas.

One of the next research steps in this field is to develop participatory indigenous knowledge databases in which the intellectual property owners maintain a stake. They are likely to use voice recognition software and digital video. Current research in this field is beginning to tackle the problem of ensuring that the owners of indigenous knowledge actively participate in the maintenance and use of such databases containing their intellectual property; for example work on participatory GIS (Harris and Weiner 1998; Jordan 1998). Qualitative databases offer the potential to arrange for primary indigenous knowledge data to remain accessible in-country, directly available not only to national researchers and development agencies, but also local resource users. The flourishing network of indigenous knowledge resource centres (Liebenstein *et al.* 1995; *Indigenous Knowledge and Development Monitor*), such as the recently founded Bangladesh Resource Centre for Indigenous Knowledge, might prove suitable institutional homes for such databases, electronically accessible throughout the country (see Sen *et al.* chapter 24). To-date they have only held secondary indigenous knowledge, as do universities, government bodies, and development agencies, stored in libraries and archives as second-hand knowledge documented in reports, books, journals and so on. Databases might grow organically as people contribute their own interviews and other material to them, advances in information technology making this increasingly possible. We have the potential of a unique living indigenous knowledge resource, available back to the owners.

Database problems and solutions

The use of databases in indigenous knowledge research may pose as many problems as it solves. They offer some exciting new methodological challenges, and put a novel spin on some old ones. The problems faced in working with databases are several, which may discourage some from using them. In the first instance they require a considerable investment of time to learn to operate and manipulate. Databases are not readily accessible. They are time consuming and labour intensive, both to master, for they demand a certain level of computing ability, and to input; and the coding and searching of data can be laborious. The intellectual returns may not warrant the investment, particularly as they are uncertain. While all research is hard work, the fact that there is no guarantee of returns for effort expended, beyond what a human brain familiar with the data can achieve, may discourage some.

Proponents of computer-based modelling and qualitative data analysis allude to the analytical benefits of 'systematicity, objectivity and rigour' (Kelle 1997). It is debatable from a postmodern perceptive whether these benefits are achievable, but such computer storage and analysis may serve, as suggested, a strategic function in legitimising 'soft' qualitative data in the eyes of natural resources scientists and others by giving an impression of 'scientific' analysis, so assisting in the promotion of disciplinary equity in interdisciplinary research. We need to investigate the extent to which computer-assisted qualitative data analysis software manipulates local knowledge data so that they can feature in 'like-for-like' exchanges with natural resources scientists, providing parity and reciprocity (and possibly even a common language) between disciplines (Crow *et al.* 1992). It may facilitate interdisciplinarity collaboration, although the question remains whether it makes indigenous knowledge more readily accessible than the conventional ethnographic monograph. It also obliges social researchers to present their data and to be more explicit about the procedures they follow and their interpretations, something that has long hindered rigorous ethnographic enquiry (Sillitoe 1996; Hesse-Biber 1995).

The implicit assumption that data are collected, inputted and analysed in a linear sequence is a drawback (Coffey *et al.* 1996) because it works against feedback in 'action research' and 'process development' projects. It misrepresents the multiple and overlapping linkages of knowledge bearers, who will not think in a linear fashion. Linear qualitative data analysis may also inhibit interdisciplinarity, promoting multidisciplinary research characterised by the exchange of poorly integrated discipline-specific contributions. Network analysis may be more appropriate. The development of 'concept models' using the computer gives common ground between quantitative and qualitative analysts, benefiting both (Padilla 1991). Interdisciplinary computer modelling, particularly when conceptualising issues, provides a common framework that breaks down disciplinary communication barriers and develops a willingness to share knowledge, absorb others' knowledge and incorporate the acquired insights into the developing conceptual model (Patten 1994). The latest generation of CAQDAS is increasingly graphical, with easy-to-understand ways of communicating complex information, and provides an accessible method of sharing information (Fedra 1995), supporting more open debate between disciplines. Objections to the use of qualitative software are that it may encourage a survey mentality, seeking volume at the expense of in-depth investigation (Hesse-Biber 1995), and even foster a trade-off between disciplinary depth and interdisciplinary breadth.

We know that knowledge is socially and culturally embedded, that it is context dependent, and that it is dynamic. We need to avoid the danger that databases may freeze representation of local knowledge in one instance in time, by developing databases that are interactive and updatable by culture bearers. Databases have the potential to integrate qualitative and quantitative data and so further a holistic systems perspective essential to indigenous knowledge work. We can see that we face considerable methodological challenges in operationalising indigenous knowledge in development contexts, seriously challenging the idea that it comprises a stock of knowledge that we can document and analyse, and manipulate locally, let alone transfer and use elsewhere. Its understanding is no easy nor quick matter. The challenge is how to understand this kind of knowledge and relate it sympathetically to natural science in its attempt to research solutions to the problems facing poor populations in lesser developed nations, such as Bangladesh. What we are advocating is the combination of local knowledge research with that of Western science which addresses these double-binds, not ignores them. We are struggling in the use of databases to further some combination of the expert and the local in knowledge construction and interpretation, we are seeking a double interdisciplinarity, a cross-culturally sensitive one.

22 Indigenous Knowledge Fieldwork: Interaction with Natural Resource Scientists

Mahbub Alam

ANTHROPOLOGISTS BY DEFINITION always respect an insider's view of a given society or culture. This attitude should be obligatory for all who aspire to work with indigenous knowledge. If an anthropologist works alone he can react flexibly as demands dictate. But when working on indigenous knowledge issues as part of a multidisciplinary team there is less potential for this as one has to comply with the team's expectations. Furthermore natural resource scientists bring quite different work practices to the same place, which may compromise the ethnographic endeavour. Many scientists treat local people as their subordinates. Bangladeshi anthropologists may receive the same treatment as they attempt to participate so far as possible in the every day life of local people. Many natural resource researchers also believe that no one except them has the right to explore natural science. They may fear that the emphasis on indigenous knowledge of natural resources threatens their 'expert' status. When convenient, they forget that they are working in a multidisciplinary team where everyone's view should be given equal emphasis. It is in this sharing of ideas that a team spirit develops among all the members. Many scientists act as if they are superior, as reflected in their attitude within the team. Anthropology, particularly in Bangladesh, is not a long established discipline. The first anthropology department in the country was only established in 1985 at Jahangirnagar University. As a result persons from other disciplines have no clear idea about the work of an anthropologist and the majority share some misconceptions about the subject. National natural resource scientists can have some problems understanding, and accommodating to, the anthropological approach. What follows is a personal account of my year's experience in working as an ethnographer in a multidisciplinary team comprising many natural resource scientists, employed to enquire into local farmers' and fishers' indigenous knowledge.

Differences in approaches

My objective as an anthropologist was to involve myself as much as I could in rural life, trying fully to master the dialect and understand people's attitudes. I was polite and showed respect when approaching informants, and was careful not to offend in my work. But my scientist colleagues' approach was quite different. They had a university education. Villagers, mostly poor farmers and fishermen, are easily intimidated by highly educated people and readily address them as *shab* 'sir'. This acts as a barrier in accessing indigenous knowledge. If an informant feels social pressure on his shoulders then dialogue becomes awkward and difficult. Few scientists attempted to overcome this obstacle; instead they basked in their status. Their attitude reflected their assumption that they had come to the field to 'rescue' people. They subscribe to the idea that people such as themselves from the 'higher echelons' of society inevitably teach and instruct the lower orders. They do not consider the idea that they may learn something from the villagers. They are arrogant. They believe that their scientific knowledge can solve the livelihood problems of the poor. Their sense of superiority as scientists is embedded deep in the hierarchical fabric of Bengali society, inextricably linked with their higher social status. Even those few who were verbally polite clearly expressed their assumption of their higher social status in their body language and attitude.

In Bengali we have different terms for persons of different ages and status. If someone is elder or respectable we are supposed to address them as *apni* 'you', a person who is comparatively younger or holds an inferior status we may call *tumi* 'you', and the most junior or inferior person we call *tui* 'you'. On many occasions I heard natural resource scientists working on the project calling poor and old farmers *tumi* or *tui*, which was inappropriate and damaging to the close relations vital to my indigenous knowledge research.

I found them addressing their enumerators in the same way. These were a few local people employed by the project to assist in the collection of information, some of whom were valuable informants of mine. One scientist even treated them as his *chakar* 'servants', using them to run his personal errands, which insulted them. He told some men to wash his vehicle, a symbol of his higher status, and to move it to a safer place for the night. Another time he instructed some enumerators to pluck green betel nut from a high tree early in the morning, which was very slippery at that time. Some of the enumerators were offended when treated in this way. I suspect he did this sort of thing out of ignorance, believing in his natural superiority as an academic. It was, however, totally inappropriate for a project that purported to promote a participatory approach to research. My work was also affected by this sort of behaviour. While I was trying to develop a close rapport with people in which I could learn, they were undermining my efforts with their concern to demonstrate their social status when in the field. Villagers used to frequently visit our field house. Some of the team's scientists complained about these visitors. They thought of the field house as their office, and correspondingly believed that we should control people's access there just as minions only enter their university and institute offices when they summon them to undertake same menial task. They suggested a 'strong administration' would be suitable for the field house. This shocked me. They did not realise the importance of the field house in my ethnographic research or its purpose as a place of informal 'work'. During their brief but numerous visits to the field they wished to consider it their office, a place of restricted access that would support their 'officer' status.

Interference and dominance

The natural resource scientists on the team also insisted on giving me advice about exploring indigenous knowledge. I listened to them, but rarely replied for I was literally lost for words, amazed at their attitudes. Some of them were conducting various kinds of participatory rural appraisal activities but their approach was at best, 'hit and run'. They guessed about cropping calendars, daily activities and other matters rather than consulting people closely. This would have required considerably more work with low status villagers and would have been demeaning to their status. Their attitude and approach to this kind of work was not genuine and I also found their methods very mechanised. A great deal of their information did not correspond with my experiences in the area. I think that they based their research largely on preconceived scientific models about how the world is, which they were imposing throughout rural Bangladesh without regard to local reality. Some of them were extremely deterministic. They did not spare the time to listen to what people had to say about their own lives. They acted as if they had already grasped the answers to local problems. Their approach therefore demonstrated no respect for the manner in which local people lived their lives. Some of them even claimed to know all the anthropology necessary for indigenous knowledge research and tried to teach me how I should go about researching it.

In the mean time my supervisors in anthropology were advising me about how to conduct explorations in indigenous knowledge. This helped me overcome my confusion and doubt, for I was myself being made to feel small and intellectually inadequate, as I could not pretend to have knowledge that promised to solve the poor villagers pressing problems. Their instructions guided me in asking appropriate questions about how people perceive their environment, and not to assume prior understanding. The scientists found it difficult to appreciate the inherent flexibility necessary for indigenous knowledge research, and the need to remain as open-minded as possible. I think they found it a hopelessly unstructured method of research, unlikely to further the understanding of anything, and therefore deserving their disdain when compared to their rigorous tried-and-tested methodologies. My supervisors also helped me to enquire into a range of issues of interest to our natural scientist colleagues: how local people identified different kinds of soils, how they determine their cropping practices, how they learn and make decisions about what to grow where and when and so on. I was inspired to explore people's thinking processes. The experiences of working as part of a multidisciplinary team were not all negative, however, for observing and listening to the natural resource researchers helped me to determine what sort of thing I should avoid. It helped me recognise the important differences between the work of the natural resource scientist and that of the indigenous researcher.

Whilst staying at the field house I had several responsibilities for local project management in addition to conducting my indigenous knowledge research. These activities helped me to build a good rapport with the villagers. The down side was that some of the natural resource scientists failed to appreciate the significance of my management functions to my relationship with villagers. Some of them even thought I was there just to assist them. They tried to dominate me like a villager; after all in their eyes I was demeaning myself by trying to work closely with them. This extended to intellectual domination. They gave me instructions to collect information on particular topics that they considered to be indigenous knowledge. For example one of them told me to collect all the proverbs of Khana, a folk poet who produced a huge number of rhymes about agricultural practices more than a thousand years ago. I suspect this was intended as a put down, suggesting that indigenous knowledge research concerns are ephemeral like the documentation of folk rhymes. Farmers are fully aware of many of Khana's works. However, people's contemporary agricultural activities are so complex and changed that her rhymes do not do them justice at all. A millennium separates her works from today, and thus it does not relate to the present reality. To the scientist, however, indigenous knowledge amounts to little more than the proverbs of Khana. He failed to see local knowledge extending beyond these proverbs.

In the beginning I had several problems reconciling what farmers were saying with the 'superior' knowledge of scientists. They and I seemed to appear ill informed. The local farmers for example called all the HYV varieties *irri* (after the International Rice Research Institute). According to the crop scientists, this reflected the illiteracy and ignorance of the people. There are many HYV varieties bred by BRRI (Bangladesh Rice Research Institute) that the farmers regularly cultivate. I was in the same position as the farmers, since I was not aware either of the differences between the varieties. The natural scientists considered this ignorant. I attempted to find out why farmers apparently did not have individual variety names. Some of them told me that when, during the Pakistan period, the *irri* varieties were first introduced the government appointed officers to oversee their adoption. It also introduced deep tube wells with paid staff to manage them. They provided the farmers with seeds of different varieties and the farmers were unaware which variety they were receiving; they were not told 'this is BR6 seed' and 'that is BR13 seed'. All they heard repeatedly was the word *irri* for HYV paddies. People did not forget this name and subsequently, when other HYV paddies were introduced the local farmers also labelled them *irri*. Those who introduced the seed did not deem it necessary to inform farmers of varietal names. It is therefore no surprise that they are ignorant of their technical labels. Instead they have invented local names for some of these new varieties. In this way farmers identify HYV varieties among themselves. Their knowledge may not match that of the university-educated natural resource scientists but the implications are not that they are unaware of differences. The scientists may not recognise the local classification but this does not justify them considering the people's way of thinking foolish.

Another episode concerned the conduct of a detailed soil survey by soil scientists with the help of the village enumerators. One scientist tried to tell me about the different properties of soils and how they reflect the fertility of the land. He was using quite a lot of technical terms and was trying to teach them to me. He was checking the soil for plasticity, stickiness etc. I did not follow his words, however, for I had also been exploring some local ideas about soils. People were telling me many things that I found did not fit in neatly with the soil scientists' ideas. One day an informant was telling me about the *ras* of the soil, the literal meaning of which is 'sap'. According to some farmers it comes with the floodwater. It is deposited on the surface and comes through from underground. The *ras* directly concerns the fertility of the land. Although some farmers have other ideas, the majority of them support this perception of *ras*. When I asked the soil scientist his opinion about *ras* he labelled it without hesitation 'soil moisture'. But the local people's understanding of *ras* is somewhat different; it is not simply moisture.

Yet another episode concerned fishing technology. One day I found the scientist who was working on aquatic resources interviewing a fisherman about the use of different fishing gear. I had recently been researching the same thing. When he found the detailed descriptions I had about fishing gear and its usage, he said somewhat dismissively "oh you are doing *shahitaya* (literature work)". I guessed from his answer what he thought about my contribution to the project; although our work was similar, my method could not produce anything more useful than bookish results of no practical use.

Conclusion

Influential villagers were not overtly concerned by the visitors. The poor, by contrast, were apprehensive and showed them great respect. Some of them feared the outsider scientists because they believed them to have power and influence. However some privately had the opposite attitude. For example several of my informants questioned the potential of the scientists' work to benefit them. Some of them became sceptical about the value of the work of the natural resource scientists. One day a farmer pointed out to me, while he was being interviewed, that the things that the soil scientists were doing with the enumerators were wrong. He said that when a farmer ploughs and plants the land, he is aware of the different kinds of soils in particular places across his field. But the scientists were collecting soil from only one part of his land, and would therefore gain an unrepresentative picture. In this regard the farmer was more critically aware than the scientist. I was pleased that local people were watching everything so closely and really appreciated the fact that they could argue for the benefit of their indigenous knowledge. This sense of solidarity boosted my confidence too.

In this chapter I have described my experiences researching indigenous knowledge on a natural resources development project from a personal point of view. My interaction with the natural resource scientists working on the project affected me considerably. It confirmed the view that interdisciplinary teamwork is not easy. The attitude of my science colleagues towards myself and to indigenous knowledge helped me to focus on what I had to do and what I should avoid. The slights sometimes hurt me. But the experience has also brought me to a better understanding of what indigenous knowledge comprises, its strength and the need to integrate it effectively into the development agenda.

23 When a Bangladeshi 'Native' is Not a Bangladeshi 'Native'

Zahir Ahmed

INDIGENOUS KNOWLEDGE RESEARCH involves fieldwork. This chapter explores some of the implications. It concerns experiences in the 'field', which relate to theoretical issues centred around the 'crisis of ethnographic representation', and assesses the politics of fieldwork in a Bangladesh village. The paper is divided into three parts. Firstly, a brief overview of the postmodern agenda on the politics of representation and textual analysis. Secondly, an exploration of the implications of conducting research 'at home' situating myself in the text, presenting my social and intellectual background, and my relationships with different respondents. Thirdly, reflecting on my experiences in the field, I examine my position as an 'indigenous' person. Any researcher, 'indigenous' or not, cannot avoid subjectivity for their background and identity informs relations with their subjects.

Fieldwork: practice

My fieldwork was conducted among farming households in a coastal community of Noakhali district, South-east Bangladesh, researching farmer behaviour, indigenous knowledge[1] and agroeconomic relations. It was conducted over a period of eleven months commencing from November 1995 to October 1996. I worked in a *char* (river sandbank) community located 14 km south of Maijdee in Sadar thana. Swadhingram is a relatively new area of Noakhali *char*, formed since 1968, from the tidal floodplain of the Meghna River. The land comprises medium highland and the soil is moderately saline. It is flood-prone. The population in 1997 consisted of approximately 1000 persons, distributed in 150 households. The majority of people have migrated from Ramgoti, 30 km away, because of river erosion. In 1968-69, the government of Bangladesh provided *khas* land (untitled land, land defined as falling under state ownership) to settle the migrants. The migrants have to struggle continuously against *jotdars* (landlords), *lathyals* (thugs) and government officials to establish their land rights. There is much conflict over land ownership. The land issue is so sensitive that farmers receive any stranger such as myself with suspicion. About 60% of farmers are both owner-occupiers and sharecroppers, another 30% are sharecroppers, and the others are landless. Absentee landlordship is prevalent, with a high proportion of annual sharecropping. The community depends on a single *aman* crop of local rice (two varieties: *rajashaile* and *kajalsaile*) grown from July to December. Many men migrate to Chittagong to find work after the *amon* crop harvest. In the *rabi* (winter crops and vegetables) and *aus* (local rice grown in the rainy season) seasons 70%-80% of land is fallow. The *rabi* crops include lentils, chilli, cowpea, mung beans, linseed, sweet potato and eggplant.

Fieldwork: theory

My main technique was 'participant observation' with more emphasis on observation than participation. I 'participated' while I was engaged in agriculture extension training for both government and non-government extension services. The training helped me to appreciate at the field level what extensionists think and do. I was an observer when staying with Swadhingram farmers. Rather than trying to get them to share 'their' experience with me, I observed their daily agricultural activities. My 'nativeness' helped me to understand their daily activities and knowing the 'cultural grammar', I engaged more readily in narrative analysis.

My fieldwork and writing of ethnography inevitably concern my relationships with others. Any ethnography concerns representation, and the problematic nature of the anthropological voice and authority (Hymes 1969; Spencer 1989). Modern ethnography has been criticised for its colonial/theoretical perspective (Asad 1973). It constructs the Orient as inferior and the Occident as superior (Said 1989, 1993). We need to unveil the politics of ethnography. Most ethnographic research has been devoted to the production and reproduction of a particular dominant discourse. We have what Said calls the 'thunderous silence over the ethnographic subject'.

Conventional ethnography, it is argued, represents overwhelmingly a Western discourse that is embedded in relations of power that favour a particular worldview, 'essentialising' others. Postmodern ethnography, variously designated experimental ethnography, interpretative anthropology, textualist or reflexive ethnography, highlights many fundamental problems of conventional anthropological research, and claims to solve them (Marcus and Fisher 1986; Marcus and Cushman 1982; Clifford and Marcus 1986). Post modernists emphasise how ethnographic writing legitimises its authority and authenticity through textual devices. They attempt to disperse authority, establish a dialogue and let the 'native' voice be heard. But many problems remain. The focus on the text exclusively concentrates on the product and not the process of ethnographic writing. The way in which they make dialogue explicit is questionable, largely because few members of a society are drawn into the ethnographic writing. One may ask to what extent those few drawn in are representative (Sutcliff 1993)? Any sort of account, textual or not, involves dominance, the author ultimately making data understandable, the interpretation influenced by his/her background (Johannsen 1992; Sutcliff 1993). How can the ethnographer give the 'native' voice back? We need to recognise the limitations implicit in any methodology, by making them more explicit in the ethnographic accounts. It involves the politics of fieldwork (Page 1988; Tedlock 1991), the politics of the text (Clifford 1988; Clifford and Marcus 1986) and the politics of context (Fox 1991).

What is the correct ethnographic stance on the question of representation? The issue of representation might be solved if the anthropologist does his/her research at 'home' (Rabinow 1986). The anthropologists should shift their attention from the exotic 'other' to their own society and engage in 'indigenous ethnography' (Clifford 1986). According to Clifford, "Insiders study their own cultures offering new angles of vision and depths of understanding, their accounts are empowered and restricted in unique ways" (1986:9). But they can still easily be treated as 'outsider'. Are the power relations involved in doing ethnography 'at home' any less problematic? During my own fieldwork my 'nativeness' became somewhat blurred and my relationships with informants were constantly negotiated.

The indigenous researcher

Who am I to do this ethnography? During fieldwork I remained distanced from the 'others' by power relations, biases and subjectivity. My social background resulted in different relationships with my two groups of informants: agriculture extension staff and the Shadhingram farmers. My identity varied with agriculture extensionists according to their official position. My middle class background, as a university teacher, was similar to that of high officials. Other staff members, who worked at the field level, were unsure and treated me as their 'boss'. When extension demonstrations occurred in the field my activities with farmers, i.e. sitting smoking *biris*, wearing a *lungi*, and going bare foot, affected my relationship with extension officials who were sometimes embarrassed and confused. I was frequently asked why I was spending time in observing the farmers' activities. An official advised me to use his office for talking to extension 'contact farmers', who were considered knowledgeable in comparison to other Shadhingram farmers. My relations with the field extension workers gradually eased because we all worked locally, talked together and approached the same farmers, albeit with quite different objectives.

My presence at the extension office and in the field was embarrassing to the extension workers. A block supervisor has to submit a monthly report, in collaboration with the Thana officer, to the head office, detailing their activities. They were afraid of disclosing what they were supposed to do and what they actually did. In the district headquarters office, where most training is conducted for block supervisors, conversations were restrained, as they would not freely discuss their progress. In the later stages of my fieldwork, I was not received cordially by the extensionists either at the headquarters level or in the field. The higher officials were worried about their lack of activities in the field, which they were supposed to visit every 15 days. The field officers should talk with 'contact' farmers on a weekly basis. Both felt uncomfortable because they feared I would disclose their irregularities.

My academic background including my nativeness undoubtedly affected my relationship with high government officials like the Deputy Commissioner and District Revenue officer. At the start of my fieldwork, when I sought permission from the Deputy Commissioner to enter the field, he advised me not to conduct my research in Shadhingram because of the land disputes, which could interrupt my study. The establishment of rights over newly formed *khas* (untitled) land is frequently disputed. Government officials play a pivotal role in distributing land. The official not surprisingly discouraged me from working there because of malpractices favouring *jotdars* (landlords) instead of the landless.

Before discussing my relationships with the farmers, it is necessary to describe who 'they' were and the context in which their identity has been constructed. Before I began my fieldwork, my knowledge of *char* farmers was based upon stereotypes. From early childhood my home was in central Noakhali, where I was regularly exposed to images of *char* people as having inferior language abilities, being greedy, liars, never wearing shoes, eating too much chilli and so on. They are treated as '*charua*' (people of the *char*), '*nicher lok*' (people of the low land), '*dhokhiner lok*' (people of the south, close to Meghna River), '*chore*' (sharecropping thieves) and so on. Each term has its own meaning in relation to land tenancy and geographical location, defining the *char* people as 'inferior', needy and poor compared to the 'superior', rich and wealthy town people.

The *char* people depend on town-dwelling land officials and landlords who own the land. Thus a patron-client relationship exists between the two worlds. My position associated with town people placed me in a difficult position. During fieldwork I observed that any stranger who came to the area was soon asked 'what is your reason for coming here?' If a stranger entered a field, the farmer would be curious. If she/he stayed for a while, the farmer would become worried and suspicious. It was because of disputed land rights. My entry into the field was treated with suspicion because I was a researcher (*gobeshok*), *uttorer lok* (town person), university teacher, and Londoner (*bilat ferot*). My social position was negotiated as equivalent to the local council chairman and rich farmers with a similar background and wealth, children's education, town connections and so on. People assumed initially that, like other NGO staff, I would bring a project to the area. Since the formation of the *char*, many 'development' projects had been introduced. Also, as no academic research had been conducted in the area, people did not understand what I was doing. I explained that I had come to learn something about agriculture in order to pass an exam in the UK. Some rich farmers, including the members of the local council, were convinced but still hoped that my work would bring a project.

My relationship with large farmers and *jotdars* (landlords) was often difficult and they tried to avoid me by appearing busy and hiding in their houses. They frequently told me to talk to their *kamla* (daily labourers) about anything I wanted to know about agriculture. They were clearly worried about their land holdings, which are based on fictitious documents. These farmers are powerful not only in wealth and labour but also because of connections with local council networks and government officials. Many rich farmers asked me to clarify my position in public. I stood in front of the community shelter and told the villagers that they had every right to be concerned about what I was doing. I was alluding to their fear of exposure. I made it known throughout the village what my intentions were and further stated that if my presence proved harmful I would leave their village. This proposal was treated cordially and was perhaps treated as a courageous step.

Throughout my stay my relationships with poor farmers were more relaxed. Although, at the outset, they were suspicious about my presence, later they became more supportive and friendly. But my purpose perplexed them. I was frequently asked who was providing my food and who was paying me to conduct such a fruitless job. One farmer commented 'I do not understand what you are going to learn from me. Is it such an important thing that you need to learn, as there are lots of things in the world to be learnt'. The landless, having no fear of losing land talked freely in spite of the landlords' rumours that I would take over all the land. Poor farmers welcomed me. I attended their festivals, wore a *lungi*, chatted in the tea stall, sharing their pains and pleasures in everyday life. Farmers visited me to smoke a *biri*, chat, have tea and accompany me to the market. I was even welcome at times of crisis such as drought or floods and was also welcome in the shelter, the centre point of the village.

I was comfortable living with poor farmers. They realised that I had no intention of harming them. They started to think of me as one of 'them'. I would attend Friday *jummha* prayer, the religious discussions called *milad* and *mahfil*, wedding ceremonies, the weekly *shalish* (local court), and funerals. I also assisted them to get admission to hospital and taught their children in primary school when the teacher was absent. I established good relationships with the children through these activities. Sometimes they helped me to gain access to their homes in spite of their fathers' reluctance.

Relations with local religious office holders were not good. My encounter with the local *Imam* (religious leader) jeopardised my fieldwork; local power relations were intertwined with him. He tried to prevent my research. From the beginning the *Imam* warned me to correct my behaviour as I was misguiding the farmers by crossing religious boundaries. I should not ask farmers sensitive questions regarding migration, settlement and above all land issues; nobody owns the land, it is all *porer jomi* (Allah's land). According to the *Imam*, I should enquire into straightforward agricultural activities, and no more. The *Imam*, inspired by religious responsibility, told me that he had to decide what was good and bad for the people:

> Allah has determined peoples' *rizik* (fate) in this world. People are being instructed to utilise resources to continue their livelihood. Swadhingram peoples' *rizik* had been determined in Ramgoti, from where they migrated. It was not their intention to come here, as it was beyond their control. It is ridiculous to ask such questions: where did you come from, why did you migrate and so on.

I became depressed and confused as to what to do. A farmer who assisted me throughout my stay reported several times that rich farmers and the *Imam* were critical of my presence and my behaviour. He advised me to stop asking questions on sensitive issues, to stop using a tape recorder, camera and video. I decided to 'correct' my behaviour and enquire only into agricultural activities. I took some video footage of soil degradation, the negative consequences of chemical fertilisers, women's seed germination process and so on, and asked some female relatives to video this among some friendly farming households. Again the *Imam* objected, preventing me from using video as I was destroying '*purdah*'(veil) inside the household; and so I stopped using this equipment. One day a farmer informed me that the *Imam* was asking *musulli* (pious people) not to co-operate with me as I would bring misery to their lives. The request was made during Friday prayer. I was fortunate that there was no support from the people, especially from the poor farmers. One or two wealthy farmers tried to support the *Imam* but there was resistance from people, including some school teachers. (The *Imam* had a strong affiliation with the wealthy farmers as they lodged and fed him). The poor farmers said that it was because the *Imam* was a *kharizi*, i.e. he belonged to a religious sect, and was inclined to be suspicious about activities such as my own. What are the implications of this sort of resistance for a 'native' researcher? Did I simply see it as a research encounter? What does this encounter entail and what should it mean?

Reflections on fieldwork

What did being 'native' mean and was I really an insider? These are some of the questions that need to be unwrapped in order to understand the insider/outsider dichotomy. I believe that my ethnographic role was contested, resisted and negotiated by 'the natives', although I was carrying a 'native' stamp. Indeed, my local identity may have hindered my fieldwork. My Muslim identity became increasingly blurred and was of no great advantage. It did not discourage the *Imam* from treating me as a *herangi* (Christian) who worked for *bideshi* (foreigners). My male gender also caused dilemmas. In order to conduct culturally all-encompassing research I had to cover female work, but in a society where '*purdah*' (veil) prevails, access was hampered. My background, identity, and objectives placed me in a position beyond my control.

My identity as a teacher and Londoner prompted people to believe I would go back to England to disclose their lives. My position resulted in me being treated as an 'outsider' who could not represent them. I followed a 'dialogical process' (Page 1988), negotiating gender, ethnicity and class identification. My ethnographic encounter with the *Imam* was such an interactive process, giving me a chance to assess 'self' in relation to the 'other's' expressed view. My methodology as an 'indigenous' ethnographer was called into question. As an insider however, I was better equipped to understand my social world and I had a tremendous amount of background information. My prior knowledge of the region gave me certain advantages. For example, I know the local language and the cultural traditions, which made my work easier. But I had problems, even linguistic ones with local dialect, intonation and relation to actions. There are significant cultural differences between mainland and *char* land. It is also hard for the 'outsider' to grasp these cultural significance's, because the meaning of words in action concern tacit aspects of peasants' life. I was more familiar with these from my childhood.

It is not that an outsider cannot understand the cultural knowledge of 'others', nor that the native ethnographer is able to articulate it more precisely. It is a question of different views. Little serious work has been conducted by 'native' ethnographers in Bangladesh, with some exceptions (e.g. Ahmed 1995; Islam 1999), and many have not produced such sensitive ethnographies as some 'outsiders'. Some 'outsider' ethnographers (Gardner 1995; White 1992) have spent long periods of time in rural villages in Bangladesh. The advantage of viewing the culture for the first time may have enabled them to see certain aspects of the culture, which because of enculturation the 'native' ethnographer might miss. It is necessary to ask whether the distinction between 'native' and 'outsider' ethnography is really correct, as the 'native' may be treated as an 'outsider'. There is no way that either native or outsider can avoid subjectivity — their background, education, class privilege, gender, race may all differ from their subjects. I may be an 'indigenous ethnographer' as a Bangladeshi who had access to certain information, but despite the advantages of being 'native', there was an enormous distance between myself and my respondents who clearly perceived me differently, perhaps as an 'outsider'. The reality was that my identity varied depending on context.

The *char* people treated an urban researcher as an 'outsider' who could not represent them. My position differed significantly from the traditional patron-client relationship. The generic term 'native' does not consider various local identities like *shouhurey* (town people), *boro lok* (rich man), *goenda* (detective) etc. My political and social position presented a separate identity to 'them'. But power relations are not all one way. The *Imam* and the village meeting where I was asked to state the objectives of my study are critical as examples of reversals of power relations. They were asking me to become the object of their scrutiny and assessment, instead of the other way around. Once I overheard people whispering '*indur dhukche amder gramey*' (the rat entered the village). Clearly this represented a strong objection to the 'native' researcher.

There is no guarantee that a 'native' researcher can achieve a more authentic perspective. For instance, Srinivash's social world was also quite different from his respondents' in terms of his caste, urban background, class privilege and so on. According to Narayan (1993), Srinivash was not treated as a native anthropologist because "... he was an educated urbanite and Brahman male and the power of his narrative ethnography lies very much in Srinivash's sensitivity to the various ways in which he interacted with members of the community, some times aligned with particular groups, some times set apart" (Narayan 1993:675). We have to recognise the limitations of our methodology, and make these more explicit in our ethnographic accounts and support a shift from 'participant observation' to 'observation of participation' (Tedlock 1991).

Relations of class work powerfully in Bangladesh to replicate 'them' and 'us' relationships of exploitation and domination, between upper class town people and excluded rural people, between rich farmers and poor ones. I ask whether it is possible in this context to escape the position of being a privileged 'outsider'.

Acknowledgements

I thank K. Gardner, A. Whitehead and A. Marie Goetz for helpful comments.

Notes

1 The term 'indigenous knowledge' has many synonyms: indigenous technical knowledge (ITK), peoples' science, indigenous agricultural knowledge (IAK), local knowledge, traditional knowledge, ethnoscience, and indigenous ecological knowledge. Though it has political connotations, I use the term 'indigenous knowledge' because of its wide use in the literature (Ahmed 1995; Sillitoe 1998a).

CONCLUSION

24 The Bangladesh Resource Centre for Indigenous Knowledge and Its Network

Sukanta Sen, Ben Angell and Anna Miles

FOR DECADES DEVELOPMENT PRACTICES have been evolving with debates about ways in which the equality gap between the developed, developing and undeveloped countries of the world can be narrowed. Despite moves towards participatory and indigenous knowledge based forms of development led by those such as Chambers (1997), in which local people are consulted during various project phases, the emphasis in development is still often with western ideas and technologies. Indigenous knowledge includes local technologies and local adaptations of technology, anything that has its origins within a particular area, and is the product of a long process of innovation, experimentation and interaction with the local environment. According to this definition indigenous knowledge should be abundant. However, due to cross-cultural influences and past development practices, much knowledge has been lost and many of the rich habitats upon which the knowledge was based have been irretrievably damaged. In Bangladesh recent figures from the International Union of Conservation on Nature and Natural Resources show that only 6% of the country's natural vegetation remains. With the natural resources of the country under such threat it is time indigenous knowledge was seen as a valuable resource in development thinking before more is lost. Local people have lived with their environment and adapted to it over hundreds of years and know more about their lifestyles than those looking in from the outside ever could. It would be foolish not to use this wealth of knowledge when instigating development programmes.

The need for the inclusion of indigenous knowledge in the development process to achieve sustainability is gaining recognition. Its importance in Bangladesh has not been overlooked and interest in indigenous knowledge is growing, both in the realms of academia and development agencies. Integrated Action Research and Development (IARD) is an organisation that has identified the potential of indigenous knowledge in development. With so many non-government and Government bodies working in development in Bangladesh and so many research papers being produced, IARD has become aware of the need for some form of structure if indigenous knowledge is to be used effectively in the country's development. Indigenous knowledge as a development concept is still in its infancy and whilst it is gaining momentum, remains little known, with independent bodies working in the field unaware of each other's existence.

It is because of this disjointed growth in awareness of the uses for indigenous knowledge that IARD established the Bangladesh Resource Centre for Indigenous Knowledge (BARCIK) in April 1997. Since its inception BARCIK has been assisting in the preservation, documentation and dissemination of indigenous knowledge in a variety of development-related fields including agriculture, healthcare and environmental conservation. It also lobbies for the inclusion of indigenous perspectives and practices in development activities. One of the most important steps BARCIK has taken to achieve its goals is the formation of an indigenous knowledge network for Bangladesh.

The work of BARCIK

The primary objectives of BARCIK since its inception are:

- To raise awareness through the documentation and dissemination of indigenous knowledge (seeing indigenous knowledge as a dynamic resource).
- To make indigenous knowledge available to development agencies, grassroots organisations, development professionals, research institutions and individual researchers.
- To facilitate and encourage participatory and sustainable approaches to development and environmental conservation featuring indigenous knowledge, to promote the transition from indigenous knowledge as marginal knowledge to indigenous knowledge as mainstream knowledge.

BARCIK presently has three main vehicles for meeting its objectives. The first of these is the quarterly publication of an international journal, *Grassroots Voice*. This publication focuses on indigenous knowledge related research and development-relevant articles. It also provides information on organisations working in the field of indigenous knowledge and gives listings of forthcoming events both in Bangladesh and internationally that have an indigenous knowledge component. It is hoped that this will not only raise awareness of the potential of indigenous knowledge in development, bringing discussion of its uses into the public arena but also put those working in the field into contact with one another.

The second activity of BARCIK is the building up of a resource library relating to indigenous knowledge and its use in development and conservation. The library houses both Bengali and English publications. The resources range from books to research papers and reports from both academics and development agencies. The aim is to establish a comprehensive resource centre that is a useful tool for all those interested in indigenous knowledge and to provide a central point for the collection and dissemination of current indigenous knowledge related activities and research.

The third vehicle is the Indigenous Knowledge Network of Bangladesh. This aims to provide a structure for the flow of information so that awareness of indigenous knowledge is raised and to enable individuals working in the area to work together. In order for this to occur the network has three main activities: (1) lobbying Government and development bodies to convince them of the need for the incorporation of indigenous knowledge in development; (2) collecting and documenting indigenous knowledge; and (3) facilitating communication between individuals and organisations working in similar areas so that shared strategies can be adopted for the promotion of indigenous knowledge in development. BARCIK acts as a clearing-house for the network, which aims to increase its membership to range from academics to development workers, extension workers and farmers. The network now consists of an executive committee of 7 members, with a web of other members spreading out from this. The aim is to develop regional subcommittees in all districts of Bangladesh.

BARCIK is a growing and dynamic organisation and in addition to the above activities, has a number of future projects planned to further the documentation and dissemination of indigenous knowledge and establish its place firmly within development. The planned activities have a grassroots focus reflecting the need to embrace the local population. These activities include:

- The publication of a journal in Bengali *Trinamul Uddog* (Grassroots Initiatives). This publication will cover articles, case studies and information on grassroots level development. The journal will target extension workers, farming communities and local development workers.
- The publication of a bimonthly Open File on various development issues through the compilation of relevant information published in daily newspapers and journals. This will be made available to extension workers and researchers.
- The establishment of regional networks and committees to raise awareness of the value of indigenous knowledge locally.
- The publication of Information Booklets on specific aspects of indigenous knowledge and its uses in development. These will be disseminated to NGOs, extension workers and academic institutions. The publications will be both in Bengali and English.
- The establishment of a BARCIK World Wide Web site to participate in indigenous knowledge discourse internationally.

The creation of an indigenous knowledge network

The national workshop 'The State of Indigenous Knowledge in Bangladesh', from which this volume originates, marked the launching of the network (see Sillitoe, Introduction).[1] In addition to raising awareness of the need for the inclusion of indigenous ideas and techniques in development, the workshop was designed to assess the demand for an indigenous knowledge network in Bangladesh. During the first day a stakeholder analysis was conducted, in which the participants were divided into agreed stakeholder groups (nine in total: academics in agriculture; researchers in agriculture; forestry researchers; biological scientists; social scientists; government research institute staff; researchers in health and medicine; NGO researchers; and development researchers). On the second day a session was allocated to a business meeting to discuss the future of the network.

A number of questions were asked in the stakeholder analysis including some that related to the idea of an indigenous knowledge network. Of particular interest were the questions 'what constraints are there to the use of indigenous knowledge in your institutions at the moment?' and 'how could an indigenous knowledge network in Bangladesh assist your work?' The information given in response by the various stakeholder groups is presented in Table 24.1. The comments highlighted the demand for an indigenous knowledge network and the areas in which it should work. Over 90% of those attending the workshop expressed a wish to join a network. In response to the information gathered, BARCIK established the Indigenous Knowledge Network of Bangladesh.

In Figure 24.1 double-headed arrows indicate flows of information and single headed arrows represent lobbying pressure. BARCIK will act as a storehouse for indigenous knowledge, which is collected by network members and their colleagues from willing informants in their area. This information is then accessible to all other members and may be published in our quarterly journal, *Grassroots Voice*. The idea is that if an extension worker or NGO is searching for a sustainable, cost-effective and locally suitable technology or practice, then BARCIK will be able to help them to come up with a solution sensitive to Bangladeshi indigenous practices. The network further promotes our objectives by providing a forum for the development of shared strategies. At network meetings members can share information and expertise, discuss ideas and direct the network's activities.

Table 24.1:	Stakeholder group responses on indigenous knowledge network

Stakeholder Group	1) What constraints are there to the use of indigenous knowledge in your institutions at the moment?	2) How could an indigenous knowledge network in Bangladesh assist your work? Give suggestions.
Academics in agriculture	Lack of trained personnel and training, lack of financial support, lack of faith in indigenous knowledge.	Identify and document indigenous technologies and technical knowledge, expand research opportunities, maintain communication between concerned parties.
Active researchers in agriculture	Indigenous knowledge is not yet well documented or classified. There is apathy toward indigenous knowledge because of ignorance of its application in today's world.	All units of the National Agriculture Research System (NARS) and the Bangladesh Agriculture Academy could join the network, adding to a shared vision of indigenous knowledge.
Forestry	There is no financial support for organisations wishing to undertake research into the developmental potential of indigenous knowledge and technologies.	Timing of network appropriate, it will be able to expand on BARCIK's continuing collection and dissemination of indigenous knowledge, it will reduce unnecessary duplication of efforts and resources, aiding in the promotion of appropriate technology.
Academics in biological sciences	Fieldwork facilities, networking, trained personnel and funding are inadequate.	Maintain contact with others working in the field, foster ideas and support, create awareness, lobby policymakers, planners and politicians, identify appropriate indigenous technologies, attract donor support.
Social scientists	Lack of funding for research.	Educate, inform, assist in securing funding, share knowledge and technologies.
Government research institution staff	Explaining indigenous knowledge can be difficult, individuals may not wish/be able to communicate ideas or practices, there is official and hierarchical resistance to the use of indigenous knowledge.	Help to meet other workers in the field, help to get new ideas and appropriate methodologies, provide access to indigenous technologies and indigenous technical knowledge, raise general awareness about such knowledge and its value.
Researchers in health and medicine	Though interest in indigenous knowledge is growing, funding to support it is not forthcoming.	Research indigenous practices, share knowledge, demonstrate technologies, provide influence, educate and secure funding.
NGO researchers	Lack of methodology for the generation of indigenous knowledge and practices, inadequate information, lack of support-policy, institutional, financial.	Provide access to indigenous knowledge, assist in the creation of a shared vision, lobby for policy change, support organisations and enhance capacity.
Development researchers	Funding, training, lack of planning at policy level.	Link with programmes at all levels (grassroots, national, international). Accumulate literature from national and international sources.

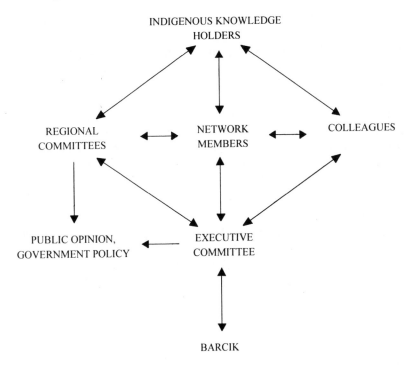

Figure 24.1   *Bangladesh Resource Centre for Indigenous Knowledge network structure*

BARCIK and its network now represent a potential access point to indigenous knowledge. *Grassroots Voice* disseminates the most recent research findings of those working in the field in Bangladesh and other parts of South Asia to an international readership. BARCIK has a computerised database holding information on organisations working with indigenous knowledge and their activities. We can see that BARCIK and its network is set up to gather and disseminate indigenous knowledge across Bangladesh and to lobby for its inclusion in development projects across the country.

Conclusion

The Bangladesh Resource Centre for Indigenous Knowledge does not stand alone in this new sphere of development work but is part of a global indigenous knowledge network. In particular it has close contacts with both South Asian and Southeast Asian networks between which information is exchanged. The global nature of BARCIK is reflected through its various links to academic institutions in Europe.

BARCIK aims to maintain a grassroots level focus through its activities and not confine its work to the realms of academia. The use of indigenous knowledge in development must involve local people and BARCIK will promote this. Indigenous knowledge is a precious resource, which we cannot afford to lose. Slowly we are starting to realise the potential of this development resource that has been for so long neglected, even actively destroyed. BARCIK through its activities is helping to place indigenous knowledge at the cutting edge of development thought and practice in Bangladesh.

To function effectively and gather a large body of knowledge BARCIK needs sustained contact with indigenous knowledge users. Current lack of funding and personnel are a problem. However with the creation of an indigenous knowledge network BARCIK has the potential to facilitate this work. In return the network members are supplied with many of the services that were reported deficient in the stakeholder analysis. The network provides access to indigenous knowledge, assists in the creation of a shared vision, lobbies for policy change, links with various programmes at all levels (grassroots/national/international). It works to raise awareness that for development to be sustainable people's beliefs, practices and knowledge must be recognised. It is hoped that readers of this book will be motivated to contact and support BARCIK in this important work.

Notes

1 BARCIK gratefully acknowledges the co-operation of the Department for International Development (UK) and its 'Socioeconomic Methodologies' programme, and Voluntary Services Overseas for assisting in its foundation and establishment of the network.

References

Abedin, M.Z. and M.A. Quddus. 1990*a*. Agroforestry systems in Bangladesh with particular reference to economics and tenurial issues. Paper presented at the *Expert Consultation on Agroforestry in the Asia-Pacific Region*, held May 15-18 1990, FAO Regional Office, Bangkok, Thailand, 49pp.

Abedin, M.Z. and M.A. Quddus. 1990*b*. Household fuel situation, homegardens and agroforestry at six agroecologically different locations of Bangladesh. In: M.Z. Abedin, C.K. Lai and M.O. Ali (eds) *Homestead Plantation and Agroforestry in Bangladesh*, pp. 19-53. Bangladesh Agricultural Research Institute, Joydebpur, Gazipur, Bangladesh.

Abedin, Z. and F. Haque. 1991. Learning from farmer innovations and innovator workshops: experiences from Bangladesh. In: B. Haverkort, J. van der Kamp and A. Waters-Bayer (eds) *Joining Farmers Experiments: Experiences in Participatory Technology Development*, pp. 161-169. Intermediate Technology Publications, London.

Abedin, Z., S. Aktar and S. Alam. 1988. Uses of multipurpose trees on the small farms of low-rainfall Ganges floodplain soils of Bangladesh. In: D. Withington, K.G. MacDicken, C.B. Sastry and N.R. Adams (eds) *Multipurpose Tree Species for Small farm Use*, pp. 31-47. Winrock Internal for Agricultural Development, Arlington, Virginia, U.S.A.

Agrawal, A. 1995. Dismantling the divide between indigenous and scientific knowledge. *Development and Change*, 26: 413-439.

Ahmed, M. 1992. Status and potential of aquaculture in small waterbodies (ponds and ditches) in Bangladesh. *ICLARM Tech. Rep.* 37, 36pp.

Ahmed, M. 1997. Socioeconomic and policy issues in the floodplain fisheries of Bangladesh. In: C. Tsai and M.Y Ali (eds) *Openwater Fisheries of Bangladesh*, pp. 89-98. Bangladesh Centre for Advanced Studies. University Press Limited, Dhaka.

Ahmed, N. 1953. Fish fauna of East Pakistan. *J. Sei*, 1: 18-24.

Ahmed, N. 1955. *Fishing Craft of East Pakistan*. East Pakistan Government Press, Dhaka.

Ahmed, N. 1970. *Fishing Gear of East Pakistan*. East Pakistan Government Press, Dhaka.

Ahmed, N.U. *et al.* 1996. *Achievement of Gender Research and Training Project: Proceedings of a Workshop*. Bangladesh Agricultural Research Council (BARC), Dhaka, Bangladesh.

Ahmed, W. 1974. *Folk Culture of Bangladesh*. University Press Limited, Dhaka.

Ahmed, Z.U. 1995. *Indigenous Knowledge and Development Discourse: The Case of Bangladesh*. Unpublished MA dissertation, University of Sussex.

Aktar, M.S., M.Z. Abedin and M.A. Quddus. 1992. Trees in crop fields under agroforestry system. *Bangladesh Journal of Training and Development*, 5(2): 115-119.

Alam, S.S., M.Y. Ali and C. Tsai. 1997. Fishing gears of floodplain fisheries in Bangladesh: A case study of *Chanda*, BSKB and Halti beels. In: C. Tsai and M.Y. Ali (eds) *Openwater Fisheries of Bangladesh*, pp. 137-152. Bangladesh Centre for Advanced Studies, University Press Limited, Dhaka.

Alamgir, K. 1997. Cultivation of yam — a very profitable crop. *Sthayiatayashil Krishsi* (Sustainable Agriculture Newsletter) October-December 1997, p. 6. BARRA, Dhaka.

Aldenderfer, M. and H.D.G. Maschner (eds). 1996. *Anthropology, Space, and Geographic Information Systems*. Oxford University Press, Oxford.

Ali, M.A. 1997. Use of mulch to conserve soil moisture for potato preservation. In: *Indigenous Technologies of Agriculture in Bangladesh*, pp. 58-59. Bangladesh Academy of Agriculture (BAA), Dhaka.

Ali, M.Y. 1997. *Fish, Water and People: Reflections on Inland Openwater Fisheries Resources of Bangladesh*. University Press Limited, Dhaka.

Alim, A. 1981. *Growth of Soil and the Furrow*. Juthi Printing Press, Kalabagan, Dhaka.

Altieri, M.A. 1987. *Agroecology: The Scientific Basis of Alternative Agriculture*. Intermediate Technology Publications, London.

Anders, M.M. and R.A. Mueller. 1995. Managing communication and research task perceptions in interdisciplinary crops research. *Qtly. J. International. Agric.*, 34: 53-69.

Anti-Slavery Society. 1984. The Chittagong Hill Tracts, militarization, oppression and the Hill tribes. *Indigenous Peoples and Development Series*: 2. Anti-Slavery Society, London.

Antweiler, C. 1998. Local knowledge and local knowing: an anthropological analysis of contested 'cultural products' in the context of development. *Anthropos*, 93: 469-494.

Asad, T. (ed). 1973. *Anthropology and the Colonial Encounter*. Ithaca Press, London.

Atran, S. 1990. *Cognitive Foundations of Natural History: Towards an Anthropology of Science*. Cambridge, Cambridge University Press.

Bagg, J. 1992. Introduction to database systems for anthropologists. *Bulletin of Information on Computing in Anthropology*, 8.

Bakshi, B.K. 1976. *Forestry Pathology: Principles and Practice in Forestry*. Forest Research Institute and Colleges, Dehra Dun.

Bandyopandhy, A.K. and G.S. Shah. 1998. Traditional knowledge on veterinary practices and human health care. *Grassroots Voice*, 1(3): 18-27.

Bangladesh Academy of Agriculture (BAA). 1997. *Indigenous Technologies of Agriculture in Bangladesh*. Bangladesh Academy of Agriculture, Dhaka.

Bangladesh Agricultural Research Council (BARC). 1982. *Indigenous Agricultural Tools and Equipment of Bangladesh*. Bangladesh Agricultural Research Council, Dhaka.

Bangladesh Bureau of Statistics. 1995. *1994 Statistical Yearbook of Bangladesh*. Bangladesh Bureau of Statistics, Ministry of Planning, Dhaka.

Bangladesh Bureau of Statistics. 1997. *Statistical Bulletin of Bangladesh*, May 1997. Bangladesh Bureau of Statistics, Ministry of Planning, Dhaka.

Bangladesh Bureau of Statistics. 1998. *Statistical Bulletin of Bangladesh*. Bangladesh Bureau of statistics, Ministry of Planning, Dhaka.

Baral, P. 1998. Convocation of Peasants and Weavers. *Chinta*, 7(2), Shayamoli, Dhaka.

BARCIK. 1998. Bangladesh Resource Centre for Indigenous Knowledge. Mimeo Flyer, Lalmatia, Dhaka.

Barnes, B. 1974. *Scientific Knowledge and Sociological Theory*. Routledge Kegan Paul, London.

Barr, J.J.F. R. Payton and P. Sillitoe. 1996a. *Preliminary Investigation of Agricultural Diversification and Farmers Practices in Bangladesh Floodplain Production Systems Involving Rice-Fish Production*. Centre for Land Use and Water Resources Research, University of Newcastle, U.K.

Barr, J.J.F., R. Payton and P. Sillitoe. 1996b. *Natural Resources and Indigenous Knowledge Research on the Floodplains of Bangladesh*. Proceedings of O.D.A. Research Project Workshop, May 1996, Dhaka.

Barr, J.J.F. 1998. Systems investigation of livelihood strategies and resource use patterns on Bangladesh floodplains. *Proceedings of the Association of Farming Systems Research and Extension, 15th Symposium*. Pretoria, South Africa Vol. 2, pp. 994-1003.

Bawden, R. 1992. Of systemics and farming systems research: a critique. In: K. Raman and T. Balaguru (eds) *Farming Systems Research in India: Strategies for Implementation*, pp. 124-138. NAARM, Hyderabad.

Bawden, R. 1995. On the systems dimension in FSR. *Journal for Farming Systems Research-Extension*, 5(2): 1-18.

Benbrook, C. and F. Mallinckrodt. 1994. *Indicators of Sustainability in the Food and Fibre Sector*. Discussion paper prepared for the Sustainability Indicators e-mail conference, 20 April 1994.

Bentley, J. 1989. What farmers don't know can't help them: the strengths and weaknesses of indigenous technical knowledge. *Agriculture and Human Values*, 3: 25-31.

Berkes, F. 1998. *Community Based Fisheries Management (CBFM) Project. Project Evaluation Mission*. International Centre for Living Aquatic Resources Management (ICLARM), Dhaka, Bangladesh.

Bhaskar, R. 1986. *Scientific Realism and Human Emancipation*. Verso, London.

Bhaskar, R. 1994. *Dialectic: The Pulse of Freedom*. Verso, London.

Bhuiyan, A.A. 1994. Social forestry as a development strategy. In: M.R. Ahmed (ed) *Social Forestry and Community Development*, pp. 23-46. Proceedings of a National workshop, October 5-10 1991, Institute of Forestry, Chittagong University, Chittagong, Bangladesh.

Biggs, S.D. 1989. *Resource-Poor Farmer Participation in Research: A Synthesis of Experiences from Nine NARS*. OFCOR, Comparative Study Paper No.3, ISNAR.

Biggs, S.D. and E. Clay. 1981. Sources of innovation in agricultural technology. *World Development*, 9(4): 321-36.

Birmingham, D.R. 1998. Learning local knowledge of soils: a focus on methodology. *Indigenous Knowledge and Development Monitor*, 6(2): 7-10.

Biswas, M.R. and M.A.S. Mandal (eds). 1993. *Irrigation Management for Crop Diversification in Bangladesh*. University Press Limited, Dhaka.

Blaikie, P., K. Brown, L. Tang, P. Dixon and P. Sillitoe. 1997. Knowledge in action: local knowledge as a development resource and barriers to its incorporation in natural resources research and development. *Journal of Agricultural Systems*, 55(2): 217-237.

Bloch, M.E.F. 1998. *How We Think They Think: Anthropological Approaches to Cognition, Memory and Literacy*. Westview Press, Boulder.

Blyth, R.E. 1998. *An Ethnographical Description of the Fish and Fisheries of Two Floodplains Sites in Rural Bangladesh*. M.Sc. dissertation. Institute of Aquaculture, Stirling University, U.K.

Boa, E.R. and M.A. Rahman. 1983. *Bamboo Blight in Bangladesh: An Important Disorder of Bamboo*. Overseas Development Administration, London, U.K., 24pp.

Boa, E.R. and M.A. Rahman. 1987. Bamboo blight and the bamboos of Bangladesh. *Forest Pathology Series*, Bulletin 1. Forest Research Institute, Chittagong, 42pp.

Bose, S. and A. Jalal. 1998. *Modern South Asia*. Routledge, London.

Bourdieu, P. 1977. *Outline of a Theory of Practice*. MacMillan, London.

Brammer, H. 1996. *The Geography of the Soils of Bangladesh.* University Press Limited, Dhaka.

Brammer, H. 1997. *Agricultural Development Possibilities in Bangladesh.* University Press Limited, Dhaka.

Breuker, J.A. and B.J. Wielinga. 1987. Use of models in the interpretation of verbal data. In: A. Kidd (ed) *Knowledge Acquisition for Expert Systems: A practical Handbook.* Plenum Press, New York.

Brokensha, D. 1986. *Local Management Systems and Sustainability.* Paper presented at the annual meeting of the Society for Economic Anthropology, Riverside.

Brokensha, D. 1998. Comment. *Current Anthropology,* 39: 236-237.

Brokensha, D., D.M. Warren and O. Werner (eds). 1980. *Indigenous Knowledge Systems and Development.* University Press of America, Lanham, U.S.A.

Budelman, A. (ed). 1996. *Agricultural R&D at the Crossroads: Merging Systems Research and Social Actor Approaches.* Royal Tropical Institute. KIT Press, Amsterdam.

Capra, F. 1996. *The Web of Life: A New Synthesis of Mind and Matter.* Harper Collins, London.

Carney, D. 1998*a.* Approaches to sustainable livelihoods for the rural poor. *ODI Poverty Briefing* 2. Overseas development Institute, London.

Carney, D. 1998*b. Sustainable Rural livelihoods: What Contribution Can We Make?* DFID, London.

CBFM. 1998. *CBFM Project 1997 Progress Report.* Community Based Fisheries Management Project, International Centre for Living Aquatic Resources Management, Dhaka.

Cernea, M.M. (ed). 1985. *Putting People First: Sociological Variables in Development Projects.* Oxford University Press, Oxford.

Chadwick, M., D. Mallick and S.S. Alam.1998. *Understanding Indigenous Knowledge: Its Role and Potential in Water Resources in Bangladesh.* Environment Centre, University of Leeds, U.K. and BCAS, Dhaka.

Chakma, S. 1992. *Chakma Parichiti.* Bangang publication, Rangamati, Bangladesh.

Chakma, S. 1993. *Parbattaya Chattagram-er Upajati O Sanskriti.* Bangang publication, Rangamati, Bangladesh.

Chambers, R. 1979. Rural development: whose knowledge counts? *Institute of Development Studies Bulletin* (10)2. IDS, Brighton.

Chambers, R. 1983. *Rural development: Putting the Last First.* Longman, London.

Chambers, R. 1986. Normal professionalism, new paradigms and development. *Institute of Development Studies Discussion Paper* 227. IDS, Brighton.

Chambers, R. 1993. *Challenging the Professions.* Intermediate Technology Publications, London.

Chambers, R. 1995. *Participatory Rural Appraisal. Recent Developments in Rural Appraisal: From Rapid to Relaxed and Participatory.* Notes for an Aga Khan Foundation Workshop, Ottawa.

Chambers, R. 1997. *Whose Reality Counts? Putting the First Last.* Intermediate Technology Publications, London.

Chambers, R., and J. Jiggins. 1986. Farming systems research: a parsimonious paradigm. *Institute of Development Studies Discussion Paper* 220. IDS, Brighton.

Chambers, R., A. Pacey and L.A. Thrupp (eds). 1989. *Farmer First: Farmer Innovation and Agricultural Research.* International Technology Publication Limited, London.

Chaudhuri, N.C. 1998. *The Autobiography of an Unknown Indian.* Picador, London.

Checkland, P.B. and J. Scholes. 1990. *Soft Systems Methodology in Action.* Wiley, New York.

Childe, G.V. 1971. Origin of agriculture. In: S. Struever (ed) *Prehistoric Agriculture.* Natural History Press, Gardu city, New York.

Chowdhury, D.N., S.M. Elias and N.U. Ahmed. 1996. Indigenous technologies used mostly by women in Bangladesh. Paper presented at the *Achievements of the Gender Research and Training Project* workshop, May 25-26 1996. Bangladesh Agricultural Research Council (BARC), Dhaka, Bangladesh.

Chowdhury, J.U. 1996. *Flood Control in a Floodplain Country: Experiences of Bangladesh.* IFCDR, Dhaka.

Chowdhury, M.K., M.A. Razzaque, A.B.M. Mahbubul, R.D. William, E.H. Gilbert and R.N. Mallick. 1993. *Methodological Guidelines for Farming Systems Research and Development in Bangladesh.* Bangladesh Agricultural Research Council and Winrock International, Dhaka.

Chowdhury M.K. *et al.* 1993. *Agroforestry Farming Systems Linkages in Bangladesh.* BARC, Winrock International, Dhaka.

Chowdhury, R.I., M.M.R. Miah, M. Hossain, A.F.H. Chowdhury and A.H.G. Quddus (eds). 1979. *Tribal Leadership and Political Integration: A Study of Chakma and Mongs Tribes of Chittagong Hill Tracts.* University of Chittagong, Chittagong.

Clarke, G. 1962. *World Prehistory.* Cambridge University Press, Cambridge.

Clifford, J. 1986. Introduction: partial truths. In J. Clifford and G.E. Marcus (eds) *Writing Culture: The Poetics and Politics of Ethnography*, pp. 1-26. University of California Press, Berkeley.

Clifford, J. 1988. *The Predicament of Culture: Twentieth Century Ethnography, Literature, and Art.* Harvard University Press, Cambridge, MA.

Clifford, J. and G.E. Marcus (eds). 1986. *Writing Culture: The Poetics and Politics of Ethnography.* University of California Press, Berkeley.

CNRS. 1996. *Community-Based Fisheries Management and Habitat Restoration Project.* Annual Report July 1995-June 1996. Centre for Natural Resources Studies, Dhaka, Bangladesh.

Coffey, A., B. Holbrook and P. Atkinson. 1996. Qualitative Data Analysis: Technologies and Representations. *Sociological Research Online,* 1(1): http://www.socresonline.org.uk/socresonline/1/1/4.html

Cohen, A.P. 1994. *Self-Consciousness: An Alternative Anthropology of Identity.* Routledge, London.

Collinson, M. 1981. A low cost approach to understanding small farmers. *Agricultural Administration.* 8 (6): 433-450.

Conklin, H.C. 1954. An ethnoecological approach to shifting cultivation. *Transactions of the New York Academy of Science,* 17: 133-42.

Conway, G.B. and E.B. Barbier. 1990. *After The Green Revolution: Sustainable Agriculture for Development.* Earthscan, London.

Cooke, W. 1899. The hill tribes of the central Indian hills. *Journal of the Anthropological Institute of Great Britain and Ireland,* 1(NS): 220-248.

Cornwall, A., I. Guijt and A. Welbourn. 1993. Acknowledging process: challenges for agricultural research and extension methodology. *Institute of Development Studies Discussion Paper* 333. IDS, Brighton.

Croll, E. and D. Parkin (eds). 1992. *Bush Base, Forest Farm: Culture Environment and Development*. Routledge, London.

Crouch, B.R. 1991. The problem census: farmer-centred problem identification. In: B. Haverkort, J. van der Kamp and A. Waters-Bayer (eds) *Joining Farmers Experiments: Experiences in Participatory Technology Development*. pp. 171-182. ILEIA Readings in Sustainable Agriculture. Intermediate Technology Publications, London.

Crow, G.M., L. Levine and N. Nager. 1992. Are three heads better than one? Reflections on doing collaborative interdisciplinary research. *Am. Educ. Res. J.*, 29(4): 737-753.

Dallmayr, R. 1996a. Global development? Alternative voices from Delhi. *Alternatives*, 21: 259-282.

Dallmayr, R. 1996b. *Beyond Orientalism: Essays on Cross-Cultural Encounters*. SUNY Press, Albany.

Dalmacio, M.V. 1989. Agroforestry for forest land management systems in Bangladesh. *Working Paper* 21, FAO, Assistance to the Forestry Sector Phase II, BGD/85/085, Dhaka.

Das, C. 1995. Politics of theorizing in a postmodern academy. *American Anthropologist*, 97(2): 269-281.

De Walt, B.R. 1994. Using indigenous knowledge to improve agriculture and natural resource management. *Human Organization*, 53(2): 123-131.

Dent, J.B., M.J. McGregor and G. Edwards-Jones. 1996. The interaction between soil and social scientists in rural land use planning. In: R.J. Wagenet and J. Bouma (eds) *The Role of Soil Science in Interdisciplinary Research*. SSSA Special Publication No. 45, pp. 113-122. Soil Science Society of America and American Society of Agronomy, Madison.

Denzin, N.K. and Y.S. Lincoln (eds). 1994. *Handbook of Qualitative Research*. Sage, London.

Dixon, P., J.J.F. Barr and P. Sillitoe. 1998. Methodological issues in incorporating local knowledge into natural resources research and development. *Proceedings of the Association for Farming Systems Research and Extension, 15th Symposium*, Nov. 1998, Pretoria, S. Africa, Vol.4.

DOF (Department of Fisheries). 1994. *Souvenir on Fish Fortnight*. Ministry of Fisheries and Livestock, Bangladesh. 112pp.

Doha, S. 1973. Fishes of the districts of Mymensingh and Tangail. *Bangladesh J. Zool.* 1(1): 1-10.

Dreze, J. and A. Sen. 1989. *Hunger and Public Action*. Clarendon Press, Oxford.

Ellis, F. 1998. Household strategies and rural livelihood diversification. *Journal of Development Studies*, 35 (1): 1-29.

Escobar, A. 1995. *Encountering Development: The Making and Unmaking of the Third World*. Princeton University Press, New Jersey.

Eyre, R. 1979. *Ronald Eyre on the Long Search*. Fount Paperbacks, London.

Fairhead, J.R. 1991. *Indigenous Technical Knowledge and Natural Resources Management in Sub-Saharan Africa: A Critical Overview*. Natural Resources Institute, Chatham, Kent, U.K.

FAO (Food and Agriculture Organization of the United Nations). 1995. *Dimensions of Need*. An Atlas of Food and Agriculture Report.

FAO. 1998. *The State of Food and Agriculture: Rural Non-Farm Income in Developing Countries*. FAO, Rome.

FAP (Flood Action Plan). 1993. *FAP 17 Village Studies*: 1-7. Dhaka, Bangladesh.

Fardon, R. (ed). 1995. *Counterworks: Managing the Diversity of Knowledge*. Routledge, London.

Farouk, S.M. and M.U. Salam. 1996. Sustainable agriculture in Bangladesh: addressing issues through human resource development. *Journal of Rural Development*, 26(1): 1-21.

Farrington, J. 1998. Organizational roles in farmer participatory research and extension: lessons from the last decade. *Natural Resources Perspectives*, 27, ODI, London.

Farrington, J. and A. Martin. 1988. Farmer partipation in agricultural research: a review of concepts and practices. *ODA Agricultural Administration Unit Occasional Paper* No. 9, Overseas Development Institute, London.

Fedra, K. 1995. Decision support for natural resources management: models, GIS, and expert systems. *AI Applications*, 9(3): 3-19.

Fergusson, J. 1994. *The Anti-Politics Machine: 'Development', Depoliticization and Bureaucratic Power in Lesotho*: Cambridge University Press, Cambridge.

Feyerabend, P. 1988. *Against Method*. Verso, London.

Fielding, N.G. and R.M. Lee. 1998. *Computer Analysis and Qualitative Research*. Sage Publications, London.

Fisher, M., O. Kortendick and D. Zeitlyn. 1997. The Avenir des Peuples des Forêts Tropicales Content Code System. *CSAC Monograph 13*. Centre for Social Anthropology and Computing, University of Kent at Canterbury.

Foster, R.J. (ed). 1995. *Nation Making: Emergent Identities in Postcolonial Melanesia*. Michigan University Press, Ann Arbor.

Foucault M. 1980. *Power/Knowledge: Selected Interviews and Other Writings*. Harvester, Brighton.

Fox, R. (ed). 1991. *Recapturing Anthropology: Working in the Present*. School of American Research Press, Santa Fe, N.M.

FPCO. 1995. *Bangladesh Water and Flood Management Strategy* (Draft). Flood Plan Co-ordination Organisation, Ministry of Water Resources, Dhaka.

Gadgil, M., F. Berkes and C. Folke. 1993. Indigeneous knowledge for biodiversity conservation. *Ambio*, 22: 151-156.

Gain, P. (ed). 1998a. *Bangladesh. Environment: Facing the 21st Century*. Society for Environment and Human Development (SEHD), Bangladesh.

Gain, P. 1998b. *The Last Forests of Bangladesh*. Society for Environment and Human Development (SEHD), Dhaka.

Gardner, K. 1995. *Global Migrants, Local Lives: Travel and Transformation in Rural Bangladesh*. Oxford University Press, Oxford.

Gardner, K. and D. Lewis. 1996. *Anthropology, Development and the Post-Modern Challenge*. Pluto Press, London.

Gibbon, D. 1994. Farming systems research/extension: background concepts, experience and networking. In: J.B. Dent and M.J. McGregor (eds) *Rural and Farming Systems Analysis: European perspectives*, pp. 3-18. CAB International, Wallingford.

Gilbert, E., D. Norman and F. Winch. 1980. Farming systems research: a critical appraisal. *MSU Occasional Paper* No. 6, Michigan.

Gill, G.J. and S.A. Motahar. 1982. Social factors affecting prospects for intensified fish farming in Bangladesh. *Bangladesh Journal of Agricultural Economics*, 1-2, 1-23.

Giri, A. 1997. Transcending disciplinary boundaries: creative experiments and the critiques of modernity. *Madras Institute of Development Studies Working Paper*, 150.

Gladwin, T. 1970. *East is a Big Bird*. Harvard University Press, Cambridge, MA.

Glaser, B.G. and A.L. Strauss. 1967. *The Discovery of Grounded Theory*. Aldine Press, Chicago.

Gonzalez, R.M. 1995. KBS, GIS and documenting indigenous knowledge. *Indigenous Knowledge and Development Monitor*, 3(1): 5-7.

Goody, J. (ed). 1968. *Literacy in Traditional Societies*. Cambridge University Press, Cambridge.

Goody, J. and I.P. Watt. 1963. The consequences of literacy. *Comparative Studies in History and Society*, 5: 304-45.

Government of Bangladesh. 1995. *The National Environment Management Action Plan (NEMAP)* (5 vols.). Ministry of Environment & Forests, Dhaka.

Government of Bangladesh. 1996. *The New Agricultural Extension Policy (NAEP)*. Ministry of Agriculture, Dhaka.

Greenland, D.J. 1997. *The Sustainability of Rice Farming*. CAB International, Wallingford and International Rice Research Institute, Manila.

Greenland, D.J., G. Bowen, H. Eswaran, R. Rhoades and C. Valentin. 1994. *Soil, Water and Nutrient Management Research: A New Agenda*. International Board for Soil Research and Management, Bangkok.

Grenier, L. 1998. *Working with Indigenous Knowledge: A Guide for Researchers*. IDRC, Ottawa.

Griffin, K. 1979. *The Political Economy of Agrarian Change: An Essay on the Green Revolution*. Macmillan, London.

Grillo, R.D. 1998. *Pluralism and the Politics of Difference: State, Culture and Ethnicity in Comparative Perspective*. Clarendon Press, Oxford.

Grillo, R.D. and R.L. Stirrat (eds). 1997. *Discources of Development: Anthropological Perspectives*. Berg, Oxford.

Haggart, K. 1994. *Rivers of Life*. Panos, London; BCAS, Dhaka.

Handy C.B. 1985. *Understanding Organisations*. Penguin, Harmondsworth.

Haque, M. 1997. *Ethnic Insurgency and National Integration: A Study of Selected Ethnic Problems of South Asia*. Lancer Books, New Delhi.

Harris, T. and D. Weiner. 1998. Empowerment, marginalization and community integrated GIS. *Cartography and Geographic Information Systems*, 25: 67-76.

Hart, A. 1986. *Knowledge Acquisition for Expert Systems*. London, U.K.

Hassan, S. 1996. Rainwater harvesting: an eco-specific intervention for Bangladesh. *Social Science Review*, XIII(1). Dhaka University Studies, Dhaka.

Haverkort, B. 1991. Farmers' experiments and participatory technology development. In: B. Haverkort, J. van der Kamp and A. Waters-Bayer (eds) *Joining Farmers Experiments: Experiences in Participatory Technology Development*, pp. 3-16. Intermediate Technology Publications, London.

Haverkort, B., J. van der Kamp and A. Waters-Bayaer (eds). 1991. *Joining Farmers' Experiments: Experiences in Participatory Technology Development*. Intermediate Technology Publications, London.

Hesse-Biber, S. 1995. Unleashing Frankenstein's Monster? The use of computers in qualitative research. In: R.G. Burgess (ed) *Computers and Qualitative Research. Studies in Qualitative Methodology*, Volume 5, pp. 25-41. JAI Press, London.

Hobart, M. (ed). 1993. *An Anthropological Critique of Development: The Growth of Ignorance*. Routledge, London.

Hossain, A. 1990. The development of farming systems research in Bangladesh. In: S. Huq, A.A. Rahman and G.R. Conway (eds) *Environmental Aspects of Agricultural Development in Bangladesh*, pp. 27-37. University Press Limited, Dhaka.

Hossain, M. 1991. *Agriculture in Bangladesh. Performance: Problems and Prospects*. University Press Limited, Dhaka.

Hossain, M.M., M.S. Kabir, P.M. Thompson, M.N. Islam and M.M. Kadir. (in press). Overview of the Community Based Fisheries Management Project. In: H.A.J. Middendorp, P.M. Thompson and R.S. Pomeroy (eds) *Sustainable Inland Fisheries Management in Bangladesh*. ICLARM Conf. Proc. 58. ICLARM, Manila.

Hossain, S.M.A. and A.B.M.M. Alam. 1993. Farmers Ingenuity and Indigenous Knowledge. In: *Developing Sustainable Farming Systems. Farming System Research: A Training Manual*. Bangladesh Agricultural University, Mymensingh.

Howes, M. and R. Chambers. 1980. Indigenous technical knowledge: analysis, implications and issues. In: D. Brokensha, D.M. Warren and O. Werner (eds) *Indigenous Knowledge Systems and Development*, pp. 225-52. University Press of America, Lanham.

Hunt, A.E. 1899. Ethnographical notes on the Murray Islands, Torres Straits. *Journal of the Anthropological Institute of Great Britain and Ireland*, 1(NS): 5-19.

Huq, A.M. 1986. *Plant Names of Bangladesh*. Bangladesh National Herbarium, BARC, Dhaka.

Huq, N. and C.R. Das. 1989. *The Flood of 1988: People's Survival. 7 Case Studies from Gheor*. Research and Evolution Division, BRAC, Bangladesh.

Huq, S. and A. Rahman. 1994. An environmental profile of Bangladesh. In A.A. Rahman, R. Haider, S. Huq and E.G. Jansen (eds) *Environment and Development in Bangladesh* (Chapter 2). University of Dhaka Press, Dhaka.

Hussain, M.S. 1992. *Soil Classification: With Special Reference to the Soils of Bangladesh*. University of Dhaka Press, Dhaka.

Hussain, M.S. *et al.* 1991. *Agroforestry Research Planning for the High Barind Tract, Rajshahi, Bangladesh: Report of a Diagnosis and Design Survey*. In: E. Torquebiau (ed). International Council for Research in Agroforestry (ICRAF), Nairobi, Kenya.

Hymes, D. 1969. *Reinventing Anthropology*. Panthern, New York.

IDS. 1989. Farmers knowledge, innovations and relation to science. In: R. Chambers, A. Pacey and L.A. Thrupp (ed) *Farmer First: Farmer Innovation and Agricultural Research*, pp. 31-38. Intermediate Technology Publications, London.

Indigenous Knowledge and Development Monitor. 1995, 1996. Correspondence on indigenous knowledge and science.

Indigenous Knowledge and Development Monitor. Network Newsletter, produced by NUFFIC, The Hague, Netherlands. [http://www.nuffic.nl/IKDM].

International Rice Research Institute (IRRI). 1992. *Programme Planning for 1993*. Los Banos, Laguna, Philippines.

Islam, M. (ed). 1990. *Folk Literature of Tangail Districts*. Public Library, Dhaka.

Islam, F. 1999. *Informal Sector and Women: A Study of a Dhaka Slum*. Unpublished PhD thesis, University of Sussex, U.K.

Islam, M.M. 1996. *Farmers Use of Indigenous Technical Knowledge (ITK) in the Context of Sustainable Agricultural Development*. M.S. thesis, Department of Agricultural Extension Education, Bangladesh Agricultural University, Mymensingh.

Islam, M.M. and M.M. Rahman. 1989. Homestead farming in rural Bangladesh. *Jr. Economic Affairs*, xxiv(2): 89-99.

Ison, R.L., P.T. Maiteny and S. Carr. 1997. Systems methodologies for sustainable natural resources research and development. *Agricultural Systems*, 55(2): 257-272.

ITDG. n.d. Food, *Livelihood and Freshwater Ecology: The Significance of Small Indigenous Fish Species*. Intermediate Technology Development Group, Dhaka, Bangladesh.

Jansen, E.G. 1990. *Rural Bangladesh: Competition for Scare Resources*. University Press Limited, Dhaka.

Jansen, E.G., A.T. Doman, A.M. Jerve and N. Rahman. 1989. *The Country Boats of Bangladesh: Social and Economic Development and Decision-Making in Inland water Transport*. Intermediate Technology Publications, London.

Janssen, W. and P. Goldsworthy. 1996. Multidisciplinary research for natural resource management: conceptual and practical implications. *Agricultural Systems*, 51: 259-279.

Jazairy, I., M. Alamgir and T. Panuccio. 1992. *The State of World Rural Poverty*. Intermediate Technology Publications, London.

Jhingran, G.A. 1997. Stock enhancement in the floodplain fisheries of Northeastern Bangladesh. In: C. Tsai and M.Y. Ali (eds) *Openwater Fisheries of Bangladesh*, pp. 183-198. Bangladesh Centre for Advanced Studies. University Press Limited, Dhaka.

Johannsen, A.M. 1992. Applied anthropology and postmodern ethnography. *Human Organization*, 51(1): 71-81.

Johnson, L. and N.E. Johnson. 1987. Knowledge illicitation involving teachback interviewing. In A. Kidd (ed) *Knowledge Acquisition for Expert Systems: A Practical Handbook*. Plenum Press, New York, U.S.A.

Jordan, G.H. 1998. A public participation GIS for community forestry user groups in Nepal: putting people before the technology. In: *Report of the National Centre for Geographic Information and Analysis Varenius Workshop on Empowerment, Marginalization and Public Participation GIS*, held October 15-17 1998, Santa Barbara, California. http://www.ncgia.ucsb.edu/varenius/ppgis/PPGIS98_rpt.html

Joshi, L. 1998. *Incorporating Farmers' Knowledge in the Planning of Interdisciplinary Research and Extension*. PhD thesis. School of Agricultural and Forest Science, University of Wales, Bangor.

Karim, Z. 1994. Needs and priorities of NARS for the management of natural resources: Bangladesh. In: P. Goldsworthy and F.W.T. Penning de Vries (eds) *Opportunities, Use and Transfer of Systems Research Methods in Agriculture to Developing Countries*, pp.105-125. Kluwer, The Netherlands.

Karim, Z. 1998. *Symposium on Vision for Agricultural Research and Development*. Bangladesh Agricultural Research Council, Farmgate, Dhaka.

Keesing, R.M. 1992. *Custom and Confrontation: The Kwaio Struggle for Cultural Autonomy*. Chicago University Press, Chicago.

Kelle, U. 1997. Theory building in qualitative research and computer programs for the management of textual data. *Sociological Research Online*, 2(2): http://www.socresonline.org.uk/socresonline/2/2/1.html

Kelle, U. 1999. The Impact of QSR NUD*IST on research and researchers. Keynote speech at the conference *Strategies in Qualitative Research: QSR NUD*IST software and methodological issues*, held 24th February 1999, Institute of Education, University of London.

Khan, A.Z.M.O. 1998. Soil, water and crops. Article published in *The Daily Star*.

Khan, M.S. 1994. Biodiversity in plants. In: A.A. Rahman, R. Haider, S. Huq and E.G. Jansen (eds) *Environment and Development in Bangladesh,* Vol. 2, pp. 196-216. University Press Limited, Dhaka.

Khan, S. 1987. *Folklore of Bangladesh.* Bangla Academy, Dhaka.

Kothari, R. 1988. *Rethinking Development: In Search of Humane Alternatives.* Ajanta, Delhi.

Kuhn, T.S. 1962. *The Structure of Scientific Revolutions.* University Press, Chicago.

Langton, J. 1998. Whalers paddle into deep water. *The Sunday Telegraph,* 27th September.

Lévi-Strauss, C. 1966. *The Savage Mind.* Weidenfeld and Nicholson, London.

Lewis, D.J., R. Gregory and G.D. Wood. 1993. Indigenous extension: farmers, fish seed traders and poverty-focused aquaculture in Bangladesh. *Development Policy Review.*

Lewis, D.J., G.D. Wood and R. Gregory. 1996. *Trading the Silver Seed: Local Knowledge and Market Mortalities in Aquacultural Development.* University Press Limited, Dhaka.

Liebenstein, G.W., L.J. Von, Slikkerveer and D.M. Warren. 1995. CIRAN: networking for indigenous knowledge. In: D.M Warren, L.J. Slikkerveer and D. Brokensha (eds) *The Cultural Dimension of Development: Indigenous Knowledge Systems,* pp. 441-444. Intermediate Technology Publications, London.

Lightfoot, C., O. De Guia, A. Aliman and F. Ocado. 1989. Systems diagrams to help farmers decide in on-farm research. In: R. Chambers, A. Pacey and L.A. Thrupp (eds) *Farmer First: Farmer Innovation and Agricultural Research,* pp. 93-100. Intermediate Technology Publications, London.

Lindholm, C. 1997. Logical and moral dilemmas of postmodernism. *Journal of the Royal Anthropological Institute,* 3: 747-760.

Lipton, M. and R. Longhurst. 1989. *New Seeds and Poor People.* Unwin Hyman, London.

Long, N. (ed). 1989. *Encounters at the Interface: A Perspective on Social Discontinuities in Rural Development.* Agricultural University, Wageningen.

Long, N. and A. Long (eds). 1992. *Battlefields of Knowledge: The Interlocking of Theory and Practice in Social Research and Development.* Routledge, London.

Long, N., and J.D. van der Ploeg. 1994. Heterogeneity, actor and structure: towards a reconstitution of the concept of structure. In: D. Booth (ed) *Rethinking Social Development: Theory, Research and Practice,* pp. 62-89. Longman, London.

Magno, V.C. 1986. *Community Forestry Handbook.* ADB Community Forestry Project, Bangladesh, FAO/UNDP Project 028, Field document 1. Ministry of Agriculture, Forest Department and FAO, Dhaka.

Mahabubullah. 1983. *Socioeconomic Factors Affecting the Utilization of Village Ponds for Fish Culture.* Bangladesh Institute of Development Studies (BIDS), Dhaka; Bangladesh Centre for Development Research (CDR), Copenhagen, Denmark.

Malinowski, B. 1922. *Argonauts of the Western Pacific.* Routledge and Kegan Paul, London.

Malinowski, B. 1939. The present state of studies in culture contact: some comments on an American approach. *Africa,* 12: 27-47.

Malinowski, B. 1945. *The Dynamics of Culture Change.* (Edited by P. Kaberry). Yale University Press, New Haven.

Mamun, M.Z. 1996. Awareness, preparedness and adjustment measures of riverbank erosion-prone people: a case study. *Disasters,* 20(1).

Mandal, M.A.S. and S.C. Dutta (eds). 1995. *Crop Diversification: Findings From a Field Research Programme.* University Press Limited, Dhaka.

Mannan, M.A., N. Alam, A. Ullah and M. Hossain. 1990. *Homestead Vegetables Production Program*. BARC, Dhaka, (mimeo).

Marcus, G.E. and D. Cushman. 1982. Ethnographies as text. *Annual Review of Anthropology*, 11: 25-69.

Marcus, G.E. and M. Fisher. 1986. *Anthropology as Cultural Critique*. University of California, Chicago.

Marsden, D. 1994. Indigenous management and the management of indigenous knowledge. In: I. Scoones and J. Thompson (eds) *Beyond Farmer First: Rural Peoples' Knowledge, Agricultural Research and Extension Practise*, pp. 52-57. Intermediate Technology Publications Limited, London.

Mascaro, J. 1970. *The Bhagavad Gita.* Penguin, Harmondsworth.

Mathias, E. 1994. *Importance and Use of Indigenous Knowledge in Sustainable Development*. Module No. 3, Technology Development and Dissemination. International Course on Regenerative Agriculture, October 3-28 1994. International Institute of Rural Resonstruction (IIRR), Silang, Philippines.

Mazid, M.A. 1993. Aquaculture Development in Bangladesh. *Bangladesh Observer*, September 26 1992.

Mazid, M.A. and M.V. Gupta. 1995. Research and information needs for fisheries development and management. Paper presented in the national Workshop on *Fisheries Resources Development and Management*, 29 October-1 November 1995, Dhaka, Bangladesh.

Mazumder, D. 1998. *The Context of Developing Small Native Species (SNS) for Aquaculture in Bangladesh: Local Environmental Change, Markets and Farmer Perceptions*. Report submitted to Centre for Environmental Technology, Imperial College of Science, Technology and Medicine, London.

Mehmet, O. 1995. *Westernizing the Third World: The Eurocentricity of Economic Development Theories*. Routledge, London.

Miles, M.B. and A.M. Huberman. 1994. *Qualitative Data Analysis: An Expanded Sourcebook*, 2nd edition. Sage Publications, Thousand Oaks, CA.

Millet-e-Mustafa, M. 1998. Towards an understanding of indigenous knowledge. Paper presented at *The State of Indigenous Knowledge in Bangladesh* held 6-7 May, Dhaka.

Ministry of Agriculture. 1973. *Bangladesh Agriculture in Statistics*. Statistical series 1, Nov. 1973. Agroeconomic Research Section, 73, Segun Bagicha, Dhaka-1000.

Ministry of Agriculture. 1997. *A Strategy for Implementing the New Agricultural Extension Policy (NAEP)*. Ministry of Agriculture, Government of People's Republic of Bangladesh.

Moorhead, S. and P. Bhargava. 1999. *All Their Tomorrows? Steadier Livelihoods for Rajasthan's Women, Men and Children*. DFID, London; Institute of Development Studies, Jaipur.

Moris, J. 1991. *Extension Alternatives in Tropical Africa*. Overseas Development Institute, London.

Mosse, D., J. Farrington and A. Rew (eds). 1998. *Development as Process: Concepts and Methods for Working with Complexity*. Research/ODI Development Policy Studies. Routledge, London.

Muniruddin, M. 1997. Cultural practices for stimulating growth of fish. In: *Indigenous Technologies of Agriculture in Bangladesh*, pp. 124-125. Bangladesh Academy of Agriculture (BAA), Dhaka.

Murdoch, J. and J. Clark. 1994. Sustainable knowledge. *Working Paper*, 9. Centre for Rural Economy, University of Newcastle.

Nabudere, D.W. 1997. Beyond modernization and development, or why the poor reject development. *Geografiska Annaler*, 79B(4): 203-215.

Nader, L. 1996. *Anthropological Inquiry into Boundaries, Power and Knowledge*. Routledge, London.

Narayan, K. 1993. How native is a 'native' anthropologist? *American Anthropologist*, 95.

Närman, A. 1999. Getting towards the beginning of the end for traditional development aid: major trends in development thinking and its practical application over the last fifty years. In: D. Simon and A. Närman (eds) *Development as Theory and Practice*, pp. 149-180. Longman, Harlow.

NAWG. 1996. Some indigenous agroforestry technologies. *Agroforestry Newsletter*, 4. National Agroforestry Working Group, BARC, Dhaka.

Nederveen Pieterse, J. 1998. My paradigm or yours? Alternative development, post-development, reflexive development. *Development and Change*, 29(2): 343-373.

Neimeijer, D. 1995. Indigenous soil classifications: complications and considerations. *Indigenous Knowledge and Development Monitor*, 3(1): 20-21.

NEMAP. 1995. *National Environment Management Action Plan*, Vol. 2, main report. Ministry of Environment and Forest, Government of the Peoples' Republic of Bangladesh, Dhaka.

Norgaard, R.B. 1987. The epistemological basis of agroecology. In: M.A. Altieri (ed) *Agroecology: The Scientific Basis of Alternative Agriculture*. International Technology Publications, London.

Norman, D.W., F.D. Worman, J.D. Siebert and E. Modiakgotla. 1995. The farming systems approach to development and appropriate technology generation. *FAO Farm Systems Management Series*, No. 10, FAO, Rome.

Nuruzzaman, K.M. 1992. *Aquaculture Prospects and Opportunities in Bangladesh*. Bangladesh Agricultural Research Council, Dhaka.

O' Callaghan, J.R. 1996. *Land Use: The Interaction of Economics, Ecology and Hydrology*. Chapman and Hall, London.

Okali, C., J. Sumberg and J. Farrington. 1994. *Farmer Participatory Research: Rhetoric and Reality*. Intermediate Technology Publications, London.

Padilla, R.V. 1991. Using computers to develop concept models of social situations. *Qualit. Sociol.*, 14(3): 263-274.

Page, H. 1988. Dialogic principles of interactive learning in the ethnographic relationship. *Journal of Anthropological Research*, 44(2): 163-81.

Patten, B.C. 1994. Ecological systems engineering towards integrated management of natural and human complexity in the ecosphere. *Ecological Modelling*, 75/76: 653-665.

Petrie, H.G. 1976. Do you see what I see? The epistemology of interdisciplinary inquiry. *J. Aesthetic Educ.*, 10: 29-43.

Pickering, A. (ed). 1992. *Science as Practice and Culture*. Chicago University Press, Chicago.

Piggott, S. 1950. *Prehistoric India*. Pelican, London.

Planning Commission. 1997. *The Fifth Five Year Plan (1997-2002)*. Planning Commission, Ministry of Planning, Sher-e-Bangla Nagar, Dhaka.

Potter, R.B., T. Binns, J.A. Elliot and D. Smith. 1999. *Geographies of Development.* Longman, Harlow.

Prein, G. and U.H. Kuchartz. 1995. Computers and triangulation. Introduction: between quality and quantity. In: U. Kelle (ed) *Computer-Aided Qualitative Data Analysis. Theory, Methods and Practice*, pp. 152-157. Sage Publications Ltd., London.

Preston, P.W. 1996. *Development Theory: An Introduction.* Blackwell, Oxford.

Pretty, J. 1998. Social capital and sustainable livelihoods. In: *Proceedings of the Association of Farming Systems Research-Extension, 15th Symposium.* Pretoria, South Africa (Joint meeting between the IUFRO research group on agroforestry and the AFSR-E), pp. 11-21.

Purcell, T.W. 1998. Indigenous knowledge and applied anthropology: questions of definition and direction. *Human Organization* 57(3): 258-272.

Qin, J., F.W. Lancaster and B. Allen. 1997. Types and levels of collaboration in interdisciplinary research in the sciences. *J. Am. Soc. Info. Sci.*, 48(10): 893-916.

Quddus, M.A. 1996. *A Bioeconomic Modelling Approach to Planning for Improved Jackfruit (Artocarpus heterophyllus Lamk.) — Based Agrisilvicultural Practice in Bangladesh.* Ph.D. Thesis, University of the Philippines, Los Baños.

Quddus, M.A., R. Begum and G. Sarwar. 1998. Use of indigenous knowledge for sustainable development of farm forestry in Bangladesh: the VFFP experiences. *Grassroots Voice*, 1(2): 5-15.

Rabinow, P. 1986. Representation as social facts: modernity and postmodernity in anthropology. In: G.E. Marcus and J. Clifford (eds) *Writing Culture: The Poetics and Politics of Ethnography*, pp. 234-261. University of California Press, Berkeley.

Rahman, A.K. 1989. *Freshwater Fisheries of Bangladesh.* Zoological Society of Bangladesh, Dhaka.

Rahman, M.A. 1978. Isolation of fungi from blight affected bamboo in Bangladesh. *Bano Biggyan Patrika*, 7: 42-47.

Rahman, M.A. 1987a. Bamboo blight in the village groves of Bangladesh. *Proceedings of the International Bamboo Workshop*, Oct. 6-14 1985, Hang Zhou, People's Republic of China, pp. 266-270.

Rahman, M.A. 1987b. Mortality of bamboos in village groves and its control. *Krishi Katha 1394*, 1364: 223-225.

Rahman, M.A. 1988. Perspectives of bamboo blight in Bangladesh. *Indian Forester*, 114(10): 726-736.

Rahman, M.A. 1997a. Diseases of forest nurseries and plantations in Bangladesh. In: A. Alam and A. Rahul (eds) *Agroforestry: Bangladesh Perspective*, pp. 231-242. Bangladesh Agricultural Research Council, Dhaka.

Rahman, M.A. 1997b. Diseases of forest nurseries and plantations in Bangladesh. In: M.A. Rahman, W. Baksha and F.U. Ahmed (eds) *Diseases and Pests of Tree Species in Forest Nurseries and Plantations in Bangladesh*, pp. 2-10. Bangladesh Agricultural Research Council, Dhaka.

Rahman, M.A. 1997c. Tribal knowledge of plant use in Hill Tracts districts of Bangladesh. *Biodiversity Newsletter*, 1(1): 1-2.

Rahman, M.A. and M.K. Alam. 1994. Infestation intensity and vertical distribution of *Scurrula gracilifolia* Roxb. Ex. Schult. on *Gmelina arborea* Roxb. plantations. In: L.J. Carlson,

G.L. Engiquez and I. Umboth (eds*)* *Forest Pest and Disease Management*, BIOTROP Special Publication No. 53, pp. 9-16. SEAMEO BIOTROP, Bogor, Indonesia.

Rahman, M.A., A.C. Basak and B. Shayesta. 1982. Root rot of *gamar* in forest nursery and its control. *Bano Biggyan Patrika*, 11: 10-16.

Rahman, M.A. and S.K. Khisa. 1981. Bamboo blight with particular reference to *Acremonium strictum*. *Bano Biggyan Patrika*, 10: 81-93.

Rahman, M.A., M. Mohiuddin and A.U. Mridha. 1987. Dieback and canker of jackfruit (*Artocarpus heterophyllus*) in Bangladesh. *Bangladesh Journal of Plant Pathology*, 3(1,2): 61-66.

Rahman, M.M. 1986. Small scale fisheries in Bangladesh: some socioeconomic problems and issues. *Bangladesh Journal of Agricultural Economics*, IX(2): 97-110.

Rana, S.A. 1997. Use of *neem* for crop protection. *Sthayiatayashil Krishsi* (Sustainable Agriculture Newsletter), October-December 1997, BARRA, Dhaka, pp. 6-7.

Reenberg, A. and B. Paarup-Laursen. 1997. Determinants for land use strategies in a sahelian agroecosystem: anthropological and ecological geographic aspects of natural resources management. *Agricultural Systems*, 53: 209-229.

Reijntjes, C., B. Haverkort and A. Waters-Bayer (eds). 1992. *Farming for the Future: An Introduction to Low-External-Input and sustainable Agriculture*. ILEIA/Macmillan, London and Basingstoke.

Rhoades, R.E. 1987. Farmers and experimentation. *ODI Agricultural Administration (Research and Extension) Network Discussion Paper*, No. 21, Overseas Development Institute, London.

Rhoades, R.E., D.E. Horton and R.H. Booth. 1986. Anthropologist, biological scientist and economist: the three musketeers or three stooges of farming systems research? In: J.R. Jones and B.J. Wallace (eds) *Social Sciences and Farming Systems Research: Methodological Perspectives on Agricultural Development*, pp. 21-40. Westview Press, Boulder.

Richards, L. 1995. Transition work! Reflections on a three year NUD*IST project. In: R.G. Burgess (ed) *Computers and Qualitative Research: Studies in Qualitative Methodology*, Volume 5, pp. 105-140. JAI Press, London.

Richards, P. 1985. *Indigenous Agricultural Revolution*. Hutchinson, London.

Richards, P. 1989. Farmers also experiment: a neglected intellectual resource in African science. *Discovery and Innovation*, 1(1): 19-25.

Richards, P. 1993. Cultivation: knowledge or performance? In: M. Hobart (ed) *An Anthropological Critique of Development*, pp. 61-78. Routledge, London.

Richards, T. and L. Richards. 1995. Using hierarchical categories in qualitative data analysis. In: U. Kelle (ed) *Computer-Aided Qualitative Data Analysis: Theory, Methods and Practice*, pp. 80-95. Sage Publications Ltd., London.

Robertson, R. 1996. Globalization: time-space and homogeneity-heterogeneity. In: M. Featherstone, S. Lash and R. Robertson (eds) *Global Modernities*, pp. 25-44. Sage, London.

Roy, I. 1996. Integrating FSR into the National Extension System: a case of Bangladesh. *Journal for Farming Systems Research-Extension*, 6(2): 45-53.

Royal Commission on Agriculture in India. 1929. Government Central Press, Bombay, India, 1928. (Reprinted by Agricole Publishing Academy, New Delhi, 1979).

RSSN. 1990. *Annual Report of the Rural Social Science Network.* Winrock International/BARC, Dhaka.

Rundstrom, R.A. 1995. GIS, indigenous peoples, and epistemological diversity. *Cartography and Geographic Information Systems*, 22(1): 45-57.

Sachs, W. 1992. *The Development Dictionary.* Zed Books, London.

Said, E. 1989. Representing the colonized: anthropology's interlucators. *Critical Inquiry*, 15: 205-225.

Said, E. 1993. *Culture and Imperialism.* Knopf, New York.

Samiruddin, M. 1989. Vegetable seed production, processing, preservation and distribution. Paper presented to the *National Seed Technology Workshop* (Mimeo).

Schmuck, H.W. 1996. *Living with the Floods: Survival Strategies of Char-Dwellers in Bangladesh.* FDCL, Berlin.

Scoones, I. 1998. Sustainable rural livelihoods: a framework for analysis. *Working Paper 72*, Institute of Development Studies, Brighton.

Scoones, I. and J. Thompson. 1994. Knowledge, power and agriculture: towards a theoretical understanding. In: I. Scoones, J. Thompson and R. Chanbers (eds) *Beyond Farmer First: Rural People's Knowledge, Agricultural Research and Extension Practice*, pp. 16-32. Intermediate Technology Publications, London.

Scoones, I., J. Thompson and R. Chambers (eds). 1994. *Beyond Farmer First: Rural People's Knowledge, Agricultural Research and Extension Practice.* Intermediate Technology Publications, London.

Sen, A. and J. Dréze. 1999. *The Amartya Sen and Jean Dréze Omnibus.* Oxford University Press, Oxford.

Senge, P. M. 1990. *The Fifth Discipline: The Art and Practice of the Learning Organization.* Doubleday, New York.

Seshu, D.V., A.E. Eknath and R.S.V. Pullin. 1994. *International Network on Genetics in Aquaculture.* ICLARM, Manila, Philippines.

Shah, W.A. (ed). 1995. *Pond Fisheries in Bangladesh: Socio-economic Studies on NGO Participation and Development Issues.* Environment and Resources Analysis Center, Dhaka.

Shah, W.A., R. Yasmin, R. Karim and M.A. Karim. 1989. Nature and extent of women's participation in the homestead vegetables farming systems. *Farming System Research Report*, OFRD, Ishurdi.

Shah, W. A., R. Yasmin, R. Karim and M.A. Karim. 1991. Participation of rural women in the homestead vegetables farming systems of Bangladesh. *Journal of the International Association of Farming System Research and Extension*, Arizona, U.S.A.

Shahed, S.M. 1988. *Bengal Society and Culture as Reflected in Rhymes.* Dhaka University, Dhaka.

Shaner, W., P. Philipp and W. Schmehl. 1982. *Farming Systems Research and Development: Guidelines for Developing Countries.* Westview Press, Boulder (Colorado).

Sharland, R. 1991. *ITK and Extension*, Bulletin 31, University of Reading, Agricultural Extension and Rural Development Department, U.K.

Sharma, P.N. (ed). 1998. *A Compilation of Indigenous Technology Knowledge for Upland Watershed Management in Bangladesh.* Participatory Watershed Management Training in Asia Program, Kathmandu.

Siddiqui, M.R., N.R. Islam, N.U. Ahmed, N.P. Magor and A.H. Khan. 1994. *Impact of FSR on Farm Families in Bangladesh*. Rice Farming Systems Division, Bangladesh; Rice Research Institute, Gazipur.

Sillitoe, P. 1996. *A Place against Time: Land and Environment in the Papua New Guinea Highlands*. Harwood Academic, London.

Sillitoe, P. 1997. Preserving indigenous knowledge. *DFID Fisheries in Bangladesh*, 2: 12.

Sillitoe, P. 1998a. The development of indigenous knowledge: a new applied anthropology. *Current Anthropology*, 39(2): 223-252.

Sillitoe, P. 1998b. Defining indigenous knowledge. National Workshop on *The State of Indigenous Knowledge in Bangladesh*, held by BARCIK, 6-7 May 1998, Dhaka.

Sillitoe, P. 1998c. What Know Natives? Indigenous Knowledge in Development. *Social Anthropology*, 6(2): 203-220.

Sillitoe, P. 1998d. Knowing the land: soil and land resource evaluation and indigenous knowledge. *Soil Use and Management*, 14(4): 188-193.

Sillitoe, P., P.J. Dixon and J.J.F. Barr. 1998. Indigenous knowledge research on the floodplains of Bangladesh: the search for a methodology. *Grassroots Voice*, 1(1): 5-15.

Sinclair, F.L. and D.H. Walker. 1998a. A Utilitarian Approach to the Incorporation of Local Knowledge in Agroforestry Research and Extension. Typescript.

Sinclair, F.L. and D.H. Walker. 1998b. Acquiring qualitative knowledge about complex agroecosystems. Part 1: representation as natural language. *Agricultural Systems*, 56(3): 341-363.

Singh, G.B. 1987. Agroforestry in the Indian subcontinent: past, present and future. In: P.K.R. Nair and H.A. Steppler (eds) *Agroforestry: A Decade of Development*, pp. 117-136. ICRAF, Nairobi.

Sobhan, R. (ed). 1991. *Report of the Task Force on Bangladesh Development Strategies for the 1990s*. Volume 4 Environmental policy. University of Dhaka Press, Dhaka.

Sobhan, R. 1997. *Growth or Stagnation: A Review of Bangladesh's Development, 1997*. Centre for Policy Dialogue, Dhaka. University Press Limited, Dhaka.

Soussan, J., D. Mallick and M. Chadwick. 1998. *Understanding Rural Change: Socio-Economic Trends and Peoples' Participation in Water Resources Management in Bangladesh*. Environment Centre, University of Leeds and Bangladesh Centre for Advanced Studies, Dhaka.

Sowerine, J., G. Shivakoti, U. Pradhan, A. Shukla and W. Ostrom (eds). 1994. *From Farmers' Fields to Data Fields and Back: A Synthesis of Participatory Information Systems for Irrigation and Other Resources*. Proceedings of an International Conference, held March 21-29 1993, at the Institute of Agriculture and Animal Science, Rampur, Nepal. IIMI, Columbo and IAAS, Rampur.

Spencer, J. 1989. Anthropology as a kind of writing. *Man*, 24: 145-64.

Stolke, V. 1995. Europe: new boundaries, new rhetorics of exclusion. *Current Anthropology*, 36: 1-24.

Street, B.V. (ed). 1993. *Cross-Cultural Approaches to Literacy*. Cambridge University Press, Cambridge.

Survival International. 1998. *Tribale* catalogue. Survival International Trading, London.

Sutcliffe, R. 1993. Writing Culture: towards 'postmodern' ethnography or much ado about nothing? An exercise in writing about writing about the other. *Canberra Anthropology (An Australian Journal of Anthropology)*, 16(2): 17-44.

Swanson, E.R. 1979. Working with other disciplines. *Am. J. Agric. Econ.*, 61(5): 849-859.

Syers, J.K. and J. Bouma (eds). 1998. *Proceeding of the Conference on Resource Management Domains*, Kuala Lumpur, 26-29 August 1996. IBSRAM Proceedings No. 16. IBSRAM, Bangkok.

Tagore, R. 1995. *Selected Poems*. Penguin Books, New Delhi.

Tedlock, B. 1991. From participant observation to observation of participation: the emergence of narrative ethnography. *Journal of Anthropological Research*, 47(1): 69-94.

Tesch, R. 1990. *Qualitative Research: Analysis Types and Software Tools*. Falmer Press, New York.

Thrupp, L.A. 1989. Legitimizing local knowledge: from displacement to empowerment for Third World people. *Agriculture and Human Values*, summer, 13-24.

Toole, E.H. 1958. Storage of vegetables seeds. *USDA Leaflet* No. 220.

Toufique, K.A. 1997. Some observations on power and property rights in the inland fisheries of Bangladesh. *World Development*, 25 (3): 457-467.

Tsai, C. and L. Ali. 1985. Openwater fisheries (carp) management program in Bangladesh. *Fisheries Information Bulletin*, 2(4). BFRSS, Dhaka, Bangladesh.

Tsai, C. and M.Y. Ali (eds). 1997. *Open Water Fisheries of Bangladesh*. Bangladesh Centre for Advanced Studies, University Press Limited, Dhaka.

UBINIG. 1996. *Nayakrishi Andolon* (The New Agricultural Movement), UBINIG, Shaymoli, Dhaka.

Ullah, M. (ed). 1991. *Living With Flood: Bangladesh Experiences*. Centre For Sustainable Development (CFSD), Bangladesh.

Ullah, M. 1996. *Land, Livelihood and Change in Rural Bangladesh*. University Press Limited, Dhaka.

Uphoff, N. 1996a. *Learning from Gal Oya*. IT Publications, London.

Uphoff, N. 1996b. Understanding the world as a heterogenous whole: insights into systems from work on irrigation. *Systems Research*, 13(1): 3-12.

van Beek, W. 1993. Processes and limitations of Dogon agricultural knowledge. In: M. Hobart (ed) *An Anthropological Critique of Development: The growth of Ignorance*, pp. 43-60. Routledge, London.

VFFP. 1997. Vegetative propagation of eucalyptus. *Shekor*, August-October 1997, quarterly newsletter of the Village and Farm Forestry Program, Swiss Agency for Development and Cooperation, Dhaka.

VFFP. 1998a. Vegetative propagation of *chambal* (*Albizia richardiana*). *Shekor*, November 1997-January 1998, quarterly newsletter of the Village and Farm Forestry Program, Swiss Agency for Development and Cooperation, Dhaka.

VFFP. 1998b. Control of an epidemic disease of *sissoo* trees. *Shekor*, February-April 1998, quarterly newsletter of the Village and Farm Forestry Program, Swiss Agency for Development and Cooperation, Dhaka.

VFFP. 1998c. Bio-pesticide: *Bishkatali*. *Shekor*, May-July 1998, quarterly newsletter of the Village and Farm Forestry Program, Swiss Agency for Development and Cooperation, Dhaka.

Waldrop, M.M. 1992. *Complexity: The Emerging Science at the Edge of Order and Chaos*. Penguin, London.

Walker, D.H. and F.L. Sinclair. 1998. Acquiring qualitative knowledge about complex agroecosystems. Part 2: formal representation. *Agricultural Systems*, 56(3): 365-386.

Walker, D.H., F.L. Sinclair and G. Kendon. 1995. A knowledge-based systems approach to agroforestry research and extension. *AI Applications*, 9(3): 61-72.

Walker, D.H., F.L. Sinclair, G. Kendon, D. Robertson, R.I. Muetzelfeldt, M. Haggith, and G.S. Turner. 1994. *Agroforestry Knowledge Toolkit: Methodological Guidelines, Computer Software and Manual for AKT1 and AKT2, Supporting the Use of a Knowledge-Based Systems Approach in Agroforestry Research and Extension*. School of Agricultural and Forest Science, University of Wales, Bangor.

Walker, D.H., F.L. Sinclair and R. Muetzelfeldt. 1991. *Formal Representation and Use of Indigenous Ecological Knowledge about Agroforestry Practices: A Pilot Phase Report*. School of Agricultural and Forest Sciences, University of Wales, Bangor, U.K.

Warren, D.M. 1991. Using indigenous knowledge in agricultural development. *Discussion Paper* No. 127, The World Bank, Washington DC, U.S.A.

Warren, D.M. and K. Cashman. 1988. Indigenous knowledge for sustainable agriculture and rural development. *Gatekeeper Series* No. SA10, Sustainable Agriculture programme, International Institute for Environment and Development, London.

Warren, D.M., L.J. Slikkerveer and D. Brokensha (eds). 1995. *The Cultural Dimensions of Development: Indigenous Knowledge Systems*. Intermediate Technology Publications, London.

Waters, M. 1998. *Globalization*. Routledge, London.

Weitzman, E.A. and M.B. Miles. 1995. *Computer Programs for Qualitative Data Analysis*. Sage Publications, Thousand Oaks, C.A.

Wennergren, E.B., C.H. Anholt and M.D. Whitaker. 1984. *Agricultural Development in Bangladesh*. Westview Press, Boulder, Colorado, U.S.A.

Whickam, T.W. 1993. *Farmers Ain't No Fools: Exploring the Role of Participatory Rural Appraisal to Access Indigenous Knowledge and Enhance Sustainable Development Research and Planning: A Case Study of Dusun Pausan, Bali, Indonesia*. M.A.Thesis, University of Waterloo, U.M.I., Ann Arbor.

White, S.C. 1992. *Arguing with the Crocodile: Gender and Class in Bangladesh*. Zed Books Ltd., London.

Wilcock, D. and R. English. 1994. Indicators linking national policy and local sustainability: approaches by the USAID Agricultural Policy Analysis Project (APAP). Paper for presentation at the SANREM CRSP Conference on *Indicators of Sustainability*, August 1-5 1994, Arlington, Virginia, Mimeo, 21pp.

Wilson, K. and G.E.B. Morren Jnr. 1990. *Systems Approaches for Improvement in Agriculture and Resource Management*. MacMillan, London.

Winkelmann, D. 1976. *The Adoption of New Maize Technology in Plan Puebla, Mexico*. International Maize and Wheat Improvement Centre (CIMMYT).

Wolfe, J., C. Bechard, P. Cizek and D. Cole. 1992. *Indigenous Western Knowledge and Resources Management System*. University School of Rural Planning and Development, University of Guelph, Canada.

Woodward, K. 1997. *Identity and Difference*. Sage Publications (Open University Culture, Media and Identities series, Volume 3) London.

Wright, S. and S. Nelson (eds). 1995. *Power and Participatory Development: Theory and Practice*. Intermediate Technology Publications, London.

Zaman, S.M.H. 1993. Agricultural development and sustainability of wetlands. In: A. Nishat and Z. Hossain (eds) *Freshwater Wetlands in Bangladesh: Issues and Approaches for Management.* IUCN, The World Conservation Union, Dhaka, Bangladesh.

Zaman, S.M.H. 1997. Sustainable development of food crops in relation to conservation and use of plant genetic resources of Bangladesh. A Keynote paper in the *National Workshop on Plant Genetic Resources of Bangladesh*, 26-29 August 1997, National Committee on Plant Genetic Resources, International Plant Genetic Resources Institute (IPGRI), Bangladesh Agricultural. Research Council (BARC), Farmgate, Dhaka.

Zuberi, M.I. 1997a. Present state of the ethnoveterinary system in North-western Bangladesh, *Proceedings of the International Conference on Ethnoveterinary Medicine*, 4-6 November 1997, MDMTC, BAIF Development Research Foundation, Pune, India.

Zuberi, M.I. 1997b. *Medicinal Plant Diversity: Present State and Conservation Needs in Bangladesh.* Country Report, IDRC Expert Group Meeting, IDRC, New Delhi, India.

Zuberi, M.I. 1998. Indigenous knowledge and sustainable development in Bangladesh. Paper presented at *The State of Indigenous Knowledge in Bangladesh*, held by BARCIK, 6-7 May, Dhaka.

Index